Learning Visual Basic .NET

Jesse Liberty

Beijing · Cambridge · Farnham · Köln · Paris · Sebastopol · Taipei · Tokyo

Learning Visual Basic .NET
by Jesse Liberty

Copyright © 2003 O'Reilly & Associates, Inc. All rights reserved.
Printed in the United States of America.

Published by O'Reilly & Associates, Inc., 1005 Gravenstein Highway North, Sebastopol, CA
95472.

O'Reilly & Associates books may be purchased for educational, business, or sales promotional
use. Online editions are also available for most titles (*safari.oreilly.com*). For more information,
contact our corporate/institutional sales department: (800) 998-9938 or *corporate@oreilly.com*.

Editor:	Valerie Quercia
Production Editor:	Darren Kelly
Cover Designer:	Emma Colby
Interior Designer:	David Futato
Production Services:	Nancy Crumpton

Printing History:

October 2002:	First Edition.

ISBN: 0-596-00386-2

[C]

Table of Contents

Preface

In July 2000, Microsoft announced the release of its new .NET platform, which represented a major change in the way people think about programming. .NET facilitates object-oriented Internet development. Visual Basic .NET (VB.NET) is a programming language that was adapted from its predecessor, Visual Basic 6, specifically for the purpose of writing applications for the .NET platform. This new version of the Visual Basic language is well suited for developing distributed web applications.

About This Book

Learning Visual Basic .NET is a primer on the VB.NET language, in the context of the .NET development environment, and also on object-oriented programming. This book focuses on the fundamentals of the VB.NET programming language, both syntactical and semantic. After mastering these concepts, you should be ready to move on to a more advanced programming guide that will help you create large-scale web and Windows applications. Chapter 19 provides a number of suggestions for your continued study of VB.NET and .NET development.

Who This Book Is For

Learning Visual Basic .NET was written for programmers with little or no object-oriented programming experience, as well as for novice programmers. Those coming from another language may have a slight advantage, but I've tried to provide an on-ramp for beginners as well, by defining all terms, demonstrating the relationships among the various constructs, and reviewing key concepts along the way.

How the Book Is Organized

Chapter 1, *Visual Basic .NET and .NET Programming*, introduces you to the VB.NET language and the .NET platform.

Chapter 2, *Getting Started with VB.NET*, presents a simple application that prints the words "Hello World" to a console window and gives a line-by-line analysis of the code.

Chapter 3, *Object-Oriented Programming*, explains the principles behind and goals of this programming methodology, including the three pillars of object-oriented programming: encapsulation, specialization, and polymorphism.

Chapter 4, *Visual Studio .NET*, introduces the Integrated Development Environment (IDE) designed specifically for .NET; using the IDE can greatly simplify how you write applications.

Chapter 5, *VB.NET Language Fundamentals*, introduces the basic syntax and structure of the VB.NET language, including the intrinsic types, variables, statements, and expressions.

Chapter 6, *Branching*, describes some of the ways you can change the order in which methods are called within a program. Statements such as If, ElseIf, and Select Case will be considered, along with the concept of loops, which are created using such keywords as Do, Do While, and Loop While.

Chapter 7, *Operators*, describes some of the symbols that cause VB.NET to take an action, such as assigning a value to a variable and arithmetically operating on values (adding, subtracting, etc.).

Chapter 8, *Classes and Objects*, introduces the key concepts of programmer-defined types (classes) and instances of those types (objects). Classes and objects are the building blocks of object-oriented programming.

Chapter 9, *Inside Methods*, delves into the specific programming instructions you'll write to define the behavior of objects.

Chapter 10, *Basic Debugging*, introduces the debugger integrated into the Visual Studio .NET Integrated Development Environment.

Chapter 11, *Inheritance and Polymorphism*, explores two of the key concepts behind object-oriented programming and demonstrates how you might implement them in your code.

Chapter 12, *Structures*, introduces the structure or struct, a programmer-defined type similar to a class, but with specific and more limited functionality.

Chapter 13, *Interfaces*, explains how you can define a set of behaviors (an interface) that any number of classes might implement.

Chapter 14, *Arrays*, introduces the array, an indexed collection of objects, all of the same type. Arrays are one of the collection types recognized by VB.NET.

Chapter 15, *Collection Interfaces and Types*, describes some of the other VB.NET collections, including stacks and queues.

Chapter 16, *Strings*, discusses the manipulation of strings of characters, the VB.NET String class, and regular expression syntax.

Chapter 17, *Throwing and Catching Exceptions*, explains how to handle errors and abnormal conditions that may arise in relation to your programs.

Chapter 18, *Applications and Events*, discusses how to write code to respond to programming occurrences like mouse clicks, keystrokes, and other events. The chapter also introduces some of the basic concepts of application programming.

Building serious commercial applications is beyond the scope of a primer like *Learning Visual Basic .NET*. But Chapter 19, *Afterword*, describes where you might go to learn more about VB.NET and .NET programming, including other books, web sites, newsgroups, and so forth.

Conventions Used in This Book

The following font conventions are used in this book:

Italic
> Used for pathnames, filenames, program names, Internet addresses, such as domain names and URLs, and new terms where they are defined.

Constant Width
> Used for command lines and options that should be typed verbatim, VB.NET keywords, and code examples.

Constant Width Italic
> Used for replaceable items, such as variables or optional elements, within syntax lines or code.

Constant Width Bold
> Used for emphasis within program code.

Pay special attention to notes set apart from the text with the following icons:

> This is a tip. It contains useful supplementary information about the topic at hand.

> This is a warning. It helps you solve and avoid annoying problems.

Support

As part of my responsibilities as author, I provide ongoing support for my books through my web site.

> *http://www.LibertyAssociates.com*

On this web site, you'll also find the complete source code for all the examples in *Learning Visual Basic .NET*, as well as access to a book-support discussion group with a section set aside for questions about VB.NET. Before you post a question, however, please check the FAQ (Frequently Asked Questions) list and the errata file on my web site. If you check these files and still have a question, then please go ahead and post to the discussion center.

The most effective way to get help is to ask a precise question or even to create a small program that illustrates your area of concern or confusion. You may also want to check the various newsgroups and discussion centers on the Internet. Microsoft offers a wide array of newsgroups, and Developmentor (*http://www.develop.com*) has wonderful .NET email discussion lists as does Charles Carroll at *http://www.asplists.com*.

We'd Like to Hear from You

We have tested and verified the information in this book to the best of our ability, but you may find that features have changed (or even that we have made mistakes!). Please let us know about any errors you find, as well as your suggestions for future editions, by writing to:

> O'Reilly & Associates, Inc.
> 1005 Gravenstein Highway North
> Sebastopol, CA 95472
> (800) 998-9938 (in the United States or Canada)
> (707) 829-0515 (international/local)
> (707) 829-0104 (fax)

We have a web page for this book where we list examples and any plans for future editions. You can access this information at:

> *http://www.oreilly.com/catalog/learnvbnet*

You can also send messages electronically. To be put on the mailing list or request a catalog, send email to:

> *info@oreilly.com*

To comment on the book, send email to:

> *bookquestions@oreilly.com*

For more information about this book and others, as well as additional technical articles and discussion on the VB.NET and the .NET Framework, see the O'Reilly & Associates web site:

http://www.oreilly.com

and the O'Reilly .NET DevCenter:

http://www.oreillynet.com/dotnet

ONDotnet.com provides independent coverage of fundamental, interoperable, and emerging Microsoft .NET programming and web services technologies.

Acknowledgments

To ensure that *Learning Visual Basic .NET* is accurate, complete, and targeted at the needs and interests of programmers, I enlisted the help of some of the brightest people I know, including Dan Hurwitz, Seth Weiss, and Sue Lynch.

John Osborn signed me to O'Reilly, for which I will forever be in his debt. Darren Kelly, Claire Cloutier, and Tatiana Diaz helped make this book better than what I'd written. Rob Romano created a number of the illustrations and improved the others. Tim O'Reilly provided support and resources, and I'm grateful. A special thank you to Val Quercia, who added great value to this book, as she has to so many others. If this book is clear and understandable, it is due to her vigilance.

CHAPTER 1

Visual Basic .NET and .NET Programming

Learning Visual Basic .NET was written to introduce the .NET version of the Visual Basic language specifically, and the .NET development platform more generally, to programmers with little or no object-oriented programming experience. Along the way, you will learn a great deal about writing high-quality, industrial-strength programs for .NET.

In this brief introduction, you will learn the basics of the Visual Basic .NET language. You will also learn some of the concepts integral to object-oriented programming, which has revolutionized how web and Windows applications are developed.

The goal of this book is to go beyond the syntax of VB.NET (the keywords and punctuation of the language) to examine the semantics of .NET programming with VB.NET (the meaning and structure of the code). VB.NET and the .NET Framework are built on the concepts of object-oriented design and programming, and these concepts will be explained as the book progresses to provide a deeper insight into how .NET programs are organized.

Visual Basic and .NET

Long, long ago, and far, far away, in a little-known universe of primitive computing, there was a language called Basic, which stood for Beginner's All-purpose Symbolic Instruction Code. Basic was designed to be as simple and accessible as possible for those unfamiliar with programming.

In 1991 Microsoft unveiled Visual Basic and changed the way graphical user interfaces were written. Visual Basic can lay claim to being one of the most popular programming languages ever invented.

Visual Basic .NET (VB.NET) is a reengineering of this venerable language, which departs in significant ways from earlier versions of Visual Basic. In fact, some early adopters of VB.NET started calling it VB.*NOT*. VB.NET has evolved into a full-fledged object-oriented commercial software development package. Yet VB.NET also retains some of the inherent simplicity of its predecessors.

VB.NET has a number of features that help it retain backwards compatibility with Visual Basic 6 (VB6). Other features have been added specifically to adapt Visual Basic to object-oriented programming and to the .NET platform.

VB.NET provides support in the language to find bugs early in the development process. This makes for code that is easier to maintain and programs that are more reliable. VB.NET does not support many features available in other languages (e.g., pointers) that make for unsafe code.

In the past, you might have learned a language like C or Java without much concern about the platform on which you would be programming. These cross-platform languages were as comfortable on a Unix box as they were on a PC running Windows.

VB.NET, however, is a version of the Visual Basic language written specifically for .NET. While .NET may become cross-platform some day soon—a Unix port is already available—for now, the overwhelming majority of .NET programs will be written to run on a machine running Windows.

Stepchild No Longer

VB.NET represents a significant step forward for Visual Basic programmers. In the past, VB has been (unfairly) cast as a second-class "toy" language that was not up to the challenge of enterprise-level software development.

Whatever the merits of that accusation for VB6 and its predecessors, it is manifestly untrue for VB.NET. The code produced by Visual Basic .NET is (nearly) identical to that produced by C# or any other compiler designed for .NET. There is *no* performance or size penalty to writing with Visual Basic .NET.

In fact, the differences between Visual Basic .NET and C# are entirely syntactic. To illustrate, one language uses semicolons, the other does not; one language uses brackets, the other parentheses. The differences are so simple and so straightforward, that converting a C# program to Visual Basic .NET is an entirely mechanical operation, one that can be performed by a simple program—and such programs are already available on the Web.

In fact it is not far from the truth to say that at the most fundamental level there is no Visual Basic .NET language and no C# language. There is, rather, a single .NET language called MSIL (Microsoft Intermediate Language). Both Visual Basic .NET and C# compilers produce MSIL code, and the code they produce is nearly identical! The real meat of .NET programming, whether in Visual Basic .NET or in C#, is the .NET platform.

The .NET Platform

In July 2000, Microsoft announced the .NET platform, a development framework that provides a new way to create Windows applications. However, .NET goes beyond traditional Windows programming to facilitate creating web applications quickly and easily. And VB.NET is one of the premier languages Microsoft supports for development in this new and exciting .NET space.

Reports are that Microsoft is devoting 80% of its research and development budget to .NET and its associated technologies. The results of this commitment are impressive. For one thing, the scope of .NET is huge. The platform consists of three separate product groups:

- A set of languages, including Visual Basic .NET and C#; a set of development tools, including Visual Studio .NET; and powerful tools for building applications, including the *Common Language Runtime* (CLR) a platform for compiling, debugging, and executing .NET applications.
- A set of .NET Enterprise Servers, formerly known as SQL Server 2000, Exchange 2000, BizTalk 2000, and so on, that provide specialized functionality for relational data storage, email, B2B commerce, etc.
- New .NET-enabled non-PC devices, from cell phones to game boxes.

The VB.NET language can be used to develop three types of applications you can run on your Windows computer:

- Console applications display no graphics
- Windows applications use the standard Windows interface
- Web applications can be accessed with a browser

This book will focus primarily on the basics of the VB.NET language, mostly using simple console applications to illustrate language fundamentals.

The .NET Framework

Central to the .NET platform is a development environment known as the *.NET Framework*. The Framework specifies how .NET programming constructs such as intrinsic types, classes, and interfaces are implemented. You will learn about these constructs in the chapters ahead.

The .NET Framework sits on top of any flavor of the Windows operating system. The most important components of the Framework are the Common Language Runtime (CLR), described in the preceding section, and the so-called Framework Class Library (FCL), which provides an enormous number of predefined types or classes for you to use in your programs. You will learn how to define your own classes in Chapter 8. Complete coverage of all the FCL classes is beyond the scope of this book. For more information on these classes, see *VB.NET Language in a Nutshell* (Roman, Petrusha, and Lomax, O'Reilly).

The VB.NET Language

The VB.NET language is disarmingly simple, but VB.NET is highly expressive when it comes to implementing modern programming concepts. VB.NET includes all the support for structured, component-based, object-oriented programming that one expects of a modern language.

The goal of VB.NET is to provide a simple, safe, object-oriented, Internet-centric, high-performance language for .NET development. VB.NET is simple because there are relatively few keywords. This makes it easy to learn and easy to adapt to your specific needs.

 Keywords are special words reserved by the language and that have a specific meaning within all VB.NET programs. Keywords include If, While, For, and so forth. You'll learn about these keywords in the coming chapters.

VB.NET is considered safe because it provides support in the language to find bugs early in the development process. This makes for code that is easier to maintain and programs that are more reliable.

VB.NET provides full support for object-oriented programming. This book will explain not only how to write object-oriented programs, but will explain why object-oriented programming has become so popular. The short answer is this: programs are becoming increasingly complex, and object-oriented programming techniques help you manage that complexity.

VB.NET was developed for .NET, and .NET was designed for developing web and web-aware programs. The Internet is a primary resource in most .NET applications.

Finally, VB.NET was designed for professional high-performance programming.

The Structure of VB.NET Applications

At the most fundamental level, a VB.NET application consists of *source code*. Source code is human-readable text written in a text editor. A text editor is like a word processor, but it puts no special characters into the file to support formatting, only the text. A classic text editor is Notepad.

Example 1-1 shows an example of a very simple source code file.

Example 1-1. A source code file

```
Module HelloWorld
    ' every console app starts with Main
    Sub Main()
      System.Console.WriteLine("Hello world!")
    End Sub
End Module
```

This program is explained in detail in Chapter 2. For now, observe that the program itself is readable: it is in normal text. The words may be strange and the layout unusual, but there are no special characters; just the normal text produced by your keyboard.

Once you write your program in an editor, you must compile it. For that you need a compiler. You will learn how to use the VB.NET compiler in Chapter 2. Once compiled, your program must be run and tested.

While you *can* perform all of these tasks using Notepad (or another text editor) and various command-line tools, your programming life will be much easier if you use the Integrated Development Environment (IDE) called Visual Studio .NET. VS.NET was designed with .NET development in mind and greatly simplifies the writing of VB.NET program code.

The Development Environment

The Visual Studio .NET Integrated Development Environment provides enormous advantages to the VB.NET programmer. This book tacitly assumes that you'll use Visual Studio .NET for your work. However, the discussion focuses more on the language and the platform than on the tools.

Nonetheless, Chapter 4 provides a good introduction to the IDE in some detail. Chapter 10 returns to the IDE to examine the debugger, which will help you find and correct problems in your code.

CHAPTER 2
Getting Started with VB.NET

You can use VB.NET to create three different types of programs:

- Web applications
- Windows applications
- Console applications

The .NET platform is web-centric. The VB.NET language was developed to allow .NET programmers to create very large, powerful, high-quality web applications quickly and easily. The .NET technology for creating web applications is called ASP.NET.

ASP.NET, the next generation from ASP (Active Server Pages), is composed of two Microsoft development technologies: Web Forms and Web Services. While the development of fully realized web applications using these technologies is beyond the scope of this book, learning the basics of the VB.NET language will certainly get you started in the right direction. VB.NET is generally acknowledged to be one of the languages of choice for ASP.NET development.

Typically, you'll create an ASP.NET application when you want your program to be available to end users on any platform (e.g., Windows, Mac, Unix). By serving your application over the Web, end users can access your program with any browser.

When you want the richness and power of a native application running directly on the Windows platform, alternatively you might create a desktop-bound Windows application. The .NET tools for building Windows applications are called Windows Forms; a detailed analysis of this technology is also beyond the scope of this book.

However, if you don't need a Graphical User Interface (GUI) and just want to write a simple application that talks to a console window (i.e., what we used to call a DOS box), you might consider creating a console application. This book makes extensive use of console applications to illustrate the basics of the VB.NET language.

Web, Windows, and console applications are described and illustrated in the following pages.

Console applications

A console application runs in a console window, as shown in Figure 2-1. A console window (or DOS box) provides simple text-based output.

Console applications are very helpful when learning a language because they strip away the distraction of the Graphical User Interface. Rather than spending your time creating complex windowing applications, you can focus on the details of the language constructs, such as how you create classes and methods, how you branch based on runtime conditions, and how you loop. All these topics will be covered in detail in coming chapters.

Figure 2-1. A console application

Windows applications

A Windows application runs on a PC's desktop. You are already familiar with Windows applications such as Microsoft Word or Excel. Windows applications are much more complex than console applications and can take advantage of the full suite of menus, controls, and other widgets you've come to expect in a modern desktop application. Figure 2-2 shows the output of a simple windows application.

Figure 2-2. A Windows application

ASP.NET applications

An ASP.NET application runs on a web server and delivers its functionality through a browser, typically over the Web. ASP.NET technology facilitates developing web applications quickly and easily. Figure 2-3 shows a message from a simple ASP.NET application.

Although most commercial applications will be either Windows or ASP.NET programs, console applications have a tremendous advantage in a VB.NET primer. Windows and ASP.NET applications bring a lot more overhead; there is great complexity in managing the window and all the events associated with the window. (Events are covered in Chapter 18.) Console applications keep things simple, allowing you to focus on the features of the language.

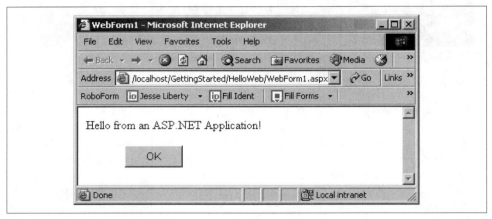

Figure 2-3. An ASP.NET application

This book does not ever go into all the myriad details of building robust Windows and ASP.NET applications. For complete coverage of these topics, please see *Programming ASP.NET* and *Programming .NET Windows Applications* both by Jesse Liberty and Dan Hurwitz (O'Reilly).

What's in a Program?

A program consists of English-language instructions called *source code*. The syntax for these instructions is strictly defined by the language. Source code consists of a series of statements. A statement is an instruction to the complier. Each instruction must be formed correctly, and one task you'll face when learning VB.NET will be to learn the correct syntax of the language. For example, in VB.NET every statement ends with a carriage return or linefeed.

Each instruction has a semantic meaning that expresses what it is you are trying to accomplish. Although you must follow the syntax, the semantics of the language are far more important in developing effective object-oriented programs. This book will provide insight into both the syntax and the semantics of good VB.NET programs.

You will save the source code you write in a text file. You can write this source code file using any simple text editor (such as Notepad), or you can use the Visual Studio .NET Integrated Development Environment (IDE). Visual Studio .NET is described in Chapter 4.

Once you write your program, you compile it using the VB.NET compiler. The end result of compiling the program is an application.

Your First Program: Hello World

In this chapter, you will create a very simple application that does nothing more than display the words "Hello World" to your monitor. This basic console application is the traditional first program for learning any new language; it demonstrates some of the basic elements of a VB.NET program.

Once you write your "Hello World" program and compile it, this chapter will provide a line-by-line analysis of the source code. This analysis gives something of a preview of the language, the fundamentals of which are described much more fully in Chapter 5.

As explained earlier, you can create VB.NET programs with any text editor. You can, for example, create each of the three programs shown previously (in Figure 2-1, Figure 2-2, and Figure 2-3) with Notepad. To demonstrate that this is possible, you'll write your very first VB.NET program using Notepad.

Begin by opening Notepad and typing in the program exactly as shown in Example 2-1.

Example 2-1. Hello World in Notepad

```
Module HelloWorld
    ' every console app starts with Main
    Sub Main()
        System.Console.WriteLine("Hello world!")
    End Sub
End Module
```

That is the entire program. Save it to your disk as a file called *helloworld.vb*.

We'll examine this program in some detail in just a moment. First, however, it must be compiled.

The Compiler

Once you save your program to disk, you must compile the code to create your application. Compiling your source code means running a compiler and passing in the source code file. You run the compiler by opening a command prompt (DOS box) and entering the program name *vbc*. Then you "pass in" your source code file by entering the filename on the command line, as in the following:

```
vbc helloworld.vb
```

The job of the compiler is to turn your source code into a working program. It turns out to be just slightly more complicated than that, because .NET uses an intermediate language called Microsoft Intermediate Language (MSIL, sometimes abbreviated to IL). The compiler reads your source code and produces IL. The .NET Just In Time (JIT) compiler then reads your IL code and produces an executable application in memory.

Microsoft provides a command window (through Visual Studio .NET) with the correct environment variables set. Open a command window by selecting the following menu items in this order:

```
Start -> Programs -> Microsoft Visual Studio .NET
-> Visual Studio.NET Tools -> Visual Studio .NET Command Prompt
```

Then navigate to the directory in which you created your code file and enter the following command:

```
vbc helloworld.vb
```

The Microsoft VB.NET compiler compiles your code; when you display the directory you'll find the compiler has produced an executable file called *helloworld.exe*. Type *helloworld* at the command prompt, and your program will execute, as shown in Figure 2-4.

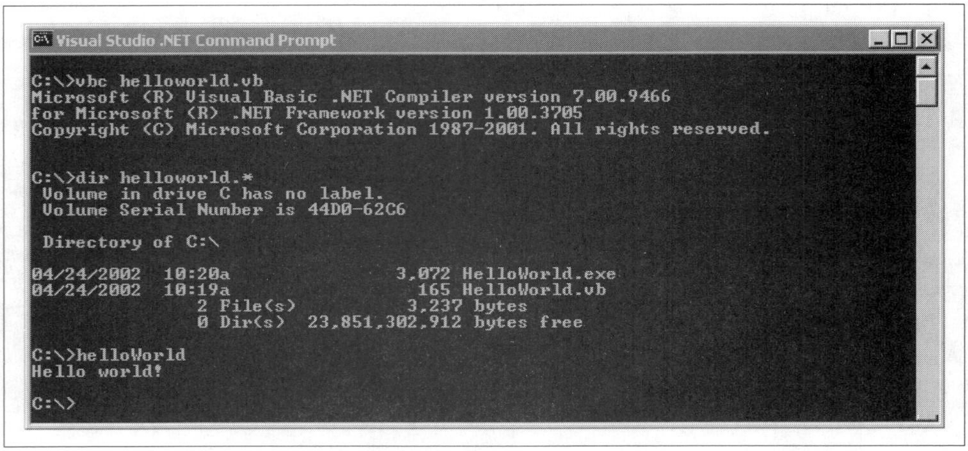

Figure 2-4. Compiling and running Hello World

Presto! You are a VB.NET programmer. That's it, close the book, you've done it. Okay, don't close the book; there are details to examine, but take a moment to congratulate yourself. Have a cookie.

Granted, the program you created is one of the simplest VB.NET programs imaginable, but it is a complete VB.NET program, and it can be used to examine many of the elements common to VB.NET programs.

Examining Your First Program

The single greatest challenge when learning to program is that you must learn everything before you can learn anything. Even this simple "Hello World" program uses many features of the language that will be discussed in coming chapters, including classes, namespaces, statements, static methods, objects, strings, inheritance, blocks, libraries, and even something called polymorphism!

It is as if you were learning to drive a car. You must learn to steer, accelerate, brake, and understand the flow of traffic. Right now we're going to get you out on the highway and just let you steer for a while. Over time you'll learn how to speed up and slow down. Along the way you'll learn to set the radio and adjust the heat so that you'll be more comfortable. In no time you'll be driving, and then won't your parents begin to worry.

Line-by-Line Analysis

Hang on tight; we're going to zip through this quickly and come back to the details in subsequent chapters. The first line in the program defines a programming unit known as a *module*. In this case, the module is named HelloWorld:

```
Module HelloWorld
```

You begin each module definition using the Module keyword, as in the preceding code line. Likewise, you end each module definition with the line:

```
End Module
```

Within the module definition, you write other programming constructs. For instance, you might define what is called an *object*. An object is an individual instance of a thing. Every object belongs to a more general category known as a *class*. While a class defines a type, each instance of that type is an object (much as Car defines a type of vehicle, and your aging rust-bucket is an individual instance of Car).

In VB.NET there are thousands of classes. Classes are used to define Windows controls (buttons, list boxes, etc.), as well as types of things (employees, students, telephones, etc.) in the program you are writing. Some classes you create yourself; some you obtain from the .NET Framework. Each class must be named. Classes are the core of VB.NET and object-oriented programming.

For now, keep in mind that modules are actually related to classes. Technically, modules are a holdover from the previous generation of the VB language, VB6. In order to adapt VB6 for object-oriented programming, VB.NET converts modules to classes for you. You'll learn about classes in Chapter 3 and about modules and classes in Chapter 8.

Within the HelloWorld module, you define a *method* called Main(). A method is a small block of code that performs an action. The Main() method is the "entry point" for every VB.NET console application; it is where your program begins. Within the HelloWorld module, the Main() method is defined from lines 3 through 5. Notice the Sub keyword signals the beginning of the subroutine and the End Sub line concludes the method:

```
Sub Main()
    System.Console.WriteLine("Hello world!")
End Sub
```

Typically, one method calls another. The called method will do work, and it can return a value to the calling method. In VB.NET, methods come in two flavors: a method that returns a value is called a *function*; a method that does not return a value is called a *sub* (for subroutine). (Function and subroutine are old, non-object-oriented terms for these kinds of methods.) You'll see how methods call one another and return values in Chapter 9.

Main() is called by the operating system (when the program is invoked). Every method name is followed by opening and closing parentheses:

```
Sub Main()
```

As the parentheses imply, it is possible to pass values into a method so that the method can manipulate or use those values. These values are called *parameters* or *arguments* to the method. In this case, Main() has no arguments. (Method arguments are covered in Chapter 9.)

Within Main() is a single line of code:

```
System.Console.WriteLine("Hello world!")
```

WriteLine() is a method that is called by the Main() method; more about WriteLine() shortly. The Console is an object that represents your screen. In this case, each Console object belongs to the Console class. In VB.NET, classes can exist within a more comprehensive grouping known as a *namespace*.

In the HelloWorld program, the Console class is defined within the System namespace. The Console class has a method, WriteLine(), that displays a line of text to the screen. The complete identification for the WriteLine() method includes the class and namespace to which it belongs:

```
System.Console.WriteLine("Hello world!")
```

The WriteLine() method declares a single parameter, the text string you want to display. When you pass in a string to the method, the string is an argument. In our sample program, the string "Hello world!" corresponds to the parameter the method expects; thus, the string is displayed to the screen.

If you will be using many objects from the same namespace, you can save typing by telling the compiler that many of the objects you'll be referring to are in that namespace. You do so by adding an Imports declaration to the beginning of your program:

```
Imports System
```

Once you add this line, you can use the Console class name without explicitly identifying its namespace (System). Thus, if you add the preceding Imports declaration, you can rewrite the contents of Main() as follows:

```
Console.WriteLine("Hello world!")
```

The compiler will check the namespace you identified (System), and it will find the Console class defined there.

Since the method (or sub) is defined within the module, you do not close the module until you have closed the method. Thus, the program ends with the sequence:

```
    End Sub
End Module
```

This discussion has omitted a single line in our program. Just before the start of the Main() method appears a comment (here in bold):

```
' every console app starts with Main
Sub Main()
    System.Console.WriteLine("Hello world!")
```

A comment is just a note to yourself. You insert comments to make the code more readable to programmers. You can place comments anywhere in your program that you think the explanation will be helpful; they have no effect on the running program.

In VB.NET, comments begin with a single quotation mark. The quote indicates that everything to the right on the same line is a comment and will be ignored by the VB.NET compiler.

Whew! That was a lot to take in all at once! Don't panic; all of the concepts introduced here are explained in detail in later chapters.

CHAPTER 3
Object-Oriented Programming

Windows and web programs are enormously complex. Programs present information to users in graphically rich ways, offering complicated user interfaces, complete with drop-down and pop-up menus, buttons, listboxes, and so forth. Behind these interfaces, programs model complex business relationships, such as those among customers, products, orders, and inventory. You can interact with such a program in hundreds, if not thousands of different ways, and the program must respond appropriately every time.

To manage this enormous complexity, programmers have developed a technique called object-oriented programming. It is based on a very simple premise: you manage complexity by modeling its essential aspects. The closer your program models the problem you are trying to solve, the easier it is to understand (and thus to write and to maintain) that program.

Programmers refer to the problem you are trying to solve and all the information you know that relates to your problem as the *problem domain*. For example, if you are writing a program to manage the inventory and sales of a company, the problem domain would include everything you know about how the company acquires and manages inventory, makes sales, handles the income from sales, tracks sales figures, and so forth. The sales manager and the stock room manager would be problem domain experts who can help you understand the problem domain.

A well-designed object-oriented program will be filled with objects from the problem domain. At the first level of design, you'll think about how these objects interact, and what their state, capabilities, and responsibilities are.

State
> A programmer refers to the current conditions and values of an object as that object's state. For example, you might have an object representing a customer. The customer's state includes the customer's address, phone number, email, as well as the customer's credit rating, recent purchase history, and so forth.

Capabilities

The customer has many capabilities, but a developer cares only about modeling those that are relevant to the problem domain. Thus a customer object might be able to buy an item, return an item, increase his credit rating, and so forth.

Responsibilities

Along with capabilities come responsibilities. The customer object is responsible for managing its own address. In a well-designed program, no other object needs to know the details of the customer's address. The address might be stored as data within the customer object, or it might be stored in a database, but it is up to the customer object to know how to retrieve and update his own address.

Of course, all of the objects in your program are just *metaphors* for the objects in your problem domain.

Metaphors

Many of the concepts used throughout this book, and any book on programming, are actually metaphors. We get so used to the metaphors we forget that they are metaphors. You are used to talking about a window on your program, but of course there is no such thing; there is just a rectangle with text and images in it. It looks like a window into your document so we call it a window. Of course, you don't actually have a document either, just bits in memory. No folders, no buttons, these are all just metaphors.

There are many levels to these metaphors. When you see a window on the screen, the window itself is just a metaphor enhanced by an image drawn on your screen. That image is created by lighting tiny dots on the screen, called *pixels*. These pixels are lit in response to instructions written in your VB.NET program. Each instruction is really a metaphor; the actual instructions read by your computer are in *Assembly* language, low-level instructions that are fed to the underlying computer chip. These Assembly instructions map to a series of 1s and 0s that the chip understands. Of course, the 1s and zeros are just metaphors for electricity in wires. When two wires meet, we measure the amount of electricity and if there is a threshold amount we call it 1, otherwise zero. You get the idea.

Good metaphors can be very powerful. The art of object-oriented programming is really the art of conceiving of good metaphors.

Creating Models

Humans are model-builders. We create models of the world to manage complexity and to help us understand problems were trying to solve. You see models all the time. Maps are models of roadways. Globes are models of the Earth. Chemical symbols are models of chemical interactions. Atomic models are representations of the interaction of subatomic particles.

Models are simplifications. There is little point to a model that is as complex as the object in the problem domain. If you had a map of the United States that had every rock, blade of grass, and bit of dirt in the entire country, the map would have to be as big as the country itself. Your road atlas of the U.S. eschews all sorts of irrelevant detail, focusing only on those aspects of the problem domain (e.g., the country's roads) that are important to solving the problem (e.g., getting from place to place). If you want to drive from Boston to New York City, you don't care where the trees are; you care where the exits and interchanges are located. Therefore, the network of roads is what appears on the atlas.

Albert Einstein once said: Things should be made as simple as possible, but not any simpler. A model must be faithful to those aspects of the problem domain that are relevant. For example, a road map must provide accurate relative distances. The distance from Boston to New York must be proportional to the actual driving distance. If one inch represents 25 miles at the start of the trip, it must represent 25 miles throughout the trip, or the map will be unusable.

A good object-oriented design is an accurate model of the problem you are trying to solve. Your design choices will influence not only how you solve the problem, but in fact they will influence how you think about the problem. A good design, like a good model, allows you to examine the relevant details of the problem without confusion.

Classes and Objects

The most important metaphors in object-oriented programming are the class and the object.

A *class* defines a new type of thing. The class defines the common characteristics of every object of that new type. For example, you might define a class Car. Every car will share certain characteristics (wheels, brake, accelerator, and so forth). Your car and my car both belong to the class of Cars; they are of type Car.

An *object* is an individual instance of a class. Each individual car (your particular car, my particular car) is an instance of the class Car, and thus is an object. An object is just a thing.

We perceive the world to be composed of things. Look at your computer. You do not see various bits of plastic and glass amorphously merging with the surrounding environment. You naturally and inevitably see distinct things: a computer, a keyboard, a monitor, speakers, pens, paper. Things.

More importantly, even before you decide to do it, you've categorized these things. You immediately classify the computer on your desk as a specific instance of a type of thing: this computer is one of the type Computer. This pen is an instance of a more general type of thing, pens. It is so natural you can't avoid it, and yet the process is so subtle, it's difficult to articulate. When I see my dog Milo, I can't help also seeing him *as a dog*, not just as an individual entity. Milo is an instance, Dog is a class.

The theory behind object-oriented programming is that for computer programs to accurately model the world, the programs should reflect this human tendency to think about individual things and types of things. In VB.NET you do that by creating a class to define a type and creating an object to model a thing.

Defining a Class

When you define a class you describe the characteristics and behavior of objects of that type. In VB.NET, you describe characteristics with *member fields*, also known as *properties*.

```
Class Dog
    Private weight As Integer  ' weight is an integer
    Private name As String     ' the Dog's name as text
```

Member fields are used to hold each objects state. For example, the state of the Dog is defined by its current weight and name. The state of an Employee might be defined by (among other things) her current salary, management level, and performance rating. Chapter 8 includes a full discussion of member fields.

You define the behavior of your new type with *methods*. Methods contain code to perform an action.

```
Class Dog
    Private weight As Integer  ' weight is an integer
    Private name As String     ' the Dog's name as text
    Public Sub bark()
       'code here to bark
    End Sub
```

 The keywords Public and Private are known as *access modifiers*, which are used to specify what classes can access particular members. For instance, public members can be called from methods in any class, while private members are visible only to the methods of the class that defines the member. Thus, objects of any class can call bark on a Dog, but only methods of Dog have access to the weight and name of the Dog. Access modifiers are discussed in Chapter 8.

A class typically defines a number of methods to do the work of that class. A Dog class might contain methods for barking, eating, napping, and so forth. An Employee class might contain methods for adjusting salary, submitting annual reviews, and evaluating performance objectives.

Methods can manipulate the state of the object by changing the values in member fields, or a method could interact with other objects of its own type or with objects of other types. This interaction among objects is crucial to object-oriented programming.

For example, a Dog method might change the state of the Dog (e.g., weight), interact with other Dogs (e.g., bark, sniff, etc.), or interact with People (e.g., beg for food). A Product object might interact with a Customer object, a Video object might interact with an EditingWindow object.

Designing a good VB.NET program is not unlike forming a good team; you look for players—or objects, in the case of a program—with different skills to whom you can assign the various tasks you must accomplish. Those players cooperate with one another to get the job done.

In a good object-oriented program, you will design objects that represent things in your problem domain. You will then divide the work of the program among your objects, assigning responsibility to objects based on their ability.

Class Relationships

The heart of object-oriented design is establishing relationships among the classes. Classes interact and relate to one another in various ways.

The simplest interaction is when a method in one class is used to call a method in a second class. For example, the Manager class might have a method that calls the UpdateSalary method on an object of type Employee. We then say that the Manager class and the Employee class are *associated*. Association among classes simply means they interact.

Some complicated types are *composed* of other types. For example, an automobile might be composed of wheels, engine, transmission, and so forth. You might model this by creating a wheel class, an engine class and a transmission class. You could then create an Automobile class, and each automobile would have four instances of the wheel class, and one instance each of the engine and transmission class. Another way to view this relationship is to say that the Automobile class *aggregates* the wheel, engine, and transmission classes.

This process of aggregation (or composition) allows you to build very complex classes from relatively simple classes. The .NET Framework provides a String class to handle text strings. You might create your own Address class out of five text strings (address line 1, address line 2, city, state, and Zip). You might then create a second class, Employee, which has as one of its members an instance of Address.

The Three Pillars of Object-Oriented Programming

Object-oriented programming is built on three sturdy pillars: *encapsulation*, *specialization*, and *polymorphism*.

Each class should be fully encapsulated; that is, it should define the state and responsibilities of that type. For example, if you create an Employee object, that Employee object should fully define all there is to know, from the perspective of your program, about each Employee. You do not, typically, want to have one class that defines the Employee's work information, and a second, unrelated class that defines the Employee's contact information. Instead, you want to encapsulate all this information inside the Employee class, perhaps by aggregating the contact information as a member of the Employee class.

Specialization allows you to establish hierarchical relationships among your classes. For example, you can define a Manager to be a specialized type of an Employee and an Employee to be a specialized type of Person. This allows you to leverage the state and abilities of an Employee object in the more specialized form of the Manager.

Polymorphism allows you to treat a group of objects in a similar way and have the objects sort out how to implement the programming instructions. For instance, suppose you have a collection of Employee objects, and you want to tell each Employee to give herself a raise. Employees get a straight 5% raise, while raises for Managers are determined by how well they've fulfilled their annual objectives. With polymorphism, you can tell each object in the collection to give itself a raise, and the right thing happens regardless of the real type of the object. That is, each employee gets 5%, while each manager gets the appropriate raise based on objectives.

Encapsulation

The first pillar of object-oriented programming is encapsulation. The idea behind encapsulation is that you want to keep each type or class discreet and self-contained. This allows you to change the implementation of one class without affecting any other class.

A class that provides a method that other classes can use is called a *server*. A class that uses that method is called a *client*. The goal of encapsulation is that you can change the details of how a server does its work without breaking anything in the implementation of the client.

This is accomplished by drawing a bright and shining line between the *public interface* of a class and its *private implementation*. The public interface is a contract issued by your class that says, I promise to be able to do this work. Specifically, you'll see that a public interface says call this method with these parameters, and I'll do this work and return this value. A client can rely on a public interface not to change. If the public interface does change, then the client must be recompiled and perhaps redesigned.

The private implementation, on the other hand, is, as its name implies, private to the server. The designer of the server class is free to change *how* it does the work promised in the public interface, so long as it continues to fulfill the terms of its implicit contract: it must take the given parameters, do the promised work and return the promised value.

For example, you might have a public method that promises as follows: Give me a dollar amount and a number of years, and I'll return the net present value. How you compute that amount is your business; if a client supplies a dollar amount and a number of years, you must return the net present value. You might implement that initially by keeping a table of values. You might change that at a later time to compute the value using the appropriate algebra. That is your business and does not affect the client. As long as you don't change the public interface (e.g., as long as you don't change the number or type of parameters expected or change the type of the return value,) your clients will not break while you change the implementation.

Specialization

The second pillar, specialization, is implemented in VB.NET by declaring that a new class derives from an existing class. When you do so, the specialized class inherits the characteristics of the more general class. The specialized class is called a *derived* class, while the more general class is known as a *base* class.

The specialization relationship is referred to as the *is-a* relationship. A dog *is a* mammal, a car *is a* vehicle. (Dog would be derived from the base class Mammal, Car from the base class Vehicle.)

Specialization allows you to create a family of objects. In Windows a button *is a* control. A listbox *is a* control. Controls have certain characteristics (color, size, location) and certain abilities (can be drawn, can be selected). These characteristics and abilities are inherited by all of their derived types. This allows for a very powerful form of reuse. Rather than cutting and pasting code from one type to another, the shared fields and methods are inherited by the derived type. If you change how a shared ability is implemented, you do not have to update code in every derived type; they inherit the changes.

For example, a Manager is a special type of Employee. The Manager adds new capabilities (hiring, firing, rewarding, praising) and a new state (annual objectives, management level, etc.). The Manager, however, also inherits the characteristics and capabilities common to all Employees. Thus a Manager has an address, a name, an employee ID, and Managers can be given raises, can be laid off, and so forth. You'll see specialization at work in Chapter 11.

Polymorphism

Polymorphism, the third pillar of object-oriented programming, is closely related to inheritance. The prefix *poly* means many; *morph* means form. Thus, polymorphism refers to the ability of a single type or class to take many forms.

The essence of polymorphism is this: at times you will know you have a collection of a general type, for example a collection of Controls. You do not know (or care) what the specific subtype each of your controls is (one may be a button, another a listbox, etc.). The important thing is that you know they all inherit shared abilities (e.g., the draw method) and that you can treat them all as controls. If you write a programming instruction that tells each control to draw itself, this is implemented properly on a per-control basis (i.e., buttons draw as buttons, listboxes draw as listboxes, etc.). You do not need to know how each subtype accomplishes this; you only need to know that each type is defined to be able to draw.

Polymorphism allows you to treat a collection of disparate derived types (buttons, listboxes, etc.) as a group. You treat the general group of controls the same way, and each individual control does the right thing according to its specific type. Chapter 11 provides more concrete examples.

Object-Oriented Analysis and Design

The steps before programming anything, other than a trivial demonstration program, are analysis and design. Analysis is the process of understanding and detailing the problem you are trying to solve. Design is the actual planning of your solution.

With trivial problems (e.g., computing the Fibonacci series[*]), you may not need an extensive analysis period, but with complex business problems, the analysis process can take weeks, or even months. One powerful analysis technique is to create what are called use-case scenarios, in which you describe in some detail how the system will be used. Among the other considerations in the analysis period are determining your success factors (how do you know if your program works) and writing a specification of your program's requirements.

Once you've analyzed the problem, you design the solution. Key to the design process is imagining the classes you will use and their inter-relationships. You might design a simple program on the fly, without this careful planning; but in any serious business application, you will want to take some time to think through the issues.

---

[*] The Fibonacci series is the values 0,1,1,2,3,5,8,13. The series is named for Fibonacci, who in 1202 investigated how fast rabbits could breed in ideal circumstances. The series works by adding the previous two numbers to get the next (thus 8 is the sum of 5+3).

There are many powerful design techniques you might use. One interesting controversy that has arisen recently is between traditional object-oriented design on the one hand* and eXtreme programming on the other.†

There are other competing approaches as well. How much time you put into these topics will depend, in large measure, on the complexity of the problems you are trying to solve and the size of your development team.

 My personal approach to managing complexity is to keep team size very small. I have worked on large development teams, and over the years I've come to believe that the ideal size is three. Three highly skilled programmers can be incredibly productive, and with three you don't need a manager. Three people can have only one conversation at a time. Three people can never be evenly split on a decision. One day I'll write a book on programming in teams of three, but this isn't it, and so we'll stay focused on VB.NET programming, rather than on design debates.

About the Examples in This Book

Object-oriented programming is designed to help you manage complex programs. Unfortunately, it is very difficult to show complex problems and their solutions in a primer on VB.NET. The complexity of these problems gets in the way of what you're trying to learn about.

The examples in this book will be extremely simple. The simplicity may hide some of the motivation for the technique, but the simplicity makes the technique clearer. You'll have to take it on faith, for now, that these techniques scale up well to very complex problems.

Most of the chapters of this book focus on the syntax of VB.NET. You need the syntax of the language to be able to write a program at all, but it's important to keep in mind that the syntax of any language is less important than its semantics. The meaning of what you are writing and why you're writing it are the real focus of object-oriented programming and thus of this book.

Don't let concern with syntax get in the way of understanding the semantics. The compiler can help you get the syntax right (if only by complaining when you get it wrong), and the documentation can remind you of the syntax, but understanding the semantics, the meaning of the construct, is the hard part. Throughout this book, I work hard to explain not only *how* you do something, but *why* and *when* you do it.

---

* See *The Unified Modeling Language User Guide*, by Grady Booch, Ivar Jacobson, and James Rumbaugh (Addison-Wesley); *The Unified Software Development Process*, by Ivar Jacobson, Grady Booch, and James Rumbaugh (Addison-Wesley); and *The Unified Modeling Language Reference Manual*, by James Rumbaugh, Ivar Jacobson, and Grady Booch (Addison-Wesley).

† See *Planning Extreme Programming* by Kent Beck and Martin Fowler (Addison-Wesley).

CHAPTER 4

Visual Studio .NET

In Chapter 2 you learned that you *can* create your VB.NET applications using Note-pad. In this chapter, you'll learn why you never *will*. Microsoft developed Visual Studio .NET (VS.NET) to facilitate the creation of Windows and web applications. You will find that this Integrated Development Environment (IDE) is a *very* powerful tool that will greatly simplify your work.

Visual Studio .NET offers many advantages to the .NET developer. The following features are discussed in this chapter:

- A modern interface using a tabbed document metaphor for source code and layout screens, and toolbars and informational windows that dock where you want them.

- Code completion, which enables you to enter code with fewer errors and much less typing.

- IntelliSense, which pops up help on every method and function call as you type.

- Dynamic, context-sensitive help, which allows you to view topics and samples relevant to the code you are writing at the moment.

- Immediate flagging of syntax errors (e.g., missing characters, misplaced braces, etc.), which allows you to fix problems as they are entered.

- The ability to compile and test programs right in the IDE.

- A built-in task list to keep track of changes you need to make.

- A Start Page that provides easy access to new and existing projects.

- Customization capability, which allows you to set user preferences for IDE appearance and behavior.

One VS.NET feature will be so important to you, even as a VB.NET novice, that it actually merits its own chapter: An integrated debugger, which enables you to step through code, observe program runtime behavior, and set breakpoints, even across multiple languages. The debugger is considered in detail in Chapter 10.

In addition to these basic capabilities, VS.NET provides a number of advanced features that will simplify the development process. These features include:

- Convenient access to multiple design and code windows.
- WYSIWYG (What You See Is What You Get) visual design of Windows forms and web forms.
- An HTML editor, which provides both Design and HTML views that update each other in real time.
- A Solution Explorer, which displays all the files that make up your solution (a collection of projects) in a hierarchical format.
- A Server Explorer, which allows you to log on to servers to which you have network access, access the data and services on those servers, and perform a variety of other chores.
- Integrated support for source control software.

Many of these advanced features are covered in detail in *Programming ASP.NET* and *Programming .NET Windows Applications* (both books cowritten by Jesse Liberty and Dan Hurwitz, published by O'Reilly).

Robert Heinlein said "TANSTAAFL: There ain't no such thing as a free lunch."* While Visual Studio .NET can save you a lot of grunt typing (and in general greatly facilitate and accelerate the development process), on the negative side the automatically generated code can obscure what is really necessary to create good working applications. It is sometimes difficult to know how Visual Studio .NET accomplishes its legerdemain. Similarly, the proliferation of mysteriously named files across your filesystem can be disconcerting when all you want to do is a simple housekeeping chore, like rename a minor part of the project.

Since most of the applications we'll build in this book are console applications designed to illustrate the basics of the language, very little obscuring code will be produced. When you go on to create Windows and web applications, however, you'll want to learn to sort through the code Visual Studio .NET generates in order to focus on the logic of your program.

The current chapter cannot possibly teach you everything about Visual Studio .NET; it is far too large and complex an application. What this chapter does is give you the basics for getting started and also point out some of the possible pitfalls.

 Keep in mind that there's no way to familiarize you with some of these features without wading into some slightly deeper waters of VB.NET programming, which will likely be a bit cloudy to you at this stage. As you get deeper into the book and learn more about the language, your understanding of VB.NET will become clearer.

---

* Robert A. Heinlein, *The Moon Is a Harsh Mistress* (St. Martin's Press).

Start Page

The Start Page is the first thing you see when you open Visual Studio .NET (unless you configure it otherwise). From here you can create new projects or open a project you worked on in a previous session. You can also find out what is new in .NET, access .NET newsgroups and web sites, search for help online, download useful code, or adjust Visual Studio .NET to your personal requirements. Figure 4-1 shows a typical Start Page.

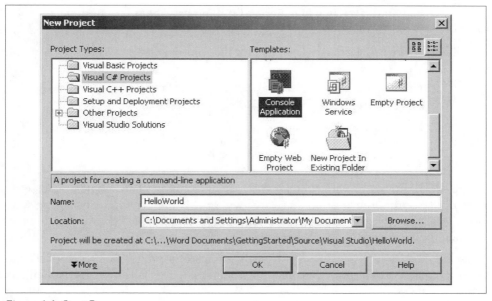

Figure 4-1. Start Page

Along the top of the application window is a set of menus and buttons. These menus and buttons are context-sensitive (i.e., they will change as the current window changes).

Along the left side of the window is a series of links to other resources, such as new developments and events in the .NET community, the MSDN online library, and free sample applications.

Projects and Solutions

A VB.NET program is built from source files, text files containing the code you write. Source code files are named with the *.vb* extension. The *helloworld.vb* file you created in Chapter 2 is a typical example.

A typical Visual Studio .NET application can have a number of other files (e.g., assembly information files, references, icons, data connections, etc.). VS.NET organizes these files into a container called a *project*.

Visual Studio .NET provides two types of containers for your source code, folders, files, and related material: the project and the solution. A project is a set of files that work together to create an executable program (*.exe*) or a dynamic link library (*.dll*). Large, complex projects may consist of multiple *.dll* files called modules.

A solution is a set of one or more related projects. Each time you create a new project, Visual Studio .NET will either add it to an existing solution or create a new solution.

Solutions are defined within a file named for the solution and have the extension *.sln*.

> The *.sln* file contains metadata, which is basically information about the data. The metadata describes the projects that compose the solution and information about building the solution. Visual Studio .NET also creates a file with the same base name as the *.sln* file, but with the filename extension *.sou* (e.g., *mySolution.sln* and *mySolution.sou*). The *.sou* file contains metadata used to customize the IDE.

There are a number of ways to open an existing solution. The simplest is to select Open Project from the Start menu (which will open a project and its enclosing solution). Alternatively, you can open a solution in Visual Studio .NET just by double-clicking the *.sln* file in Windows Explorer.

Typically, the build process results in the contents of a project being compiled into an executable (*.exe*) file or a dynamic link library (*.dll*) file. This book focuses on creating executable files.

> The metadata describing the project is contained in a file named after the project with the extension *.vbproj*. The project file contains version information, build settings, and references to other source files to include as part of the project.

Templates

When you create a new project, you get the New Project dialog box, shown in Figure 4-2.

In the New Project dialog, you select the project type (in the lefthand pane) and the template (in the right). There are a variety of templates for each project type. A template is a file that Visual Studio .NET uses to set up the initial state of your project.

For the examples in this book, you'll always choose Visual Basic Projects for the project type, and in most cases, you'll choose Console Application as the template.

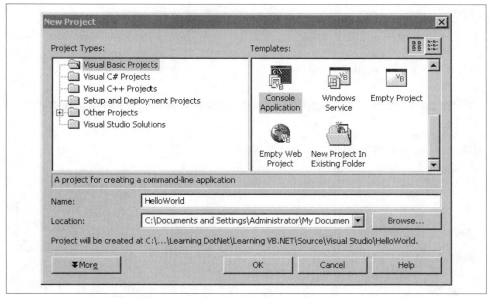

Figure 4-2. New Project dialog lets you choose a project template

Specify the name of the directory in which your project will be stored (any directory you like). At this point, you can also name your project. For the purposes of example, enter the name HelloWorld.

> Project names can contain any standard characters, except leading or trailing spaces, Windows or DOS keywords, and any of the following special characters:
>
> # % & * | \ : " < > ? /

Inside the Integrated Development Environment (IDE)

The Visual Studio .NET IDE is centered around an editor. An editor is much like a word processor, except that it produces simple text (i.e., without formatting, such as bold, italics, etc.). As you may recall, source code files are simple text files.

The Visual Studio .NET IDE also provides support for building GUIs, which are integral to Windows and web projects. The following pages introduce some of the key features of the IDE.

Layout

The IDE is a Multiple Document Interface (MDI) application. There is a main window, and within the main window are a number of smaller windows. The central window is the text editing window. Figure 4-3 shows the basic layout.

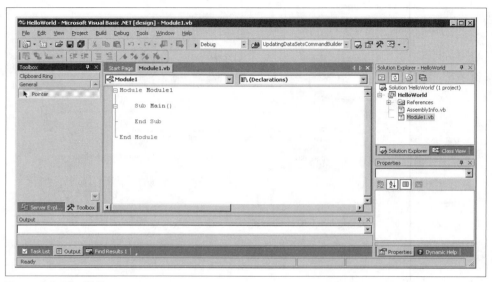

Figure 4-3. The IDE

To the left of the editing window are a number of tabbed windows that contain tools used when creating Windows and web applications. To the right of the editing window is a window called the Solution Explorer. This window shows the files in the current project and the solution to which the project belongs.

In the lower-right corner is the dynamic help window. In the lower-left corner are a number of tabbed windows, including the task list. The IDE will add tasks to this list when your program has errors that must be fixed, and you can add tasks of your own to assist you in remembering what work remains to be done.

All of these windows are resizable and dockable, and many windows share space by using tabs. They can be resized by placing the mouse cursor over the edge you want to move. The cursor will change to a double arrow resizing cursor, at which point you can drag the window edge one way or the other.

The Visual Studio .NET window has a titlebar across the top, with menus below. Under the menus are toolbars with buttons that duplicate many of the common menu commands. Nearly everything that can be done through menus can also be done with context-sensitive pop-up menus, as described shortly.

By default, the toolbars are docked along the top of the window. As with many Windows applications, they can be undocked and moved to other locations, either left free-floating or docked along other window edges. You move the toolbars by grabbing them with the mouse and dragging them where you want.

Right-clicking on the titlebar of a dockable window pops up a menu with three mutually exclusive check items that let you customize the behavior of the window:

Dockable
> Specifies that the window can be dragged and docked along any side of the Visual Studio .NET window.

Hide
> Makes the window disappear, temporarily. To see the window again—that is, to unhide it—use the View item on the main menu. (The Pushpin icon, described shortly, also affects this behavior.)

Floating
> Specifies that the window will not dock when dragged against the edge of the VS.NET window. Then the floating window can be placed anywhere on the desktop, even outside the VS.NET window.

In the upper-right corner of the main IDE window are two icons:

Pushpin
> This icon toggles the AutoHide property of the window. When the pushpin is pointing down, the window is pinned in place—that is, AutoHide is turned off. Moving the cursor off the window will not affect its visibility.
>
> When the pushpin is pointing sideways, AutoHide is turned on. Moving the cursor off the window hides the window. To see the window again, hover (or click) on the tab that is now visible along the edge where the window had been docked.

X
> The standard "close window" icon.

IntelliSense

Underlying the IDE is Microsoft's IntelliSense technology, which puts help and editing assistance (including code completion) instantly at your disposal. IntelliSense makes programmers' lives much easier. It provides real-time, context-sensitive help that appears right under your cursor.

For example, in the Hello World code shown in Chapter 2, you called the WriteLine() method for the Console object. If you write this code in VS.NET, the pop-up help will show you every available method of the Console object as soon as you type the dot (.), as shown in Figure 4-4. And if you begin to type a method—say you enter the letters "Wr"—IntelliSense jumps to the first method that matches what you've typed so far.

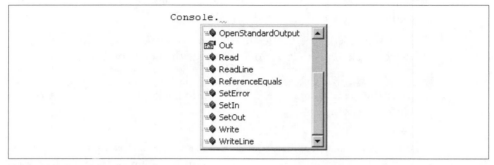

Figure 4-4. Pop-up code completion

Once you enter the method you want to call, Microsoft's pop-up help shows you the various versions of the method and helps you determine the parameters you'll need, as illustrated in Figure 4-5.

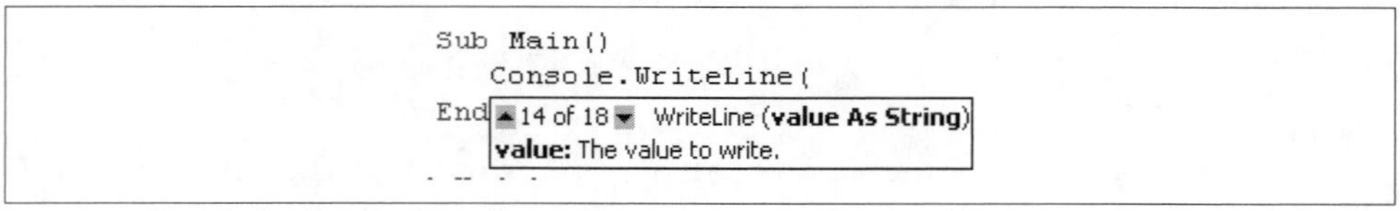

Figure 4-5. Pop-up help

Code completion automatically completes your thoughts for you, drastically reducing your typing. Drop-down lists provide all methods and properties possible in the current context, making them available at a keystroke or mouse click.

Building and Running

You can run your application at any time by selecting either Start or Start Without Debugging from the Debug menu, or you can accomplish the same results by pressing either F5 or Ctrl+F5, respectively. You can also start the program by clicking the Start icon (pictured in Figure 4-6) on the Standard toolbar.

▶

Figure 4-6. The Start icon

For console applications, the advantage of running the program with Ctrl+F5 is that Visual Studio .NET will open your application in a console window, display its results, and then add a line to press a key when you are ready, as shown in

Figure 4-7. This keeps the window open until you've seen the results and pressed a key, at which point the window will close.

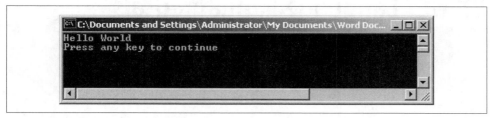

Figure 4-7. Running the application

For More Information

This brief overview of Visual Studio .NET was intended to familiarize you with the tool. There is a great deal more to know about this tool, but most of it will not be relevant to creating the simple applications in this book.

The best way to learn about the power and scope of Visual Studio .NET is to use it and to explore its various nooks and crannies. Try right-clicking in various places and explore the context-sensitive pop-up menus as well.

As you make your way through the book, you'll see various helpful features of Visual Studio .NET highlighted. All of these tips should make programming in VB.NET easier for you. The application's online help files (MSDN) provide extensive additional support.

CHAPTER 5

VB.NET Language Fundamentals

Chapter 2 demonstrates a very simple VB.NET program that prints the text string "Hello world!" to the console screen and provides a line-by-line analysis of that program. However, even that very simple program was complex enough that some of the details had to be skipped over. The current chapter begins an in-depth exploration of the syntax and structure of the VB.NET language.

Types

Every object you create or use in a VB.NET program must have a specific *type* (e.g., you must declare the object to be an integer or a string or a Dog or a Button). The type tells the compiler how big the object is and what it can do.

Types come in two flavors: those that are built into the language (intrinsic types) and types you create (classes, structs, and interfaces, discussed in Chapters 8, 12, and 13, respectively). VB.NET offers a number of intrinsic types, shown in Table 5-1.

Table 5-1. The intrinsic types

Type	Size (in bytes)	.NET type	Description
Boolean	1	Boolean	True or false.
Byte	1	Byte	Unsigned (values 0–255).
Char	2	Char	Unicode characters.
Date	8	DateTime	Midnight 1/1/0001 through 11:59:59 12/31/9999.
Decimal	12	Decimal	Fixed-precision numbers up to 28 digits and the position of the decimal point; typically used in financial calculations; requires the suffix "m" or "M."
Double	8	Double	Double-precision floating-point numbers; holds the values from approximately $+/-5.0 * 10^{-324}$ to approximately $+/-1.8 * 10^{308}$ with 15–16 significant figures.
Integer	4	Int32	Integer values between −2,147,483,648 and 2,147,483,647.
Long	8	Int64	Integers ranging from −9,223,372,036,854,775,808 to 9,223,372,036,854,775,807.

Table 5-1. The intrinsic types (continued)

Type	Size (in bytes)	.NET type	Description
Short	2	Int16	Integer values −32,768 to 32,767.
Single	4	Single	Floating-point numbers; holds the values from approximately +/−1.5 * 10^{-45} to approximate +/−3.4 * 10^{38} with 7 significant figures.
String		String	A sequence of Unicode characters.

Each type has a name (e.g., Integer) and a size (e.g., 4 bytes). The size tells you how many bytes each object of this type occupies in memory. An Integer, for example, is four bytes big. (User-defined types also have a size, measured as the sum of all their member variables.) Programmers generally don't like to waste memory if they can avoid it, but with the cost of memory these days, you can afford to be mildly profligate if doing so simplifies your program. The description field of Table 5-1 tells you the minimum and maximum values you can hold in objects of each intrinsic type.

> Each VB.NET type corresponds to an underlying .NET type. Thus, what VB.NET calls an Integer, .NET calls an INT32. This is interesting only if you care about sharing objects across languages.

When programmers talk about what an object can do, they typically mean the methods of the object. Intrinsic types have implicit methods and they can't do much. You can use them to add two numbers together, and they can display their values as strings. User-defined types can do a lot more; their abilities are determined by the methods you create, as discussed in detail in Chapter 9.

Objects of an intrinsic type are called variables. Variables are discussed in detail later in this chapter.

Numeric Types

Most of the intrinsic types are used for working with numeric values: Byte, Decimal, Double, Integer, Long, Short, and Single.

The types can be classified either as those used for integer values (whole numbers) and those used for fractional values (rational numbers). The Byte, Integer, Long, and Short types all hold whole number values.[*] (The Byte type is not used very often and won't be discussed in this book.)

Typically you decide which size integer to use (Integer, Long, or Short) based on the magnitude of the value you want to store. For example, a Short can only hold values

---

[*] Remember, the Y2K problem was caused by programmers who couldn't imagine needing to reference a year later than 1999.

from −32,768 to 32,767, while an Integer can hold values from −2,147,483,648 through 2,147,483,647.

That said, memory is fairly cheap, and programmer time is increasingly expensive; most of the time you'll simply declare your variables to be of type Integer, unless there is a good reason to do otherwise.

Among the types that hold fractional values, the Single, Double, and Decimal types offer varying degrees of size and precision. For most uses, Single will suffice. If you need to hold a really big fractional number, you might use a Double. The Decimal value type was added to the language to support accounting applications. Note that the compiler assumes that any number with a decimal point is a Double unless you tell it otherwise. How you tell it otherwise is explained in the "Variables" section, later in this chapter.

Non-Numeric Types: Boolean, Char, Date, and String

In addition to the numeric types, the VB.NET language offers four other types: Boolean, Char, Date, and String.

A Boolean value is a value that is either true or false.[*] Boolean values are used frequently in VB.NET programming as you'll see throughout this book. Virtually every comparison (e.g., is myDog bigger than yourDog?) results in a Boolean value.

The Char type is used from time to time when you need to hold a single character. The Char type can represent a simple character (e.g., A), a Unicode character (\u0041), or an escape character enclosed by single quote marks ('\n'). You'll see Chars used in this book, and their use will be explained in context.

The Date type is used to hold date and time values. This type is most useful when working with a database from which you might extract date-time values.

The String type is used to hold a series of text characters. Chapter 16 discusses the use of Strings in detail.

Types and Compiler Errors

When you create a program using VB.NET, you can specify that the type of all variables must be declared before they are used. It is generally considered to be good programming practice to do so. You require that variables must be typed by including the following line at the top of your source code file:

```
Option Explicit On
```

---

[*] The Boolean type was named after George Boole (1815–1864), an English mathematician who published *An investigation into the Laws of Thought, on Which are founded the Mathematical Theories of Logic and Probabilities* and thus created the science of Boolean algebra.

It is also a good idea to specify that VB.NET behave as a *strongly typed* language. This means that the compiler will verify that each declared type is the proper type for the object in question. In order to make VB.NET behave as a strongly typed language, you would also add the following line to the top of your source code:

```
Option Strict On
```

 Thus, by implication, most well-designed VB.NET programs will begin with the following two lines:
```
Option Explicit On
Option Strict On
```

When VB.NET is strictly typed, the compiler will complain if you try to use a type improperly. This compiler check provides important assistance when you're developing code. The compiler complains in one of two ways: it issues a warning or it issues an error.

 You are well advised to treat warnings as errors. That is, you ought to stop what you are doing and figure out why there is a warning and fix the problem. Never ignore a compiler warning.

Programmers talk about design time, compile time, and run time. Design time is when you are designing the program. Compile time is when you compile the program, and run time is (surprise!) when you run the program.

The earlier you unearth a bug, the better. It is better (and cheaper) to discover a bug in your logic at design time than later. Likewise, it is better (and cheaper) to find bugs in your program at compile time than at run time. Not only is it better; it is more reliable. A compile-time bug will fail every time you run the compiler, but a runtime bug can hide. Runtime bugs slip under a crack in your logic and lurk there (sometimes for months), biding their time, waiting to come out when it will be most expensive (or most embarrassing) to you.

It will be a constant theme of this book that you *want* the compiler to find bugs. The compiler is your friend. The more bugs the compiler finds, the fewer bugs your users will find. Using Option Strict On to make VB.NET strictly typed helps the compiler find bugs in your code. Here's how: suppose you tell the compiler that Milo is of type Dog. Sometime later you try to use Milo to display text. Oops, Dogs don't display text. Your compiler will stop with an error:

```
Dog does not contain a definition for `showText'
```

Very nice. Now you can figure out if you used the wrong object or you called the wrong method.

VS.NET actually finds the error even before the compiler does. When you try to add a method, IntelliSense pops up a list of valid methods to help you, as shown in Figure 5-1.

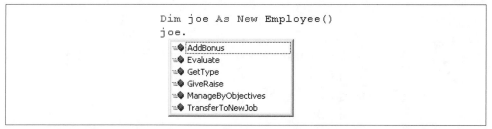

```
Dim joe As New Employee()
joe.
    AddBonus
    Evaluate
    GetType
    GiveRaise
    ManageByObjectives
    TransferToNewJob
```

Figure 5-1. IntelliSense

When you try to add a method that does not exist, it won't be in the list. That is a pretty good clue that you are not using the object properly.

Variables

A variable is an object that can hold a value:

```
Dim myVariable As Integer = 15
```

In this example, myVariable is an object/variable of type Integer. You can assign values to that object, and then you can extract those values later. You *initialize* a variable by writing a definition and then assigning a value to that variable. The previous code line defines myVariable and initializes it with the value 15. The syntax for defining a variable is as follows:

```
access-modifier identifier As type [= value]
```

Access modifiers are discussed in Chapter 8; for now you'll use `Dim`.

 The keyword `Dim` is short for dimension. This term dates back to the early days of Basic programming and is essentially vestigial.

An identifier is just an arbitrary name for a variable, method, class, or other element. In this case, the variable's identifier is myVariable. The keyword `As` signals that the term that follows is the type, in this case Integer.

Specifying Type with a Character

Rather than using a word to specify a variable's type, you can append a single character that corresponds to the type to the variable's name.

While type characters were preserved in the Visual Basic .NET language for continuity with VB6, many developers feel they should be avoided and that spelling out the type makes for clearer, easier-to-maintain code.

For example, rather than writing As Integer, you can use the suffix %, which has the same meaning. Thus, the following two lines are equivalent:

```
Dim myVariable As Integer
Dim myVariable%
```

Not every type has a corresponding character, but you are free to use the corresponding character for those types that do. The complete set is shown in Table 5-2.

Table 5-2. Type characters

Type	Type character	Usage
Decimal	@	Dim decimalValue@ = 123.45
Double	#	Dim doubleValue# = 3.14159265358979
Integer	%	Dim integerValue% = 1
Long	&	Dim longValue& = 123456789
Single	!	Dim singleValue! = 3.1415
String	$	Dim stringValue$ = "Hello world!"

Initializing Variables

You can define variables without initializing them:

```
Dim myVariable As Integer
```

You can then assign a value to myVariable later in your program:

```
Dim myVariable As Integer
'some other code here
myVariable = 15   'assign 15 to myVariable
```

You can also change the value of a variable later in the program. That is why they're called variable; their values vary.

```
Dim myVariable As Integer
'some other code here
myVariable = 15   'assign 15 to myVariable
'some other code here
myVariable = 12   'now it is 12
```

Technically, a variable is a named storage location (i.e., stored in memory) with a type. After the final line of code in the previous example, the value 12 is being stored in the named location myVariable.

Example 5-1 illustrates the use of variables. To test this program, open VS.NET and create a console application. Type in the code as shown.

Example 5-1. Using variables

```
Module Module1
    Sub Main()
        Dim myInt As Integer = 7
        Console.WriteLine("Initialized myInt: {0}", myInt)
        myInt = 5
        Console.WriteLine("After assignment myInt: {0}", myInt)
    End Sub
End Module
```

Output:
```
Initialized myInt: 7
After assignment myInt: 5
```

WriteLine()

The .NET Framework provides a useful method for displaying output on the screen in console applications: System.Console.WriteLine(). How you use this method will become clearer as you progress through the book, but the fundamentals are straightforward. You call the method, passing in a string that you want printed to the console (the screen), as in the Hello World application in Chapter 2.

You can also pass in substitution parameters. A substitution parameter is just a place holder for a value you want to display. For example, you might pass in the substitution parameter {0} and then when you run the program you'll substitute the value held in the variable myVariable, so that its value is displayed where the parameter {0} appears in the WriteLine() statement.

Here's how it works. You place a number between braces:

```
System.Console.WriteLine("After assignment, myVariable: {0}", myVariable)
```

Notice that you follow the quoted string with a comma and then a variable name. The value of the variable will be substituted into the parameter. Assuming myInt has the value 15, the statement shown previously causes the following to display:

```
After assignment, myVariable: 15
```

If you have more than one parameter, the variable values will be substituted in order, as in the following:

```
System.Console.WriteLine("After assignment, myVariable: {0} and
myOtherVariable: {1}", myVariable, myOtherVariable);
```

—continued—

> Assuming myVariable has the value 15, and myOtherVariable has the value 20, this
> will cause the following to display:
>
> ```
> After assignment, myVariable: 15 and myOtherVariable: 20.
> ```
> You'll see a great deal more about WriteLine() in coming chapters.

Example 5-1 initializes the variable myInt to the value 7, displays that value, reassigns the variable with the value 5, and displays it again.

Default Values

VB.NET does not require that you initialize your variables (though it is a very good idea to discipline yourself to do so). If you do not initialize your variable, it will be set to a default value, as shown in Table 5-3.

Table 5-3. Default values for uninitialized variables

Datatype	Default value
All numeric types (`Byte`, `Decimal`, `Double`, `Integer`, `Long`, `Short`, `Single`)	0
`Boolean`	`False`
`Date`	`01/01/0001 12:00:00 AM`
`Object`	`Nothing`
`String`	`""` (zero-length string)

Object defaults to `Nothing`. The `Nothing` keyword indicates that the variable is not associated with any object. You can assign `Nothing` to an object of any type, and the default value will be assigned to that object.

Constants

Variables are a powerful tool, but there are times when you want to manipulate a defined value, one whose value you want to ensure remains constant. A *constant* is like a variable in that it can store a value. However, unlike with a variable, the value of a constant cannot be changed while the program runs.

For example, you might need to work with the Fahrenheit freezing and boiling points of water in a program simulating a chemistry experiment. Your program will be clearer if you name the variables that store these values FreezingPoint and BoilingPoint, but you do not want to permit their values to be changed while the program is executing. The solution is to use a constant. Constants come in three flavors: *literals*, *symbolic constants*, and *enumerations*.

Literal Constants

A literal constant is just a value. For example, 32 is a literal constant. It does not have a name; it is just a literal value. And you can't make the value 32 represent any other value. The value of 32 is always 32. You can't assign a new value to 32; and you can't make 32 represent the value 99 no matter how you might try.

When you write an integer as a literal constant, you are free just to write the number. The characters 32 make up a literal constant for the Integer value 32, and you can assign them accordingly:

```
Dim myValue As Integer = 32  'assign the literal value 32
```

If you want to assign a different type, however, you will want to use the correct format. For example, to designate the value 32 as a Double (rather than as an Integer), you will append the character R, as in the following:

```
32R ' the double value 32
```

The complete list of literal formats is shown in Table 5-4.

Table 5-4. Literal formats

Type	Literal	Example
Boolean	True, False	Dim booleanValue As Boolean = True
Char	C	Dim charValue As Char = "J"C
Decimal	D	Dim decimalValue As Decimal = 3.1415D
Double	Any floating point number, or R	Dim doubleValue As Double = 3.1415
		Dim doubleValue As Double = 3.1415R
		Dim doubleValue As Double = 5R
Integer	Any integer value in range, or I	Dim integerValue As Integer = 100
		Dim integerValue As Integer = 100I
Long	Any integer value outside the range of type Integer or L	Dim longValue As Long = 5000000000
		Dim longValue As Long = 100L
Short	S	Dim shortValue As Short = 100S
Single	F	Dim singleValue As Single = 3.14F
String	""	Dim stringValue As String = "Hello world!"

Symbolic Constants

Symbolic constants assign a name to a constant value. You declare a symbolic constant using the following syntax:

```
access-modifier Const identifier As type = value;
```

Access modifiers are discussed in Chapter 8; for now you will use public.

The Const keyword is followed by an identifier (the name of the constant), the as keyword, the *type* of the constant (e.g., Integer), then the assignment operator (=), and the *value* with which you'll initialize the constant. This is similar to declaring a variable, except that you start with the keyword Const and symbolic constants *must* be initialized. Once initialized a symbolic constant cannot be altered. For example, in the following declaration, 32 is a literal constant and FreezingPoint is a symbolic constants of type Integer:

```
Public Const FreezingPoint As Integer = 32
```

Example 5-2 illustrates the use of symbolic constants.

Example 5-2. Symbolic constants

```
Module Module1
    Sub Main()
        Const FreezingPoint As Integer = 32 ' degrees Farenheit
        Const BoilingPoint As Integer = 212

        System.Console.WriteLine("Freezing point of water: {0}", FreezingPoint)
        System.Console.WriteLine("Boiling point of water: {0}", BoilingPoint)

        'FreezingPoint = 0
    End Sub
End Module
```

Example 5-2 creates two symbolic integer constants: FreezingPoint and Boiling-Point. See the sidebar "Naming Conventions" for a discussion of how to name symbolic constants.

Naming Conventions

Microsoft has promulgated white papers on how you should name the variables, constants, and other objects in your program. They define two types of naming conventions: Camel notation and Pascal notation.

In Camel notation, names begin with a lowercase letter. Multiword names (e.g., "my button") are written with no spaces and no underscore and with each word after the first capitalized. Thus, the correct name for "my button" is myButton.

Pascal notation is just like Camel notation except that the first letter is also uppercase (e.g., FreezingPoint).

Microsoft suggests that variables be written with Camel notation and constants with Pascal notation. In later chapters, you'll learn that member variables and methods are named using Camel notation, while classes are named using Pascal notation.

These constants serve the same purpose as using the *literal* values 32 and 212, for the freezing and boiling points of water, respectively, in expressions that require them. However, because the constants have names, they convey far more meaning. Also, if you decide to switch this program to Celsius, you can reinitialize these constants at compile time to 0 and 100, respectively; and all the rest of the code should continue to work.

To prove to yourself that the constant cannot be reassigned, try uncommenting the third from the last line of the preceding program (it appears in bold), by removing the quote mark:

```
FreezingPoint = 0
```

Then when you recompile, you'll receive this error:

```
Constant cannot be the target of a reassignment
```

Enumerations

Enumerations provide a powerful alternative to literal or simple symbolic constants. An enumeration is a distinct value type, consisting of a set of named constants (called the *enumerator list*).

In Example 5-2, you created two related constants:

```
Const FreezingPoint As Integer = 32 ' degrees Farenheit
Const BoilingPoint As Integer = 212
```

You might want to add a number of other useful constants to this list as well, such as:

```
Const LightJacketWeather As Integer = 60
Const SwimmingWeather As Integer = 72
Const WickedCold As Integer = 0
```

Notice, however, that this process is somewhat cumbersome; also this syntax shows no logical connection among these various constants. VB.NET provides an alternate construct, the enumeration, which allows you to group logically related constants, as in the following:

```
Enum Temperatures
    CelsiusMeetsFahrenheit = -40
    WickedCold = 0
    FreezingPoint = 32
    LightJacketWeather = 60
    SwimmingWeather = 72
    BoilingPoint = 212
End Enum
```

Every enumeration has an underlying type, which can be any integral type (Byte, Integer, Long, or Short). The technical specification of an enumeration is:

```
[access modifiers] Enum identifier [As base-type]
    enumerator-list [ = constant-expression]
End Enum
```

The optional access modifiers are considered in Chapter 8.

 In a specification statement, anything in square brackets is optional. That is, you can declare an Enum with no access modifiers or base-type, or without assigning a value. Note that the base-type is optional, even if Option Strict is On.

For now, let's focus on the rest of this declaration. An enumeration begins with the Enum keyword, which is followed by an identifier, such as:

```
Enum Temperatures
```

The base-type is the underlying type for the enumeration. That is, are you declaring constant Integers or constant Longs? If you leave out this optional value (and often you will), it defaults to Integer, but you are free to use any of the integral types (e.g., Long). For example, the following fragment declares an enumeration of Longs:

```
Enum ServingSizes As Long
    Small = 1
    Regular = 2
    Large = 3
End Enum
```

Notice that the key portion of an Enum declaration is the enumerator list, which contains the constant assignments for the enumeration, each separated by a newline. Example 5-3 rewrites Example 5-2 to use an enumeration.

Example 5-3. Using an enumeration

```
Module Module1
    Enum Temperatures
        WickedCold = 0
        FreezingPoint = 32
        LightJacketWeather = 60
        SwimmingWeather = 72
        BoilingPoint = 212
    End Enum 'Temperatures

    Sub Main()
        System.Console.WriteLine( _
            "Freezing point of water: {0}", _
            Temperatures.FreezingPoint)
        System.Console.WriteLine( _
            "Boiling point of water: {0}", _
            Temperatures.BoilingPoint)
    End Sub
End Module
```

Output:
```
Freezing point of water: FreezingPoint
Boiling point of water: BoilingPoint
```

In Example 5-3, you declare an enumerated constant called Temperatures. When you want to use any of the values in an enumeration in a program, the values of the enumeration must be qualified by the enumeration name.

You cannot just refer to FreezingPoint; instead, you use the enumeration identifier (Temperatures) followed by the dot operator and then the enumerated constant (FreezingPoint). This is called qualifying the identifier FreezingPoint. Thus, to refer to the FreezingPoint, you use the full identifier Temperatures.FreezingPoint.

Unfortunately, if you pass the name of a constant within an enumeration to the WriteLine() method, the name is displayed, not the value. In order to display the value of an enumerated constant, you must cast the constant to its underlying type (in this case, Integer), as shown in Example 5-4.

Example 5-4. Casting the enumerated value

```
Module Module1
    Enum Temperatures
        WickedCold = 0
        FreezingPoint = 32
        LightJacketWeather = 60
        SwimmingWeather = 72
        BoilingPoint = 212
    End Enum 'Temperatures
    Sub Main()
        System.Console.WriteLine( _
            "Freezing point of water: {0}", _
            CInt(Temperatures.FreezingPoint))

        System.Console.WriteLine( _
            "Boiling point of water: {0}", _
            CInt(Temperatures.BoilingPoint))
    End Sub
End Module
```

When you cast a value (in this example, using the CInt() function) you tell the compiler: "I know that this value is really of the indicated type." In this case, you are saying: "Treat this enumerated constant as an Integer." Since the underlying type is Integer, this is safe to do. See the next section, "About Casting," for more information about the use of CInt() and the other casting functions.

In Example 5-4, the values in the two enumerated constants, FreezingPoint and BoilingPoint, are both cast to type Integer; then those Integer values are passed to WriteLine() and displayed.

Each constant in an enumeration corresponds to a numerical value. In Example 5-4, each enumerated value is an integer. If you don't specifically set it otherwise, the enumeration begins at 0, and each subsequent value counts up from the previous. Thus, if you create the following enumeration:

```
Enum SomeValues
    First
    Second
    Third = 20
    Fourth
End Enum
```

the value of First will be 0, Second will be 1, Third will be 20, and Fourth will be 21.

 If Option Strict is set On, Enums are treated as formal types; that is, they are not just a synonym for another type, they are a type in their own right. Therefore an explicit conversion is required to convert between an Enum type and an integral type (such as Integer, Long, etc.).

About Casting

Objects of one type can be converted into objects of another type. This is called casting. Casting can be either narrowing or widening. The way casting is invoked is either explicit or implicit.

A widening cast is one in which the conversion is to a type that can accommodate every possible value in the existing variable type. For example, an Integer can accommodate every possible value held by a Short. Thus, casting from Short to Integer is a widening conversion.

A narrowing cast is one in which the conversion is to a type that may not be able to accommodate every possible value in the existing variable type. For example, a Short can accommodate only some of the values that an Integer variable might hold. Thus, casting from an Integer to a Short is a narrowing conversion.

In VB.NET, conversions are invoked either implicitly or explicitly. In an implicit conversion, the compiler makes the conversion with no special action by the developer. With an explicit conversion, the developer must use a special function to signal the cast. For example, in Example 5-4, you use the CInt function to explicitly cast the Enumerated value to an Integer.

The semantics of an explicit conversion are: "Hey! Compiler! I know what I'm doing." This is sometimes called "hitting it with the big hammer" and can be very useful or very painful, depending on whether your thumb is in the way.

Whether a cast is implicit or explicit is affected by the Option Strict setting. If Option Strict is On (as it always should be), only widening casts can be implicit.

The explicit cast functions follow. Refer back to Table 5-1 for information about the ranges covered by the various numeric types.

CBool()
> Converts any valid string (e.g., "True") or numeric expression to Boolean. Numeric nonzero values are converted to True, zero is converted to False.

CByte()

Converts numeric expression in range 0 to 255 to Byte. Round any fractional part.

CChar()

Returns the first character of a string as a Char.

CDate()

Converts any valid representation of a date or time to the Date type (e.g., "January 1, 2002" is converted to the corresponding Date type).

CDbl()

Converts any expression that can be evaluated as a number to a Double if it is in the range of a Double.

CDec()

Converts any expression that can be evaluated as a number to a Decimal if it is in the range of a Decimal.

CInt()

Converts any expression that can be evaluated as a number to a Integer if it is in the range of a Integer; rounds fractional part.

CLng()

Converts any expression that can be evaluated as a number to a Long if it is in the range of a Long; rounds fractional part.

CObj()

Converts any expression that can be interpreted as an Object to an Object.

CShort()

Converts any expression that can be evaluated as a number to a Short if it is in the range of a Short.

CStr()

If Boolean, converts to the string "True" or "False." If the expression can be interpreted as a date, returns a string expression of the date. For numeric expressions, the returned string represents the number.

CType()

This is a general purpose conversion function that uses the syntax:

```
CType(expression, typename)
```

where *expression* is an expression or a variable, and *typename* is the datatype to convert to. The first conversion in Example 5-4 can be rewritten from:

```
System.Console.WriteLine( _
    "Freezing point of water: {0}", _
    CInt(Temperatures.FreezingPoint))
```

to:

```
System.Console.WriteLine( _
    "Freezing point of water: {0}", _
    CType(Temperatures.FreezingPoint, Integer))
```

Strings

It is nearly impossible to write a VB.NET program without creating strings. A string object holds a series of characters.

You declare a string variable using the string keyword much as you would create an instance of any type:

```
Dim myString As String
```

You specify a *string literal* by enclosing it in double quotes:

```
"Hello World"
```

It is common to initialize a string variable that contains a string literal:

```
Dim myString As String = "Hello World"
```

Strings are covered in much greater detail in Chapter 16.

Statements

In VB.NET, a complete program instruction is called a *statement*. Programs consist of sequences of VB.NET statements. Each statement should end with a newline:

```
Dim myString As String = "Hello World"
```

You *can* combine multiple statements on a single line if you divide them with a colon. The following sample shows two code lines on a single line, with a colon marking the end of the first:

```
Dim myVariable As Integer = 5 : Dim myVar2 As Integer = 7
```

Using the colon may allow you to squeeze more than one statement on a line. However, this is generally considered to be poor programming practice because it makes the code harder to read and thus harder to maintain.

Sometimes a single code statement simply won't fit on a single line in a file. If your code will not fit on a single line, you can use the line-continuation character, the underscore (_), as in this excerpt from Example 5-4:

```
System.Console.WriteLine( _
    "Freezing point of water: {0}", _
    CInt(Temperatures.FreezingPoint))
```

Note that you must use a space before the underscore in order to continue the line. In the preceding snippet, all three lines are considered to be a single statement because you use two continuation characters, one at the end of each of the first two lines.

VB.NET statements are evaluated in order. The compiler starts at the beginning of a statement list and makes its way to the bottom. This would be entirely straightforward, and terribly limiting, were it not for branching. Branching allows you to change the order in which statements are evaluated. Chapter 7 describes branching in detail.

Whitespace

In the VB.NET language, spaces, tabs, and newlines are considered to be "whitespace" (so named because you see only the white of the underlying "page"). Extra whitespace is generally ignored in VB.NET statements. Thus, you can write:

```
Dim myVariable As Integer = 5
```

or:

```
Dim        myVariable        As        Integer        =        5
```

and the compiler will treat the two statements as identical.

The exception to this rule is that whitespace within a string is treated as literal; it is not ignored. If you write:

```
System.Console.WriteLine("Hello World")
```

each space between "Hello" and "World" is treated as another character in the string. (In this case, there is only one space character.)

Most of the time the use of whitespace is intuitive. The key is to use whitespace to make the program more readable to the programmer; the compiler is indifferent. Problems arise only when you do not leave space between logical program elements that require it. For instance, although the expression:

```
Dim myVariable As Integer = 5
```

is the same as:

```
Dim myVariable As Integer=5
```

it is not the same as:

```
DimmyVariable As Integer = 5
```

The compiler knows that the whitespace on either side of the assignment operator is extra, but the whitespace between the access modifier Dim and the variable name myVariable is *not* extra; it is required.

This is not surprising; the whitespace allows the compiler to *parse* the keyword Dim rather than some unknown term DimmyVariable. You are free to add as much or as little whitespace between Dim and myVariable as you care to, but there must be at least one whitespace character (typically a space or tab).

CHAPTER 6

Branching

A method is, essentially, a mini-program within your larger program. It is a set of statements that execute one after the other, as in the following:

```
Sub MyMethod()
End Sub
```

Methods are executed from top to bottom. The compiler reads each line of code in turn and executes one line after another. This continues in sequence until the method *branches*. Branching means that the current method is interrupted temporarily and a new method or routine is executed; when that new method or routine finishes, the original method picks up where it left off. A method can branch in either of two ways: unconditionally or conditionally.

As the name implies, unconditional branching happens every time the program is run. An unconditional branch happens, for example, whenever the compiler encounters a new method call. The compiler stops execution in the current method and branches to the newly called method. When the newly called method returns (i.e., completes its execution), execution picks up in the original method on the line just below the line where the new method was called.

Conditional branching is more complicated. Methods can branch based on the evaluation of certain conditions that occur at runtime. For instance, you might create a branch that will calculate an employee's federal withholding tax only when her earnings are greater than the minimum taxable by law. VB.NET provides a number of statements that support conditional branching, such as If, ElseIf, and Select Case. The use of these statements is discussed later in this chapter.

A second way that methods break out of their mindless step-by-step processing of instructions is by looping. A loop causes the method to repeat a set of steps until some condition is met (e.g., "Keep asking for input until the user tells you to stop or until you receive ten values"). VB.NET provides many statements for looping, including Do, Do While, and Loop While, which are also discussed in this chapter.

Unconditional Branching Statements

The simplest example of an unconditional branch is a method call. When a method call is reached, no test is made to evaluate the state of the object; the program execution branches immediately, and unconditionally, to the start of the new method.

You call a method by writing its name, for example:

```
UpdateSalary()  'invokes the method UpdateSalary
```

 It is also legal to call a VB.NET method with the optional keyword Call:

```
Call Method1()
```

However, if you do use Call on a function, the return value is discarded. Since this represents a disadvantage and there is no other advantage to this syntax, it won't be used in this book.

As explained in the introduction, when the compiler encounters a method call, it stops execution of the current method and branches to the new method. When that new method completes its execution, the compiler picks up where it left off in the original method. This process is illustrated schematically in Figure 6-1.

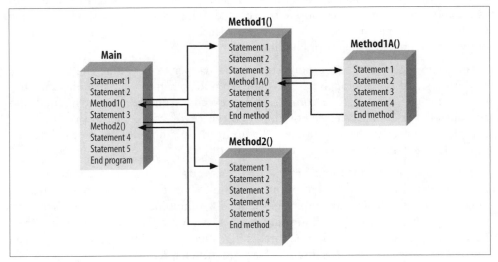

Figure 6-1. How branching works

As Figure 6-1 suggests, it is actually quite common for there to be unconditional branching several methods deep. In Figure 6-1, execution begins in a method called Main(). Statement1 and Statement2 execute; then the compiler sees a call to Method1(). Program execution branches unconditionally to the first line of

Method1(), where its first three statements are executed. At the call to Method1A(), execution again branches, this time to the start of Method1A().

The four statements in Method1A() are executed, and Method1A() returns. Execution resumes on the first statement after the method call in Method1() (Statement 4). Execution continues until Method1() ends, at which time execution resumes back in Main() at Statement3. At the call to Method2(), execution again branches; all the statements in Method2() execute, and then Main() resumes at Statement4. When Main() ends, the program itself ends.

You can see the effect of method calls in Example 6-1. Execution begins in Main() but branches to a method named SomeMethod(). The WriteLine() statements in each method assist you in seeing where you are in the code as the program executes.

Example 6-1. Branching to a method

```
Option Strict On
Imports System
Module Module1
    Sub Main()
        Console.WriteLine("In Main! Calling SomeMethod()...")
        SomeMethod()
        Console.WriteLine("Back in Main().")
    End Sub 'Main

    Sub SomeMethod()
        Console.WriteLine("Greetings from SomeMethod!")
    End Sub 'SomeMethod

End Module
```

Output:
```
In Main! Calling SomeMethod()...
Greetings from SomeMethod!
Back in Main().
```

Program flow begins in Main() and proceeds until SomeMethod() is invoked. (Invoking a method is sometimes referred to as "calling" the method.) At that point, program flow branches to the method. When the method completes, program flow resumes at the next line after the call to that method.

 You can instead create an unconditional branch by using one of the unconditional branch keywords: Goto, Exit, Return, or Throw. The first three of these are discussed later in this chapter, while the final statement, throw, is discussed in Chapter 17.

Methods and their parameters and return values are discussed in detail in Chapter 9.

Conditional Branching Statements

While methods branch unconditionally, often you will want to branch within a method depending on a condition that you evaluate while the program is running. This is known as conditional branching. Conditional branching statements allow you to write logic such as "If you are over 25 years old, then you may rent a car."

VB.NET provides a number of constructs that allow you to write conditional branches into your programs; these constructs are described in the following sections.

If Statements

The simplest branching statement is If. An If statement says, "if a particular condition is true, then execute the statement; otherwise skip it." (The condition is a *Boolean expression*. An expression is a statement that evaluates to a value. A Boolean expression evaluates to either true or false.)

The formal description of an If statement is:

```
If expression Then
    statements
End If
```

You are likely to find this kind of description of the If statement in your compiler documentation. It shows you that the If statement takes an *expression* (a statement that returns a value) and Then executes the *statements* until the End If, but only if the *expression* evaluates true.

An alternative one-line version is:

```
If expression Then statement
```

 Many VB.NET developers avoid the single-line If statement because it can be confusing and thus difficult to maintain.

Example 6-2 illustrates the use of an If statement.

Example 6-2. Using the If statement

```
Option Strict On
Imports System
Module Module1

    Sub Main()

        Dim valueOne As Integer = 10
        Dim valueTwo As Integer = 20
        Dim valueThree As Integer = 30
```

Example 6-2. Using the If statement (continued)

```
        Console.WriteLine("Testing valueOne against valueTwo...")
        If valueOne > valueTwo Then
            Console.WriteLine( _
                "ValueOne: {0} larger than ValueTwo: {1}", _
                valueOne, valueTwo)
        End If

        Console.WriteLine("Testing valueThree against valueTwo...")
        If valueThree > valueTwo Then
            Console.WriteLine( _
                "ValueThree: {0} larger than ValueTwo: {1}", _
                valueThree, valueTwo)
        End If
        Console.WriteLine("Testing is valueTwo > 15 (one line)...")
        If valueTwo > 15 Then Console.WriteLine("Yes it is")

    End Sub 'Main
End Module
```

Output:
```
Testing valueOne against valueTwo...
Testing valueThree against valueTwo...
ValueThree: 30 larger than ValueTwo: 20
Testing is valueTwo > 15 (one line)...
Yes it is
```

In this simple program, you declare three variables, valueOne, valueTwo, and valueThree, with the values 10, 20, and 30, respectively. In the first If statement, you test whether valueOne is greater than valueTwo.

```
If valueOne > valueTwo Then
    Console.WriteLine( _
        "ValueOne: {0} larger than ValueTwo: {1}", valueOne, valueTwo)
End If
```

Because valueOne (10) is less than valueTwo (20), this If statement fails (the condition returns false), and thus the body of the If statement (the statements between the If and the End If) doesn't execute.

> The test for greater than uses the greater than operator (>), which is discussed in detail in Chapter 7.

You then test whether valueThree is greater than valueTwo:

```
If valueThree > valueTwo Then
    Console.WriteLine( _
        "ValueThree: {0} larger than ValueTwo: {1}", valueThree, valueTwo)
End If
```

Since valueThree (30) *is* greater than valueTwo (20), the test returns true, and thus the statement executes. The statement in this case is the call to the WriteLine() method, shown in bold.

Finally, you use a one-line if statement to test whether valueTwo is greater than 15. Since this evaluates true, the statement that follows executes, and the words "Yes it is" are displayed.

```
If valueTwo > 15 Then Console.WriteLine("Yes it is")
```

The output reflects that the first If statement fails, but the second and third succeed:

```
Testing valueOne against valueTwo...
Testing valueThree against valueTwo...
ValueThree: 30 larger than ValueTwo: 20
Testing is valueTwo > 15 (one line)...
Yes it is
```

If . . . Else Statements

Often, you will find that you want to take one set of actions when the condition tests true and a different set of actions when the condition tests false. This allows you to write logic such as "If you are over 25 years old, then you may rent a car; *otherwise*, you must take the train."

The *otherwise* portion of the logic is executed in the Else statement. For example, you can modify Example 6-2 to print an appropriate message whether or not valueOne is greater than valueTwo, as shown in Example 6-3.

Example 6-3. The Else statement

```
Option Strict On
Imports System
Module Module1

    Sub Main( )

        Dim valueOne As Integer = 10
        Dim valueTwo As Integer = 20
        Dim valueThree As Integer = 30

        Console.WriteLine("Testing valueOne against valueTwo...")
        If valueOne > valueTwo Then
           Console.WriteLine( _
                "ValueOne: {0} larger than ValueTwo: {1}", valueOne, valueTwo)
        Else
           Console.WriteLine( _
                "Nope, ValueOne: {0} is NOT larger than valueTwo: {1}", _
                valueOne, valueTwo)
        End If
    End Sub 'Main
```

Example 6-3. The Else statement (continued)

```
End Module
```

Output:
```
Testing valueOne against valueTwo...
Nope, ValueOne: 10 is NOT larger than valueTwo: 20
```

Because the test in the If statement fails (valueOne is *not* larger than valueTwo), the body of the If statement is skipped and the body of the Else statement is executed. Had the test succeeded, the If statement body would execute and the Else statement would be skipped.

Nested If Statements

It is possible, and not uncommon, to nest If statements to handle complex conditions. For example, suppose you need to write a program to evaluate the temperature and specifically to return the following types of information:

- If the temperature is 32 degrees or lower, the program should warn you about ice on the road.

- If the temperature is exactly 32 degrees, the program should tell you that there may be ice patches.

- If the temperature is higher than 32 degrees, the program should assure you that there is no ice.

There are many good ways to write this program. Example 6-4 illustrates one approach, using nested If statements.

Example 6-4. Nested If statements

```
Option Strict On
Imports System
Module Module1

   Sub Main()
      Dim temp As Integer = 32

      If temp <= 32 Then
         Console.WriteLine("Warning! Ice on road!")
         If temp = 32 Then
            Console.WriteLine("Temp exactly freezing, beware of water.")
         Else
            Console.WriteLine("Watch for black ice! Temp: {0}", temp)
         End If 'temp = 32
      End If 'temp <= 32
   End Sub 'Main

End Module
```

Example 6-4. Nested If statements (continued)

Output:
```
Warning! Ice on road!
Temp exactly freezing, beware of water.
```

The logic of Example 6-6 is that it tests whether the temperature is less than or equal to 32. If so, it prints a warning:

```
If temp <= 32 Then
        Console.WriteLine("Warning! Ice on road!")
```

The program then uses a second If statement, nested within the first, to check whether the temp is equal to 32 degrees. If so, it prints one message ("Temp exactly freezing, beware of water."); if not, the temp must be less than 32 and an Else is executed, causing the program to print the next message ("Watch for black ice . . ."). Because the second If statement is nested within the first If, the logic of the Else statement is: "since it has been established that the temp is less than or equal to 32, and it isn't equal to 32, it must be less than 32."

 The less-than-or-equal-to operator is <=, as described in Chapter 7.

ElseIf

The ElseIf statement allows you to perform a related sequence of Ifs without nesting per se. The logic of ElseIf is that if the first If evaluates false, then evaluate the first ElseIf. The first If/ElseIf combination to evaluate true will have its statements executed (and no others will even be evaluated). If none of the statements evaluates true, the final Else clause is executed. Example 6-5 uses ElseIf to perform the same actions as Example 6-4 used nested Ifs for.

Example 6-5. ElseIf

```
Option Strict On
Imports System
Module Module1

    Sub Main()
        Dim temp As Integer = -32

        If temp > 32 Then
            Console.WriteLine("Safe driving...")
        ElseIf temp = 32 Then
            Console.WriteLine("Warning, 32 degrees, watch for ice and water")
        ElseIf temp > 0 Then
            Console.WriteLine("Watch for ice...")
        ElseIf temp = 0 Then
```

Example 6-5. ElseIf (continued)

```
      Console.WriteLine("Temperature = 0")
   Else
      Console.WriteLine("Temperatures below zero, Wicked Cold!")
   End If
 End Sub 'Main

End Module
```

Output:
```
Temperatures below zero, Wicked Cold!
```

Select Case Statements

Nested If statements and long sequences of ElseIf statements are hard to read, hard to get right, and hard to debug. When you have a complex set of choices to make, the Select Case statement is a more powerful alternative. The logic of a Select Case statement is this: "pick a matching value and act accordingly." The syntax is as follows:

```
Select [ Case ] testExpression
[ Case expressionList
   [ statements ] ]
[ Case Else
   [ else-statements] ]
End Select
```

It is easiest to understand this construct in the context of a sample program. In Example 6-6 a value of 15 is assigned to the variable targetInteger. The Select Case statement tests for the values 5, 10, and 15. If one matches, the associated statement is executed.

Example 6-6. Using Select Case

```
Option Strict On
Imports System
Module Module1

   Sub Main( )
      Dim targetInteger As Integer = 15

      Select Case targetInteger
         Case 5
            Console.WriteLine("5")
         Case 10
            Console.WriteLine("10")
         Case 15
            Console.WriteLine("15!")
         Case Else
            Console.WriteLine("Value not found")
      End Select
   End Sub 'Main
```

Example 6-6. Using Select Case (continued)

```
End Module
```

Output:
```
15!
```

The output shows that 15 matched, and the associated statement was executed, displaying the value 15. If none of the values matched, any statements following Case Else would be executed.

Note that Case also allows you to check a variable against a range of values. You can combine Case with the keywords Is and To to specify the ranges, as illustrated in Example 6-7. Note that the target value (targetInteger) has been changed to 7.

Example 6-7. Testing for a range of values

```
Option Strict On
Imports System
Module Module1

    Sub Main( )
       Dim targetInteger As Integer = 7

       Select Case targetInteger
          Case Is < 10
             Console.WriteLine("Less than 10")
          Case 10 To 14
             Console.WriteLine("10-14")
          Case 15
             Console.WriteLine("15!")
          Case Else
             Console.WriteLine("Value not found")
       End Select
    End Sub 'Main

End Module
```

Output:
```
Less than 10
```

In Example 6-7, the first test examines whether targetInteger is less than 10. You specify this by combining Case with the Is keyword followed by the less-than operator and the number 10 to specify the range:

```
Case Is < 10
```

You then use Case with the To keyword to specify a range of 10 through 14:

```
Case 10 To 14
```

The preceding Case will match any value of 10 through 14 inclusive. You are not restricted to just testing for a numeric value. You can also test for string values. In fact, you can test ranges of string values, examining whether a target value fits alphabetically within the range, as shown in Example 6-8.

Example 6-8. Testing alphabetic ranges

```
Option Strict On
Imports System
Module Module1

    Sub Main()

        Dim target As String = "Milo"
        Select Case target

            Case "Alpha" To "Lambda "
                Console.WriteLine("Alpha To Lambda executed")
            Case "Lamda" To "Zeta"
                Console.WriteLine("Lambda To Zeta executed")
            Case Else
                Console.WriteLine("Else executed")
        End Select
    End Sub 'Main

End Module
```

Output:
```
Lambda To Zeta executed
```

Example 6-8 tests whether the string "Milo" fits within the alphabetic range between the strings "Alpha" and "Lambda"; then it tests whether "Milo" fits within the range between the strings "Lambda" and "Zeta". Both ranges are inclusive. Clearly the second range encompasses the string "Milo" and the output bears that out.

You can also simply test whether one string matches another. The following case tests whether the string "Milo" is the same as the string "Fred":

```
Dim target As String = "Milo"

    Select Case target
        Case "Fred"
            Console.WriteLine("Fred")
```

But clearly "Milo" does not equal "Fred."

You can also combine a series of tests in a single Case statement, separating them by commas. Thus you could test whether "Milo" matches either of the strings "Fred" or "Joe" and also whether it falls within the (admittedly small) alphabetic range that comes before "Alpha" using the following code:

```
Dim target As String = "Milo"

    Select Case target
        Case "Fred", "Joe", Is < "Alpha"
            Console.WriteLine("Joe or Fred or < Alpha")
```

Clearly "Milo" would not match any of these cases, but changing the target string to "Aardvark" would get you somewhere.

Iteration (Looping) Statements

In many situations you will want to do the same thing again and again, perhaps slightly changing a value each time you repeat the action. This is called iteration or looping. Typically, you'll iterate (or loop) over a set of items, taking the same action on each. This is the programming equivalent to an assembly line. On an assembly line, you might take a hundred car bodies and put a windshield on each one as it comes by. In an iterative program, you might work your way through a collection of text boxes on a form, retrieving the value from each in turn and using those values to update a database.

VB.NET provides an extensive suite of iteration statements, including Do, For, and Foreach. You can also create a loop by using a statement called Goto. The remainder of this chapter considers the use of Goto, Do, and For. However, you'll have to wait until Chapter 14 to learn more about Foreach.

Creating Loops with Goto

The Goto statement was used previously as an unconditional branch in a switch statement. Its more common usage, however, is to create a loop. In fact, the Goto statement is the seed from which all other looping statements have been germinated. Unfortunately, it is a semolina seed, producer of spaghetti code and endless confusion.

Programs that use Goto statements outside of switch blocks jump around a great deal. Goto can cause your method to loop back and forth in ways that are difficult to follow.

If you were to try to draw the flow of control in a program that makes extensive use of Goto statements, the resulting morass of intersecting and overlapping lines might look like a plate of spaghetti—hence the term "spaghetti code." Spaghetti code is a contemptuous epithet; no one wants to write spaghetti code.

Most experienced programmers properly shun the Goto statement, but in the interest of completeness, here's how you use it:

1. Create a label.
2. Goto that label.

The label is an identifier followed by a colon. You place the label in your code, and then you use the Goto keyword to jump to that label. The Goto command is typically tied to an If statement, as illustrated in Example 6-9.

Example 6-9. Using Goto

```
Option Strict On
Imports System
Module Module1

    Sub Main()
        Dim counterVariable As Integer = 0

repeat:  ' the label
        Console.WriteLine("counterVariable: {0}", counterVariable)

        ' increment the counter
        counterVariable += 1
        If counterVariable < 10 Then
            GoTo repeat ' the dastardly deed
        End If
    End Sub 'Main

End Module
```

Output:
```
counterVariable: 0
counterVariable: 1
counterVariable: 2
counterVariable: 3
counterVariable: 4
counterVariable: 5
counterVariable: 6
counterVariable: 7
counterVariable: 8
counterVariable: 9
```

This code is not terribly complex; you've used only a single Goto statement. However, with multiple such statements and labels scattered through your code, tracing the flow of execution becomes very difficult.

It was the phenomenon of spaghetti code that led to the creation of alternatives, such as the Do loop.

The Do Loop

The semantics of a Do loop are "Do this work while a condition is true" or "Do this work until a condition becomes true." You can test the condition either at the top or at the bottom of the loop. If you test at the bottom of the loop, the loop will execute at least once. Every Do loop is bounded by the Loop keyword, which marks the end of the methods to be executed within the loop.

The Do loop can even be written with no conditions, in which case it will execute indefinitely, until it encounters an Exit Do statement.

Do loops come in a number of varieties, some of which require additional keywords such as While and Until. The syntax for these various Do loops follow. Note that in each case, the *Boolean-expression* can be any expression that evaluates to a Boolean value of true or false.

```
Do While Boolean-expression
    statements
Loop

Do Until Boolean-expression
    statements
Loop

Do
    statements
Loop While Boolean-expression

Do
    statements
Loop Until Boolean-expression

Do
    statements
Loop
```

In the first type of Do loop, Do While, the *statements* in the loop execute only while the *Boolean-expression* returns true. Example 6-10 shows a Do While loop, which in this case does no more than increment a counterVariable from 0 to 10, printing a statement to that effect to the console for each iteration of the loop.

Example 6-10. Using Do While

```
Option Strict On
Imports System
Module Module1

    Sub Main( )
        Dim counterVariable As Integer = 0

        Do While counterVariable < 10
            Console.WriteLine("counterVariable: {0}", counterVariable)
            counterVariable = counterVariable + 1
        Loop ' While counterVariable < 10

    End Sub 'Main
End Module
```

Output:
```
counterVariable: 0
counterVariable: 1
counterVariable: 2
counterVariable: 3
counterVariable: 4
```

Example 6-10. Using Do While (continued)

```
counterVariable: 5
counterVariable: 6
counterVariable: 7
counterVariable: 8
counterVariable: 9
```

The second version of Do, Do Until, executes until the *boolean-expression* returns true, using the following syntax:

```
Do Until Boolean-expression
    statements
Loop
```

Example 6-11 modifies Example 6-10 to use Do Until.

Example 6-11. Using Do Until

```
Option Strict On
Imports System
Module Module1

    Sub Main()
        Dim counterVariable As Integer = 0

        Do Until counterVariable = 10
            Console.WriteLine("counterVariable: {0}", counterVariable)
            counterVariable = counterVariable + 1
        Loop ' Until counterVariable = 10

    End Sub 'Main

End Module
```

The output from Example 6-11 is identical to that of Example 6-10.

> Be very careful when looping to a specific value. If the value is never reached, or skipped over, your loop can continue without end.

Do While and Do Until are closely related; which you use will depend on the semantics of the problem you are trying to solve. That is, use the construct that represents how you think about the problem. If you are solving this problem: "keep winding the box until the Jack pops up," then use a Do Until loop. If you are solving this problem: "As long as the music plays, keep dancing," then use a Do While loop.

In order to make sure a Do While or Do Until loop runs at least once, you can test the condition at the end of the loop. The following are the syntax lines to test the condition at the end, for Do While and Do Until, respectively. To distinguish them from the other variants, we'll call them Do Loop While and Do Loop Until.

```
Do
    statements
Loop While boolean-expression

Do
    statements
Loop Until boolean-expression
```

If your counterVariable were initialized to 100, but you wanted to make sure the loop ran once anyway, you might use the Do Loop While construct, as shown in Example 6-12.

Example 6-12. Do Loop While

```
Option Strict On
Imports System
Module Module1

    Sub Main()
        Dim counterVariable As Integer = 100

        Do
            Console.WriteLine("counterVariable: {0}", counterVariable)
            counterVariable = counterVariable + 1
        Loop While counterVariable < 10

    End Sub 'Main

End Module
```

Output:
```
counterVariable: 100
```

The final Do loop construct is a loop that never ends because there is no condition to satisfy:

```
Do
    statements
Loop
```

The only way to end this construct is to deliberately break out of the loop using the Exit Do statement, described in the next section.

Breaking out of a Do Loop

You can break out of any Do loop with the Exit Do statement. You *must* break out of the final Do construct:

```
Do
    statements
Loop
```

because otherwise it will never terminate. You typically use this construct when you do not know in advance what condition will cause the loop to terminate (e.g., the termination can be in response to user action).

By using Exit Do within an If statement, as shown in Example 6-13, you can basically mimic the Do Loop While construct demonstrated in Example 6-12.

Example 6-13. Using Exit Do

```
Option Strict On
Imports System
Module Module1

    Sub Main()
        Dim counterVariable As Integer = 0

        Do
            Console.WriteLine("counterVariable: {0}", counterVariable)
            counterVariable = counterVariable + 1

            ' test whether we've counted to 9, if so, exit the loop
            If counterVariable > 9 Then
                Exit Do
            End If
        Loop

    End Sub 'Main

End Module
```

Output:
```
counterVariable: 0
counterVariable: 1
counterVariable: 2
counterVariable: 3
counterVariable: 4
counterVariable: 5
counterVariable: 6
counterVariable: 7
counterVariable: 8
counterVariable: 9
```

In Example 6-13, you would loop indefinitely if the If loop did not set up a condition and provide an exit via Exit Do. However, as written, Example 6-13 exits the loop when counterVariable becomes greater than 9. You typically would use either the Do While or Do Loop While construct to accomplish this, but there are many ways to accomplish the same thing in VB.NET. In fact, VB.NET offers yet another alternative, the While loop, as described in the sidebar.

While Loops

VB.NET offers a While loop construct that is closely related to the Do While loop, albeit less popular. The syntax is:

```
While Boolean-expression
   statements
End While
```

The logic of this is *identical* to the basic Do While loop, as demonstrated by the following code:

```
Option Strict On
Imports System
Module Module1

    Sub Main()
       Dim counterVariable As Integer = 0

       While counterVariable < 10
          Console.WriteLine("counterVariable: {0}",
          counterVariable) counterVariable =
          counterVariable + 1
       End While

    End Sub 'Main

End Module

Output:
counterVariable: 0
counterVariable: 1
counterVariable: 2
counterVariable: 3
counterVariable: 4
counterVariable: 5
counterVariable: 6
counterVariable: 7
counterVariable: 8
counterVariable: 9
```

Because the While loop was deprecated in VB6, and because its logic is identical to the more common Do While loop, many VB.NET programmers eschew the While loop construct. It is included here for completeness.

The For Loop

When you need to iterate over a loop a specified number of times, you can use a For loop with a counter variable. The syntax of the For loop is:

```
For variable = expression To expression [ Step expression ]
   statements
Next [ variable-list ]
```

The simplest and most common use of the For statement is to create a variable to count through the iterations of the loop. For example, you might create an integer variable loopCounter that you'll use to step through a loop ten times, as shown in Example 6-14. Note that the Next keyword is used to mark the end of the For loop.

Example 6-14. Using a For loop

```
Option Strict On
Imports System
Module Module1

    Sub Main()

        Dim loopCounter As Integer
        For loopCounter = 0 To 9
            Console.WriteLine("loopCounter: {0}", loopCounter)
        Next

    End Sub 'Main

End Module
```

Output:
```
loopCounter: 0
loopCounter: 1
loopCounter: 2
loopCounter: 3
loopCounter: 4
loopCounter: 5
loopCounter: 6
loopCounter: 7
loopCounter: 8
loopCounter: 9
```

The variable (loopCounter) can be of any numeric type. For example, you might initialize a Single rather than an Integer and step up through the loop from 0.5 to 9, as shown in Example 6-15.

Example 6-15. Loop with a Single counter

```
Option Strict On
Imports System
Module Module1

    Sub Main()

        Dim loopCounter As Single
        For loopCounter = 0.5 To 9
            Console.WriteLine("loopCounter: {0}", loopCounter)
        Next

    End Sub 'Main
```

Example 6-15. Loop with a Single counter (continued)
```
End Module
```

Output:
```
loopCounter: 0.5
loopCounter: 1.5
loopCounter: 2.5
loopCounter: 3.5
loopCounter: 4.5
loopCounter: 5.5
loopCounter: 6.5
loopCounter: 7.5
loopCounter: 8.5
```

The loop steps up by one on each iteration because that is the default step value. The next step would be 9.5, which would be above the upper limit (9) you've set. Thus, the loop ends at loopCounter 8.5.

You can override the default step value of 1 by using the keyword Step. For example, you can modify the step counter in the previous example to .5, as shown in Example 6-16.

Example 6-16. Adjusting the step counter
```
Option Strict On
Imports System
Module Module1

    Sub Main()

       Dim loopCounter As Single
       For loopCounter = 0.5 To 9 Step 0.5
          Console.WriteLine("loopCounter: {0}", loopCounter)
       Next

    End Sub 'Main

End Module
```

Output:
```
loopCounter: 0.5
loopCounter: 1
loopCounter: 1.5
loopCounter: 2
loopCounter: 2.5
loopCounter: 3
loopCounter: 3.5
loopCounter: 4
loopCounter: 4.5
loopCounter: 5
loopCounter: 5.5
loopCounter: 6
loopCounter: 6.5
```

Example 6-16. Adjusting the step counter (continued)

```
loopCounter: 7
loopCounter: 7.5
loopCounter: 8
loopCounter: 8.5
loopCounter: 9
```

Controlling a For Loop Using Next

Finally, you can modify multiple variables on each Next statement. This allows you to nest one For loop within another. You might, for example, use an outer and an inner loop to iterate through the contents of collections, as described in Chapter 15. A simple example of this technique is shown in Example 6-17.

Example 6-17. Multiple updates with one Next statement

```
Option Strict On
Imports System
Module Module1

    Sub Main()

        Dim outer As Integer
        Dim inner As Integer

        For outer = 3 To 6
            For inner = 10 To 12
                Console.WriteLine("{0} * {1} = {2}", _
                    outer, inner, outer * inner)
        Next inner, outer

    End Sub 'Main

End Module
```

Output:
```
3 * 10 = 30
3 * 11 = 33
3 * 12 = 36
4 * 10 = 40
4 * 11 = 44
4 * 12 = 48
5 * 10 = 50
5 * 11 = 55
5 * 12 = 60
6 * 10 = 60
6 * 11 = 66
6 * 12 = 72
```

As an alternative to updating both counters in the same Next statement, you can provide each nested For loop with its own Next statement:

```
For outer = 3 To 6
    For inner = 10 To 12
```

```
        Console.WriteLine("{0} * {1} = {2}", _
            outer, inner, outer * inner)
    Next inner
Next outer
```

When you update a single value in a Next statement, you are free to leave off the variable you are updating. Thus, the previous code is identical to the following code:

```
For outer = 3 To 6
    For inner = 10 To 12
        Console.WriteLine("{0} * {1} = {2}", _
            outer, inner, outer * inner)
    Next
Next
```

In both cases, the output will be identical to that of Example 6-17.

 VB.NET programmers generally prefer using individual Next statements rather than combining Next statements on one line because it makes for code that is easier to understand and to maintain.

CHAPTER 7

Operators

An *operator* is a symbol (e.g., =, +, >, etc.) that causes VB.NET to take an action. That action might be an assignment of a value to a variable, the addition of two values, or a comparison of two values, etc.

In the previous chapters, you've seen a number of operators at work. For example, in Chapter 5 you saw the assignment operator used. The single equal sign (=) is used to assign a value to a variable, in this case the value 15 to the Integer variable myVariable:

```
Dim myVariable As Integer = 15
```

In Chapter 6, you saw more sophisticated operators, such as the greater than comparison operator (>) used to compare two values:

```
If valueOne > valueTwo Then
```

The preceding If statement compares valueOne with valueTwo; if the former is larger than the latter, the test evaluates true, and the If statement executes.

This chapter will consider many of the operators used in VB.NET in some detail.

The Assignment Operator (=)

The assignment operator causes the operand on the left side of the operator to have its value changed to whatever is on the right side of the operator. The following expression assigns the value 15 to myVariable:

```
Dim myVariable As Integer = 15
```

Mathematical Operators

VB.NET uses seven mathematical operators: five for standard calculations (+, -, *, /, and \), a sixth to return the remainder when dividing integers (Mod), and a seventh for exponential operations (^). The following sections consider the use of these operators.

Simple Arithmetical Operators (+, -, *, /, \)

VB.NET offers five operators for simple arithmetic: the addition (+), subtraction (-), and multiplication (*) operators work as you might expect. Adding two numbers returns their sum, subtracting returns their difference, and multiplying returns their product.

VB.NET offers *two* division operators: / and \. The forward slash or right-facing division operator (/) returns a floating-point answer. In other words, this operator allows for a fractional answer; there is no remainder. Thus, if you use this operator to divide 12 by 5 (12/5), the answer is 2.4. This answer is returned as a Double. Note that if you assign the returned value to an integer variable, the decimal part is lopped off, and the result will be 2. If Option Strict is turned On (as it should be), you cannot assign the result to an integer without explicitly casting because you would lose the decimal portion of the answer.

The backslash or left-facing division operator (\) performs integer division; that is, it returns an integer value and discards any remainder. Thus, if you use the integer division operator to divide 12 by 5 (12\5), the return value is truncated to the integer 2, with VB.NET discarding the remainder of 2. However, no cast is needed (even with Option Strict On) because you've explicitly asked for the integer value. Example 7-1 illustrates integer and fractional division.

Example 7-1. Arithmetic operators

```
Option Strict Off
' must be off to allow implicit casting of quotient to an integer
Imports System
Module Module1

    Sub Main()

        Dim twelve As Integer = 12
        Dim five As Integer = 5
        Dim intAnswer As Integer
        Dim doubleAnswer As Double

        Console.WriteLine("{0} + {1} = {2}", _
            twelve, five, twelve + five)

        Console.WriteLine("{0} - {1} = {2}", _
            twelve, five, twelve - five)

        Console.WriteLine("{0} * {1} = {2}", _
            twelve, five, twelve * five)
        ' integer division
```

Example 7-1. Arithmetic operators (continued)

```
    intAnswer = twelve \ five
    doubleAnswer = twelve \ five
    Console.WriteLine("{0} \ {1} = [integer] {2}  [double] {3}", _
        twelve, five, intAnswer, doubleAnswer)

    ' division. Assign result to both an integer and a double
    ' note, option strict must be off!
    intAnswer = twelve / five
    doubleAnswer = twelve / five
    Console.WriteLine("{0} / {1} = [integer] {2}  [double] {3}", _
        twelve, five, intAnswer, doubleAnswer)

  End Sub ' End of the Main() method definition

End Module
```

Output:
```
12 + 5 = 17
12 - 5 = 7
12 * 5 = 60
12 \ 5 = [integer] 2   [double] 2
12 / 5 = [integer] 2   [double] 2.4
```

In Example 7-1, you first declare two variables named twelve and five, which are initialized to the contain the numeric values 12 and 5, respectively:

```
Dim twelve As Integer = 12
Dim five As Integer = 5
```

You then pass the sum, difference, and product of seven and five to the Console. WriteLine() method:

```
Console.WriteLine("{0} + {1} = {2}", _
    twelve, five, twelve + five)

Console.WriteLine("{0} - {1} = {2}", _
    twelve, five, twelve - five)

Console.WriteLine("{0} * {1} = {2}", _
    twelve, five, twelve * five)
```

The results are just as you would expect:

```
12 + 5 = 17
12 - 5 = 7
12 * 5 = 60
```

VB.NET allows for two types of division, standard (/) and integer (\), which produce floating-point and integer results, respectively. In addition, the type of the variable to which you assign the answer also affects the value that is ultimately saved. You cannot assign a floating-point answer to a variable of type Integer. So, even if you perform standard division and receive a fractional answer, if you assign that answer to an Integer variable, the result will be truncated—just as if you used integer division (\) to begin with! This is a bit confusing. Let's consider some examples.

First, you'll create two local variables, intAnswer and doubleAnswer, to hold two quotients:

```
Dim intAnswer As Integer
Dim doubleAnswer As Double
```

As the names imply, and the declarations confirm, intAnswer is a variable of type Integer (a whole number type) and doubleAnswer is a variable of type Double (a rational number type). The type of the variable affects whether it can hold a fractional answer—a Double can, an Integer can't.

Example 7-1 includes the following equations for integer division:

```
intAnswer = twelve \ five
doubleAnswer = twelve \ five
```

The result returned by integer division, using the (\) operator, is always an integer. Thus, it does not matter whether you assign the result of integer division to a variable of type Integer or to a variable of type Double. This is reflected in the output:

```
12 \ 5 = [integer] 2  [double] 2
```

Example 7-1 then uses the standard division operator (/), which allows for fractional answers:

```
intAnswer = twelve / five
doubleAnswer = twelve / five
```

The standard division operator returns a floating-point answer, which can be accommodated by a variable of type Double (as in your variable doubleAnswer). But assigning the result to an Integer variable (like intAnswer) implicitly casts the result to an Integer, which results in the fractional portion being discarded, as in the following output:

```
12 / 5 = [integer] 2  [double] 2.4
```

Example 7-1 implicitly casts a Double to an Integer to illustrate that the result is truncated. However, you would not normally write code like this. In fact, in order for Example 7-1 to compile as written, we've had to go against good programming practice by setting Option Strict to Off:

```
Option Strict Off
```

If you do not set Option Strict to Off, you will receive the following compile error:

```
Option Strict disallows implicit conversions from 'Double' to
'Integer'
```

Since in actual practice, Option Strict should always be On, if you need to cast, you should do so explicitly. Thus, you would set Option Strict to On, and then explicitly cast the result using one of the cast functions described in Chapter 5, as in the following:

```
intAnswer = CInt(twelve / five)
```

The modulus Operator (Mod) to Return Remainders

To find the remainder in integer division, use the modulus operator (Mod). For example, the statement 17 Mod 4 returns 1 (the remainder after integer division).

The modulus operator turns out to be more useful than you might at first imagine. When you perform modulus n on a number that is a multiple of n, the result is zero. Thus 80 Mod 10 = 0 because 80 is an even multiple of 10. This fact allows you to set up loops in which you take an action every *n*th time through the loop, by testing a counter to see if Modn is equal to zero, as illustrated in Example 7-2.

Example 7-2. Using the modulus operator (Mod)

```
Option Strict On
Imports System
Module Module1

    Sub Main()

        Dim counter As Integer

        ' count from 1 to 100
        For counter = 1 To 100
            ' display the value
            Console.Write("{0} ", counter)

            ' every tenth value, display a tab and the value
            If counter Mod 10 = 0 Then
                Console.WriteLine(vbTab & counter)
            End If

        Next counter

    End Sub ' End of Main() method definition

End Module
```

Output:
```
1 2 3 4 5 6 7 8 9 10     10
11 12 13 14 15 16 17 18 19 20    20
21 22 23 24 25 26 27 28 29 30    30
31 32 33 34 35 36 37 38 39 40    40
41 42 43 44 45 46 47 48 49 50    50
51 52 53 54 55 56 57 58 59 60    60
61 62 63 64 65 66 67 68 69 70    70
71 72 73 74 75 76 77 78 79 80    80
```

Example 7-2. Using the modulus operator (Mod) (continued)

```
81 82 83 84 85 86 87 88 89 90    90
91 92 93 94 95 96 97 98 99 100   100
```

In Example 7-2, the value of the counter variable is incremented by one each time through the For loop. Within the loop, the value of counter is compared with the result of modulus 10 (counter Mod 10). When this evaluates to zero, meaning the value of counter is evenly divisible by 10, the value is printed in the righthand column.

> This code uses the vbTab constant to represent a Tab character, as explained in Chapter 16.

The Exponentiation Operator (^)

The final arithmetic operator is the exponentiation operator (^), which raises a number to the power of the exponent. Example 7-3 raises the number 5 to a power of 4.

Example 7-3. The exponentiation operator

```
Option Strict On
Imports System
Module Module1

    Sub Main()

        Dim value As Integer = 5
        Dim power As Integer = 4

        Console.WriteLine("{0} to the {1}th power is {2}", _
            value, power, value ^ power)

    End Sub ' End of the Main() method definition

End Module
```

Output:
```
5 to the 4th power is 625
```

Relational Operators

Relational operators are used to compare two values and then return a Boolean (i.e., true or false). The greater-than operator (>), for example, returns true if the value on the left of the operator is greater than the value on the right. Thus, 5>2 returns the value true, while 2>5 returns the value false.

The relational operators for VB.NET are shown in Table 7-1. This table assumes two variables: bigValue and smallValue, in which bigValue has been assigned the value 100 and smallValue the value 50.

Table 7-1. Relational operators (assumes bigValue = 100 and smallValue = 50)

Name	Operator	Given this statement:	The expression evaluates to:
Equals	=	bigValue = 100	True
		bigValue = 80	False
Not Equals	<>	bigValue <> 100	False
		bigValue <> 80	True
Greater than	>	bigValue > smallValue	True
Greater than or equals	>= or =>	bigValue >= smallValue	True
		smallValue => bigValue	False
Less than	<	bigValue < smallValue	False
Less than or equals	<= or =<	smallValue <= bigValue	True
		bigValue =< smallValue	False

Each of these relational operators acts as you might expect. Notice that some of the operators are composed of two characters. For example, the greater than or equal to operator is created using the greater than symbol (>) and the equal sign (=). Notice that you can place these symbols in either order (>= or =>) to form the greater than or equal to operator.

In VB.NET, the equality operator and the assignment operator are represented by the same symbol, the equal sign (=). In the following code line, the symbol is used in each of these ways:

```
If myX = 5 Then myX = 7
```

The first use of the = symbol is as the equality operator ("if myX is equal to 5"); the second use is as the assignment operator ("set myX to the value 7"). The compiler figures out how the symbol is to be interpreted according to the context.

Logical Operators Within Conditionals

If statements (discussed in Chapter 6) test whether a condition is true. Often you will want to test whether two conditions are both true, or only one is true, or neither is true. VB.NET provides a set of logical operators for this, as shown in Table 7-2. This table assumes two variables, x and y, in which x has the value 5, and y has the value 7.

Table 7-2. Logical operators

Operator	Given this statement	The expression evaluates to	Logic
And	x = 3 And y = 7	False	Both must be true to evaluate true.
Or	x = 3 Or y = 7	True	Either or both must be true to evaluate true.
XOr	X = 5 XOr y = 7	False	True only if one (and only one) statement is true.
Not	Not x = 3	True	Expression must be false to evaluate true.

The And operator tests whether two statements are both True. The first line in Table 7-2 includes an example that illustrates the use of the And operator:

```
x = 3 And y = 7
```

The entire expression evaluates false because one side (x = 3) is false. (Remember that x=5 and y=7.)

With the Or operator, either or both sides must be true; the expression is false only if both sides are false. So, in the case of the example in Table 7-2:

```
x = 3 Or y = 7
```

the entire expression evaluates true because one side (y = 7) is true.

The XOr logical operator (which stands for eXtreme Or) is used to test if one (and only one) of the two statements is correct. Thus, the example from Table 7-2:

```
x = 5 XOr y = 7
```

evaluates false because both statements are true. (The XOr statement is false if both statements are true, or if both statements are false; it is true only if one, and only one, statement is true.)

With the Not operator, the statement is true if the expression is false, and vice versa. So, in the accompanying example:

```
Not x = 3
```

the entire expression is true because the tested expression (x = 3) is false. (The logic is: "it is true that it is not true that x is equal to 3.")

All of these examples appear in context in Example 7-4.

Example 7-4. The logical operators

```
Option Strict On
Imports System
Module Module1

    Sub Main()

        Dim x As Integer = 5
        Dim y As Integer = 7
```

Example 7-4. The logical operators (continued)

```
Dim andValue As Boolean
Dim orValue As Boolean
Dim xorValue As Boolean
Dim notValue As Boolean

andValue = x = 3 And y = 7
orValue = x = 3 Or y = 7
xorValue = x = 3 Xor y = 7
notValue = Not x = 3

Console.WriteLine("x = 3 And y = 7. {0}", andValue)
Console.WriteLine("x = 3 Or y = 7. {0}", orValue)
Console.WriteLine("x = 3 Xor y = 7. {0}", xorValue)
Console.WriteLine("Not x = 3. {0}", notValue)

    End Sub 'Main

End Module
```

Output:
```
x = 3 And y = 7. False
x = 3 Or y = 7. True
x = 3 Xor y = 7. True
Not x = 3. True
```

Operator Precedence

The compiler must know the order in which to evaluate a series of operators. For example, if I write:

```
myVariable = 5 + 7 * 3
```

there are three operators for the compiler to evaluate (=, +, and *). It could, for example, operate left to right, which would assign the value 5 to myVariable, then add 7 to the 5 (12) and multiply by 3 (36). Since we're evaluating from left to right, the assignment has been done, so the value 36 is thrown away. This is clearly not what is intended.

The rules of precedence tell the compiler which operators to evaluate first. As is the case in algebra, multiplication has higher precedence than addition, so 5+7*3 is equal to 26 rather than 36. Both addition and multiplication have higher precedence than assignment, so the compiler will do the math, and then assign the result (26) to myVariable only after the math is completed.

In VB.NET, parentheses are also used to change the order of precedence much as they are in algebra. Thus, you can change the result by writing:

```
myVariable = (5+7) * 3
```

Grouping the elements of the assignment in this way causes the compiler to add 5+7, multiply the result by 3, and then assign that value (36) to myVariable.

Within a single line of code, operators are evaluated in the following order:

- Mathematical
- Concatenation
- Relational/Comparison
- Logical

Relational operators are evaluated left to right. Mathematical operators are evaluated in this order:

- Exponentiation (^)
- Division and multiplication (/, *)
- Integer division (\)
- Modulus operator (Mod)
- Addition and subtraction (+,-)

The logical operators are evaluated in this order:

- Not
- And
- Or
- XOr

In some complex equations, you might need to nest parentheses to ensure the proper order of operations. For example, assume I want to know how many seconds my family wastes each morning. It turns out that the adults spend 20 minutes over coffee each morning and 10 minutes reading the newspaper. The children waste 30 minutes dawdling and 10 minutes arguing.

Here's my algorithm:

```
(((minDrinkingCoffee  + minReadingNewspaper )* numAdults ) +
((minDawdling + minArguing) * numChildren)) * secondsPerMinute.
```

Although this works, it is hard to read and hard to get right. It's much easier to use interim variables:

```
wastedByEachAdult = minDrinkingCoffee  +  minReadingNewspaper
wastedByAllAdults =  wastedByEachAdult * numAdults
wastedByEachKid =  minDawdling  + minArguing
wastedByAllKids =  wastedByEachKid * numChildren
wastedByFamily = wastedByAllAdults + wastedByAllKids
totalSeconds =  wastedByFamily * 60
```

The latter example uses many more interim variables, but it is far easier to read, understand, and (most important) debug. As you step through this program in your debugger, you can see the interim values and make sure they are correct. See Chapter 10 for more information.

A more complete listing is shown in Example 7-5.

Example 7-5. Using parentheses and interim variables

```
Option Strict On
Imports System
Module Module1

    Sub Main()
        Dim minDrinkingCoffee As Integer = 5
        Dim minReadingNewspaper As Integer = 10
        Dim minArguing As Integer = 15
        Dim minDawdling As Integer = 20

        Dim numAdults As Integer = 2
        Dim numChildren As Integer = 2

        Dim wastedByEachAdult As Integer
        Dim wastedByAllAdults As Integer
        Dim wastedByEachKid As Integer
        Dim wastedByAllKids As Integer
        Dim wastedByFamily As Integer
        Dim totalSeconds As Integer

        wastedByEachAdult = minDrinkingCoffee + minReadingNewspaper
        wastedByAllAdults = wastedByEachAdult * numAdults
        wastedByEachKid = minDawdling + minArguing
        wastedByAllKids = wastedByEachKid * numChildren
        wastedByFamily = wastedByAllAdults + wastedByAllKids
        totalSeconds = wastedByFamily * 60
        Console.WriteLine("Each adult wastes {0} minutes", wastedByEachAdult)
        Console.WriteLine("Each child wastes {0} mintues", wastedByEachKid)
        Console.WriteLine("Total minutes wasted by entire family: {0}", _
                wastedByFamily)
        Console.WriteLine("Total wasted seconds: {0}", totalSeconds)

    End Sub ' End of Main() module definition

End Module
```

Output:
```
Each adult wastes 15 minutes
Each child wasts 35 mintues
Total minutes wasted by entire family: 100
Total wasted seconds: 6000
```

CHAPTER 8

Classes and Objects

Chapter 5 discusses the intrinsic types, such as Integer, Long, and Single, that are built into the VB.NET language. As you may recall, these simple types allow you to hold and manipulate numeric values and strings. The true power of VB.NET, however, lies in its capacity to let the programmer define new types to suit particular problems. It is this ability to create new types that characterizes an object-oriented language. You specify new types in VB.NET by declaring and defining *classes*.

Particular instances of a class are called *objects*. The difference between a class and an object is the same as the difference between the concept of a Dog and the particular dog who is sitting at your feet as you read this. You can't play fetch with the definition of a Dog, only with an instance.

A Dog class describes what dogs are like: they have weight, height, eye color, hair color, disposition, and so forth. They also have actions they can take, such as eat, walk, bark, and sleep. A particular dog (such as my dog Milo) will have a specific weight (62 pounds), height (22 inches), eye color (black), hair color (yellow), disposition (angelic), and so forth. He is capable of all the actions—methods, in programming parlance—of any dog (though if you knew him you might imagine that eating is the only method he implements).

The huge advantage of classes in object-oriented programming is that classes *encapsulate* the characteristics and capabilities of a type in a single, self-contained unit. Suppose, for instance, you want to sort the contents of an instance of a Windows list box control. The list box control is defined as a class. One of the properties of that class is that it knows how to sort itself. Sorting is encapsulated within the class, and the details of how the list box sorts itself are not made visible to other classes. If you want a list box sorted, you just tell the list box to sort itself, and it takes care of the details.

So, you simply write a method that tells the list box to sort itself—and that's what happens. How it sorts is of no concern; *that* it does so is all you need to know.

As noted in Chapter 3, this is called encapsulation, which along with polymorphism and inheritance, is one of three cardinal principles of object-oriented programming. Polymorphism and inheritance are discussed in Chapter 11.

An old programming joke asks, how many object-oriented programmers does it take to change a light bulb? Answer: none, you just tell the light bulb to change itself.* This chapter explains the VB.NET language features that are used to specify new classes. The elements of a class—its behaviors and its state—are known collectively as its *class members*.

Class behavior is created by writing methods (sometimes called member functions). A method is a small routine that every object of the class can execute. For example, a Dog class might have a bark method; a list box class might have a sort method.

Class state is maintained by fields (sometimes called member variables). Fields can be primitive types (e.g., an Integer to hold the age of the dog, a set of strings to hold the contents of the list box), or fields can be objects of other classes (e.g., an Employee class may have a field of type Address).

Finally, classes may also have properties, which act like methods to the creator of the class, but look like fields to clients of the class. A client is any object that interacts with instances of the class.

Defining Classes

When you define a new class, you define the characteristics of all objects of that class, as well as their behaviors. For example, if you are creating your own windowing operating system, you might want to create screen widgets (known as controls in Windows). One control of interest might be a list box, a control that is very useful for presenting a list of choices to the user and enabling the user to select from the list.

List boxes have a variety of characteristics: height, width, location, and text color, for example. Programmers have also come to expect certain behaviors of list boxes: they can be opened, closed, sorted, and so on.

Object-oriented programming allows you to create a new type, ListBox, which encapsulates these characteristics and capabilities.

To define a new type or class, you first declare it and then define its methods and fields. You declare a class using the Class keyword. The complete syntax is as follows:

```
[attributes] [access-modifiers] Class identifier
[Inherits classname]
   {class-body}
End Class
```

---

* Alternate answer: "None, Microsoft has changed the standard to darkness."

Attributes are used to provide special metadata about a class (that is, information about the structure or use of the class) and are beyond the scope of this book. You will not need attributes for routine VB.NET programming.

Access modifiers are discussed later in this chapter. (Typically, your classes will use the keyword `Public` as an access modifier.)

The *identifier* is the name of the class that you provide. Typically, VB.NET classes are named with nouns (e.g., Dog, Employee, ListBox). The naming convention (not required, but strongly encouraged) is to use Pascal notation. In Pascal notation, you use no underbars nor hyphens, but if the name has two words (Golden Retriever) you push the two words together, each word beginning with an uppercase letter (GoldenRetriever).

The optional `Inherits` statement is discussed in Chapter 11.

The member definitions that make up the *class-body* (a discussion of which follows) are enclosed by open and closed curly braces ({}).

```
Public Class Dog
    Dim age As Integer   'the dog's age
    Dim weight As Integer  'the dog's weight
    Public Sub Bark()
       '....
    End Sub
End Class
```

All the things a Dog can do are described by methods within the class definition of Dog. The dog's attributes, or state, are described by the fields (member variables), such as age and weight.

Instantiating Objects

To make an actual instance, or object, of the Dog class, you must declare the object, and you must allocate memory for the object. These two steps combined are necessary to create, or *instantiate*, the object. Here's how you do it.

First, you declare the object by writing the access modifier (in this case, `Dim`), followed by an identifier (milo) for the object or instance of the class, the `As` keyword, and the type or class name (Dog):

```
Dim milo As Dog  'declare milo to be an instance of Dog
```

This is not unlike the way you create a local variable. Notice also that (as with variables), by convention the identifier for the object uses Camel notation. Camel notation is just like Pascal notation except that the very first letter is lowercase. Thus, a variable or object name might be myDog, designatedDriver, or plantManager.

The declaration alone doesn't actually create an instance, however. To create an instance of a class, you must also allocate memory for the object using the keyword New.

```
milo = New Dog()  'allocate memory for milo
```

You can combine the declaration of the Dog type with the memory allocation into a single line:

```
Dim milo As New Dog()
```

This declares milo to be an object of type Dog and also creates a new instance of Dog. You'll see what the parentheses are for later in this chapter in the discussion of the constructor.

In VB.NET, *everything* happens within a class. "But wait," I hear you cry, "we have been creating modules!" Yes, you've been writing code using modules, but when you compile your application, a class is created for you from that module. This is VB.NET's strategy to continue to use modules (as VB6 did) but still comply with the .NET approach that everything is a class. (See the next section, "Modules Are Classes," for further explanation).

Given that everything happens within a class, no methods can run outside of a class, not even Main(). The Main() method is the entry point for your program; it is called by the operating system, and it is where execution of your program begins. Typically, you'll create a small module to house Main():

```
Module modMain
    Public Sub Main()
        ...
    End Sub
End Module
```

The compiler will turn this module into a class for you, as explained in the next section. However, it is somewhat more efficient for you to declare the class yourself:

```
Public Class Tester
    Public Sub Main()
        Dim testObject As New Tester()
    End Sub
    ' other members
End Class
```

In the preceding code, you create the Tester class explicitly. Even though Tester was created to house the Main() method, you've not yet instantiated any objects of type Tester. To do so you would write:

```
Dim testObject As New Tester() 'make an instance of Tester
```

As you'll see later in this chapter, creating an instance of the Tester class allows you to call other methods on the object you've created (testObject).

One way to understand the difference between a class and an instance (object) of that class is to consider the distinction between the type Integer and a variable of type Integer.

You can't assign a value to a type:

```
Integer = 5  ' error
```

Instead, you assign a value to an object of that type—in this case, a variable of type Integer:

```
Dim myInteger As Integer
myInteger  = 5 'ok
```

Similarly, you can't assign values to fields in a class; you must assign values to fields in an object. Thus, you can't write:

```
Dog.weight = 5
```

This is not meaningful. It isn't true that every Dog's weight is 5 pounds. You must instead write:

```
milo.weight = 5
```

This says that a particular Dog's weight (milo's weight) is 5 pounds.

Modules Are Classes

You can see the relationship between modules and classes very easily. Begin by creating a new VB.NET console application called ModuleTest, as shown in Example 8-1.

Example 8-1. ModuleTest

```
Module Module1

    Sub Main( )
      Console.WriteLine("Hello from Module")
    End Sub

End Module
```

Using VS.NET, build this program and run it. Building the program saves an executable version on disk. Open ILDasm, which is the Intermediate Language DISassembler. ILDasm is a tool provided with the SDK that allows you to look at the Intermediate Language code produced by your program.

You might need to search for ILDasm on your disk. It is typically found in:

```
Program Files\Microsoft Visual Studio .NET\FrameworkSDK\Bin
```

Open ILDasm and make the following menu choice:

```
File->Open
```

Navigate to your *ModuleTest* directory, and then navigate into the *bin* directory. Double-click on the *.exe* file. Expand the project, and you'll find a declaration of a class. Double-click on the class, and you'll see that Module1 has been declared to be a class, as shown in Figure 8-1.

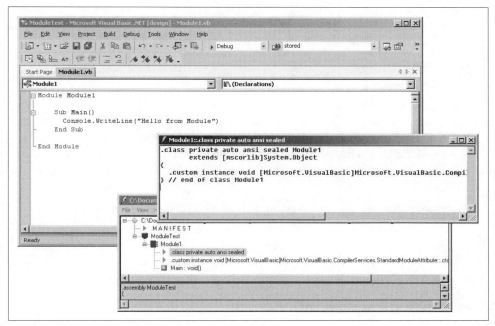

Figure 8-1. Modules are classes

Memory Allocation: The Stack Versus the Heap

Objects created within methods are called local variables. They are local to the method, as opposed to belonging to the object, as member variables do. The object is created within the method, used within the method and then destroyed when the method ends. Local objects are not part of the object's state, they are temporary value holders, useful only within the particular method.

Local variables of intrinsic types such as int are created on a portion of memory known as *the stack*. The stack is allocated and de-allocated as methods are invoked. When you start a method, all the local variables are created on the stack. When the method ends, local variables are destroyed.

These variables are referred to as *local* because they exist (and are visible) only during the lifetime of the method. They are said to have *local scope*. When the method ends, the variable goes out of scope and is destroyed.

VB.NET divides the world of types into value types and reference types. Value types are created on the stack. All the intrinsic types (Integer, Long, etc.) are value types, and thus are created on the stack.

Classes, on the other hand, are reference types. Reference types are created on an undifferentiated block of memory known as *the heap*. When you declare an instance of a reference type, what you actually are declaring is a reference. A reference is a variable that refers to another object. The reference acts like an alias for the object.

That is, when you write:

```
Dim milo As New Dog( )
```

what actually happens is that the New operator creates a Dog object on the heap and returns a reference to it. That reference is assigned to milo. Thus, milo is a reference object that refers to a Dog object on the heap. It is common to say that milo is a reference to a Dog, or even that milo is a Dog object, but technically that is incorrect. milo is actually a reference object that refers to an (unnamed) Dog object on the heap.

The reference milo acts as an alias for that unnamed object. For all practical purposes, however, you can treat milo as if it were the Dog object itself.

The implication of using references is that you can have more than one reference to the same object. To see this difference between creating value types and reference types, examine Example 8-2. A complete analysis follows the output.

Example 8-2. Creating value types and reference types

```
Option Strict On
Imports System
Public Module Module1

    Public Class Dog
        Public weight As Integer
    End Class

    Public Class Tester
        Public Shared Sub Main( )
            Dim testObject As New Tester( )
            testObject.Run( )
        End Sub

        Public Sub Run( )
            ' create an integer
            Dim firstInt As Integer = 5

            ' create a second integer
            Dim secondInt As Integer = firstInt

            ' display the two integers
            Console.WriteLine( _
```

Example 8-2. Creating value types and reference types (continued)

```
            "firstInt: {0} secondInt: {1}", firstInt, secondInt)

        ' modify the second integer
        secondInt = 7

        ' display the two integers
        Console.WriteLine( _
            "firstInt: {0} secondInt: {1}", firstInt, secondInt)

        ' create a dog
        Dim milo As New Dog( )

        ' assign a value to weight
        milo.weight = 5

        ' create a second reference to the dog
        Dim fido As Dog = milo

        ' display their values
        Console.WriteLine( _
            "Milo: {0}, fido: {1}", milo.weight, fido.weight)
        ' assign a new weight to the second reference
        fido.weight = 7

        ' display the two values
        Console.WriteLine( _
            "Milo: {0}, fido: {1}", milo.weight, fido.weight)
    End Sub

End Class

End Module
```

Output:
```
firstInt: 5 secondInt: 5
firstInt: 5 secondInt: 7
Milo: 5, fido: 5
Milo: 7, fido: 7
```

In Example 8-2, you create a class named Tester within your module. (Remember that the module itself will be converted to a class at compile time; that class will contain the Tester class.) You must mark Main() with the keyword Shared. (The Shared keyword is covered in detail in Chapter 9.)

Within Main(), you create an instance of the Tester class, and you call the Run() method on that instance:

```
Public Shared Sub Main( )
    Dim testObject As New Tester( )
    testObject.Run( )
End Sub
```

Run() begins by creating an integer, firstInt, and initializing it with the value 5. The second integer, secondInt, is then created and initialized with the value in firstInt. Their values are displayed as output:

```
firstInt: 5 secondInt: 5
```

Because Integer is a value type, a copy of the value is made, and secondInt is an independent second variable, as illustrated in Figure 8-2.

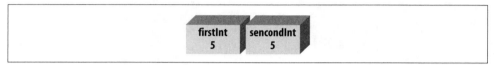

Figure 8-2. secondInt is a copy of firstInt

Then the program assigns a new value to secondInt:

```
secondInt = 7
```

Because these variables are value types, independent of one another, the first variable is unaffected. Only the copy is changed, as illustrated in Figure 8-3.

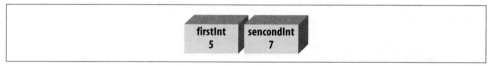

Figure 8-3. Only the copy is changed

When the values are displayed, they are now different:

```
firstInt: 5 secondInt: 7
```

Your next step is to create a simple Dog class with only one member: a public variable weight.

 Generally you will not make member variables public. The weight field was made public to simplify this example. The use of the Public keyword and other access modifiers are explained later in this chapter.

You instantiate a Dog object and save a reference to that Dog object in the reference milo:

```
Dim milo As New Dog()
```

You assign the value 5 to milo's weight field:

```
milo.weight = 5
```

You commonly say that you've set milo's weight to 5, but actually you've set the weight of the unnamed object on the heap to which milo refers, as shown in Figure 8-4.

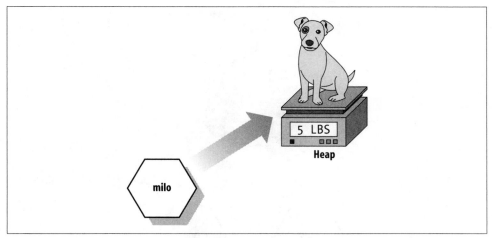

Figure 8-4. milo is a reference to an unnamed Dog object

Next you create a second reference to Dog and initialize it by setting it equal to milo. This creates a new reference to the same object on the heap.

```
Dim fido As Dog = milo
```

Notice that this is syntactically similar to creating a second Integer variable and initializing it with an existing Integer, as you did before:

```
Dim secondInt As Integer = firstInt
Dim fido As Dog = milo
```

The difference is that Dog is a reference type, so fido is not a copy of milo; it is a second reference to the same object to which milo refers. That is, you now have an object on the heap with two references to it, as illustrated in Figure 8-5.

When you change the weight of that object through the fido reference:

```
fido.weight = 7
```

you are changing the weight of the same object to which milo refers. This is reflected in the output:

```
Milo: 7, fido: 7
```

It isn't that fido is changing milo; it is that by changing the (unnamed) object on the heap to which fido refers, you are simultaneously changing the value of milo because they refer to the same unnamed object.

Creating a Time Class

Now consider a class to keep track of and display the time of day. The internal state of the class must be able to represent the current year, month, date, hour, minute, and second. You probably would also like the class to display the time in a variety of formats.

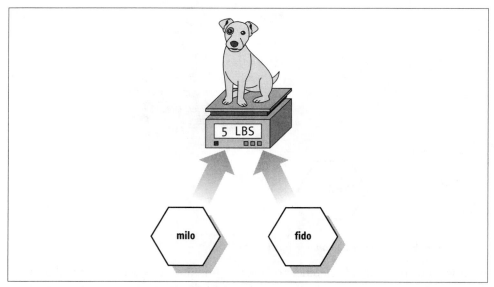

Figure 8-5. fido is a second reference to the Dog object

You might implement such a class by defining a single method and six variables, as shown in Example 8-3.

Example 8-3. The Time class

```
Option Strict On
Imports System
Public Class Time
    ' Private variables
    Private Year As Integer
    Private Month As Integer
    Private Date As Integer
    Private Hour As Integer
    Private Minute As Integer
    Private Second As Integer
    ' Public methods
    Public Sub DisplayCurrentTime()
        Console.WriteLine("stub for DisplayCurrentTime")
    End Sub 'DisplayCurrentTime
End Class 'Time

Module Module1
    Sub Main()
        Dim timeObject As New Time()
        timeObject.DisplayCurrentTime()
    End Sub

End Module
```

This code creates a new user-defined type: Time. The Time class definition begins with the declaration of a number of member variables: Year, Month, Date, Hour, Minute, and Second. The keyword Private indicates that these values can only be called only by methods of this class. The Private keyword is an access modifier, the use of which is explained later in this chapter.

Many VB.NET programmers prefer to put all of the member fields together, either at the very top or the very bottom of the class declaration, though that is not required by the language.

The only method declared within the Time class is the method DisplayCurrentTime(). The DisplayCurrentTime() method is defined as a sub-procedure, or subroutine; as explained in Chapter 2, which means it will not return a value to the method that invokes it. For now, the body of this method has been "stubbed out."

Stubbing out a method is a temporary measure you might use when you first write a program to allow you to think about the overall structure without filling in every detail when you create a class. When you stub out a method body, you leave out the internal logic and just mark the method, as done here, perhaps with a message to the console:

```
Public Sub DisplayCurrentTime()
    Console.WriteLine("stub for DisplayCurrentTime")
End Sub 'DisplayCurrentTime
```

When you create the project, VS.NET creates the module, named Module1. Within the module, you define your Main() method, and within Main() you can instantiate a Time object:

```
Module Module1
    Sub Main()
        Dim timeObject As New Time()
```

Because timeObject is an instance of Time, Main() can make use of the DisplayCurrentTime() method available with objects of that type and call it to display the time:

```
    timeObject.DisplayCurrentTime()
```

You invoke a method on an object by writing the name of the object (timeObject), followed by the dot operator (.), followed by the method name and parameter list in parentheses (in this case, empty). You'll see how to pass in values to initialize the member variables in the discussion of constructors, later in this chapter.

Access Modifiers

An access modifier determines which class methods—including methods of other classes—can see and use a member variable or method within a class. Table 8-1 summarizes the VB.NET access modifiers.

Table 8-1. Access modifiers

Access modifier	Restrictions
Public	No restrictions. Members that are marked Public are visible to any method of any class.
Private	The members in class A that are marked Private are accessible only to methods of class A.
Protected	The members in class A that are marked Protected are accessible to methods of class A and also to methods of classes derived from class A. The Protected access modifier is used with derived classes, as explained in Chapter 11.
Friend	The members in class A that are marked Friend are accessible to methods of any class in A's assembly.[a]
Protected Friend	The members in class A that are marked Protected Friend are accessible to methods of class A, to methods of classes derived from class A, and also to any class in A's assembly. This is effectively Protected *or* Friend. (There is no concept of Protected *and* Friend.)

[a] An assembly is a collection of files that appear to the programmer as a single executable (.exe) or DLL.

The Time class and its DisplayCurrentTime() method are both declared public so that any other class can make use of them. If DisplayCurrentTime() had been private, it would not be possible to invoke DisplayCurrentTime from any method of any class other than methods of Time. In Example 8-3, DisplayCurrentTime() was invoked from a method of Tester (not Time), and this was legal because both the class (Time) and the method (DisplayCurrentTime) were marked public.

It is good programming practice to explicitly set the accessibility of all methods and members of your class.

Method Arguments

The behavior of a class is defined by the methods of that class. To make your methods as flexible as possible, you can define parameters: information passed into the method when the method is invoked. Thus, rather than having to write one method when you want to sort your ListBox from A–Z and a second method when you want to sort it from Z–A, you define a more general Sort() method and pass in a parameter specifying the order of the sort.

Methods can take any number of parameters.* The parameter list follows the method name and is encased in parentheses. Each parameter's type is identified before the name of the parameter.

For example, the following declaration defines a subprocedure (thus, it returns no value) named MyMethod() which takes two parameters, an integer and a button:

---

* The terms "argument" and "parameter" are often used interchangeably, though some programmers insist on differentiating between the parameter declaration and the arguments passed in when the method is invoked.

```
Sub MyMethod (firstParam As Integer, secondParam As Button)
    ' ...
End Sub
```

Within the body of the method, the parameters act as local variables, as if you had declared them in the body of the method and initialized them with the values passed in. Example 8-4 illustrates how you pass values into a method, in this case values of type Integer and Single.

The compiler will mark your parameters as ByVal, indicating that the parameter is passed "by value."

ByVal firstParam As Integer

When a parameter is passed by value, a copy is made. This is opposed to passing "by reference." (The distinction is described in Chapter 9.) The ByVal keyword and its implications are discussed in detail in Chapter 9.

Example 8-4. Passing parameters

```
Option Strict On
Imports System
Public Class TestClass
    Sub SomeMethod( _
        ByVal firstParam As Integer, _
        ByVal secondParam As Single)

        Console.WriteLine( _
            "Here are the parameters received: {0}, {1}", _
            firstParam, secondParam)

    End Sub
End Class

Module Module1

    Sub Main()
        Dim howManyPeople As Integer = 5
        Dim pi As Single = 3.14F

        Dim tc As New TestClass()
        tc.SomeMethod(howManyPeople, pi)

    End Sub

End Module
```

Output:
```
Here are the parameters received: 5, 3.14
```

Note that, if Option Strict is On, when you pass in a Single with a decimal part (3.14), you must append the letter F (3.14F) to signal the compiler that the value is a Single, and not a Double.

The method SomeMethod() takes an Integer and a Single and displays them using Console.WriteLine(). The parameters, which are named firstParam and second-Param, are treated as local variables within SomeMethod().

In the calling method (Main), two local variables (howManyPeople and pi) are created and initialized. These variables are passed as the arguments to SomeMethod(). The compiler maps howManyPeople to firstParam and pi to secondParam, based on their relative positions in the parameter list.

Constructors

In Example 8-3, notice that the statement that creates the Time object looks as though it is invoking a method:

```
Dim timeObject As New Time();
```

In fact, a method *is* invoked whenever you instantiate an object. This method is called a *constructor*. Each time you define a class, you are free to define your own constructor, but if you don't, the compiler will provide one for you invisibly and automatically. The job of a constructor is to create the object specified by a class and to put it into a valid state. Before the constructor runs, the object is just a blob of memory; after the constructor completes, the memory holds a valid instance of the class.

The Time class of Example 8-3 does not define a constructor. As noted earlier, if you do not declare a constructor, the compiler provides one for you. The constructor provided by the compiler creates the object but takes no other action.

Any constructor that takes no arguments is called a *default constructor*. It turns out that the constructor provided by the compiler takes no arguments, and hence is a default constructor. This terminology has caused a great deal of confusion. You can create your own default constructor, and if you do not create a constructor at all, the compiler will create a default constructor for you, by default.

If you do not explicitly initialize your member variables, they are initialized to innocuous values (integers to 0, strings to the empty string, etc.). Table 8-2 lists the default values assigned to primitive types.

Table 8-2. Types and their default values

Type	Default value
Numeric (Integer, Long, etc.)	0
Boolean	false
Char	'\0' (null)
Enum	0
Reference	null

Typically, you'll want to define your own constructor and provide it with arguments, so that the constructor can set the initial state for your object. In Example 8-3, you want to pass in the current year, month, date, and so forth, so that the object is created with meaningful data.

You declare a constructor like any other member method except:

- The constructor is always named New.
- Constructors are declared using the Sub keyword (which means there is no return value).

If there are arguments to be passed, you define an argument list just as you would for any other method. Example 8-5 declares a constructor for the Time class that accepts a single argument, an object of type DateTime. (DateTime is a type provided by the .NET Framework Class Library.)

Example 8-5. Creating a constructor

```
Option Strict On
Imports System
Public Class Time
    ' Private variables
    Private Year As Integer
    Private Month As Integer
    Private Date As Integer
    Private Hour As Integer
    Private Minute As Integer
    Private Second As Integer

    ' Public methods
    Public Sub DisplayCurrentTime()
        System.Console.WriteLine("{0}/{1}/{2} {3}:{4}:{5}", _
            Month, Date, Year, Hour, Minute, Second)
    End Sub 'DisplayCurrentTime

    ' Constructor
    Public Sub New( _
ByVal theYear As Integer, _
ByVal theMonth As Integer, _
ByVal theDate As Integer, _
ByVal theHour As Integer, _
```

Example 8-5. Creating a constructor (continued)

```
ByVal theMinute As Integer, _
ByVal theSecond As Integer)

        Year = theYear
        Month = theMonth
        Date = theDate
        Hour = theHour
        Minute = theMinute
        Second = theSecond
    End Sub

End Class 'Time

Module Module1

    Sub Main()
        Dim timeObject As New Time(2005, 3, 25, 9, 35, 20)
        timeObject.DisplayCurrentTime()
    End Sub

End Module
```

Output:
3/25/2005 9:35:20

In this example, the constructor (Sub New) takes a series of integer values and initializes all the member variables based on these parameters. When the constructor finishes, the Time object exists, and the values have been initialized. When DisplayCurrentTime() is called in Main(), the values are displayed.

Try commenting out one of the assignments and running the program again. You'll find that each member variable is initialized by the compiler to 0. Integer member variables are set to 0 if you don't otherwise assign them. Remember that value types (e.g., integers) must be initialized; if you don't tell the constructor what to do, it will set innocuous values.

Initializers

It is possible to initialize the values of member variables in an *initializer*, instead of having to do so in the constructor. You create an initializer by assigning an initial value to a class member:

```
Private Second As Integer = 30
```

Assume that the semantics of the Time object are such that no matter what time is set, the seconds are always initialized to 30. You might rewrite your Time class to use an initializer so that the value of Second is always initialized, as shown in Example 8-6.

Example 8-6. Using an initializer

```
Option Strict On
Imports System
Public Class Time
   ' Private variables
   Private Year As Integer
   Private Month As Integer
   Private Date As Integer
   Private Hour As Integer
   Private Minute As Integer
   Private Second As Integer = 30

   ' Public methods
   Public Sub DisplayCurrentTime()
       System.Console.WriteLine("{0}/{1}/{2} {3}:{4}:{5}", _
           Month, Date, Year, Hour, Minute, Second)
   End Sub 'DisplayCurrentTime

   Public Sub New( _
   ByVal theYear As Integer, _
   ByVal theMonth As Integer, _
   ByVal theDate As Integer, _
   ByVal theHour As Integer, _
   ByVal theMinute As Integer)
      Year = theYear
      Month = theMonth
      Date = theDate
      Hour = theHour
      Minute = theMinute
   End Sub

End Class 'Time

Module Module1

   Sub Main()
      Dim timeObject As New Time(2005, 3, 25, 9, 35)
      timeObject.DisplayCurrentTime()
   End Sub

End Module
```

Output:
3/25/2005 9:35:30

If you do not provide a specific initializer, the constructor will initialize each integer member variable to zero (0). In the case shown, however, the Second member is initialized to 30:

```
Private Second As Integer = 30
```

Copy Constructors

A *copy constructor* creates a new object by copying variables from an existing object of the same type. For example, you might want to pass a Time object to a Time constructor so that the new Time object has the same values as the old one.

VB.NET does not provide a copy constructor, so if you want one you must provide it yourself. Such a constructor copies the elements from the original object into the new one:

```
Public Sub New(ByVal existingObject As Time)
    Year = existingObject.Year
    Month = existingObject.Month
    Date = existingObject.Date
    Hour = existingObject.Hour
    minute = existingObject.Minute
    second = existingObject.Second
End Sub
```

A copy constructor is invoked by instantiating an object of type Time and passing it the name of the Time object to be copied:

```
Dim t2 As New Time(existingObject)
```

Here an existing Time object (existingObject) is passed as a parameter to the copy constructor which will create a new Time object (), as shown in Example 8-7.

Example 8-7. Copy constructor

```
Option Strict On
Imports System
Public Class Time
    ' Private variables
    Private Year As Integer
    Private Month As Integer
    Private Date As Integer
    Private Hour As Integer
    Private Minute As Integer
    Private Second As Integer = 30

    ' Public methods
    Public Sub DisplayCurrentTime()
        System.Console.WriteLine("{0}/{1}/{2} {3}:{4}:{5}", _
            Month, Date, Year, Hour, Minute, Second)
    End Sub 'DisplayCurrentTime

    Public Sub New( _
    ByVal theYear As Integer, _
    ByVal theMonth As Integer, _
    ByVal theDate As Integer, _
    ByVal theHour As Integer, _
    ByVal theMinute As Integer)
        Year = theYear
```

Example 8-7. Copy constructor (continued)

```
        Month = theMonth
        Date = theDate
        Hour = theHour
        Minute = theMinute
        Second = theSecond
    End Sub

    Public Sub New(existingObject As Time)
        Year = existingObject.Year
        Month = existingObject.Month
        Date = existingObject.Date
        Hour = existingObject.Hour
        Minute = existingObject.Minute
        Second = existingObject.Second
    End Sub

End Class 'Time

Module Module1

    Sub Main()
        Dim timeObject As New Time(2005, 3, 25, 9, 35)
        Dim t2 As New Time(timeObject)
        timeObject.DisplayCurrentTime()
        t2.DisplayCurrentTime()
    End Sub

End Module
```

Output:
3/25/2005 9:35:30
3/25/2005 9:35:30

The Me Keyword

The keyword Me refers to the current instance of an object. The Me reference is a hidden reference to every unshared method of a class; shared methods are discussed later in this chapter. Each method can refer to the other methods and variables of that object by way of the Me reference.

The Me reference is typically used in any of three ways. The first way is to qualify instance members that have the same name as parameters, as in the following:

```
    Public Sub SomeMethod(ByVal Hour As Integer)
        Me.Hour = Hour
    End Sub
```

In this example, SomeMethod() takes a parameter (Hour) with the same name as a member variable of the class. The Me reference is used to resolve the ambiguity. While Me.Hour refers to the member variable, Hour refers to the parameter.

The argument in favor of this style, which is often used in constructors, is that you pick the right variable name and then use it both for the parameter and for the member variable. The counter-argument is that using the same name for both the parameter and the member variable can be confusing.

The second use of the Me reference is to pass the current object as a parameter to another method, as in the following code:

```
Public Sub myMethod()
    Dim someObject As New SomeType()
    someObject.SomeMethod(Me)
End Sub
```

In this code snippet, you call a method on an object, passing in the Me reference. This allows the method you're calling access to the methods and properties of the current object.

The third use of the Me reference is with indexers, which are covered in Chapter 14.

You can also use the Me reference to make the copy constructor more explicit:

```
Public Sub New(ByVal that As Time)
    Me.Year = That.Year
    Me.Month = That.Month
    Me.Date = That.Date
    Me.Hour = That.Hour
    Me.Minute = That.Minute
    Me.Second = That.Second
End Sub
```

In this snippet, Me refers to the current object (the object whose constructor is running), and That refers to the object passed in.

Using Shared Members

The properties and methods of a class can be either *instance members* or *shared members*. Instance members are associated with instances of a type, while shared members are associated with the class, and not with any particular instance. Methods are instance methods unless you explicitly mark them with the keyword Shared.

The vast majority of methods will be instance methods. The semantics of an instance method are that you are taking an action on a specific object. From time to time, however, it is convenient to be able to invoke a method without having an instance of the class, and for that you will use a shared method.

You can access a shared member through the name of the class in which it is declared. For example, suppose you have a class named Button and have instantiated objects of that class named btnUpdate and btnDelete.

Suppose that the Button class has an instance method Draw() and a shared method GetButtonCount(). The job of Draw() is to draw the current button; the job of GetButtonCount() is to return the number of buttons currently visible on the form.

You access an instance method through an instance of the class—that is, through an object:

```
btnUpdate.SomeMethod()
```

You can access a shared method in the same way:

```
btnUpdate.GetButtonCount()
```

You can also access a shared method through the class name (rather than through an instance):

```
Button.GetButtonCount()
```

This allows you to access the shared method without having an instance of the class.

A common use of shared member variables, or fields, is to keep track of the number of instances/objects that currently exist for your class. In Example 8-8, you create a Cat class. The Cat class might be used in a pet store simulation. For this example, the Cat class has been stripped to its absolute essentials. An analysis follows.

Example 8-8. Shared fields

```
Option Strict On
Imports System
Class Cat '
   Private Shared instances As Integer = 0
   Private weight As Integer
   Private name As String

   Public Sub New(ByVal name As String, ByVal weight As Integer)
      instances += 1
      Me.name = name
      Me.weight = weight
   End Sub

   Public Shared Sub HowManyCats()
      Console.WriteLine("{0} cats adopted", instances)
   End Sub

   Public Sub TellWeight()
      Console.WriteLine("{0} is {1} pounds", _
      name, weight)
   End Sub

End Class 'Cat

Module Module1

   Sub Main()
      Cat.HowManyCats()
```

Example 8-8. Shared fields (continued)

```
    Dim frisky As New Cat("Frisky", 5)
    frisky.TellWeight()
    Cat.HowManyCats()
    Dim whiskers As New Cat("Whiskers", 7)
    whiskers.TellWeight()  ' instance method
    whiskers.HowManyCats() ' shared method through instance
    Cat.HowManyCats()      ' shared method through class name
  End Sub

End Module
```

Output:
```
0 cats adopted
Frisky is 5 pounds
1 cats adopted
Whiskers is 7 pounds
2 cats adopted
2 cats adopted
```

The Cat class begins by defining a shared member variable, instances, that is initialized to 0. This shared member field will keep track of the number of Cat objects created. Each time the constructor (Sub New) runs (creating a new object), the instances field is incremented.

The Cat class also defines two instance fields: name and weight. These track the name and weight of each individual Cat object.

The Cat class defines two methods: HowManyCats() and TellWeight(). HowManyCats() is shared. The number of cats is not an attribute of any given Cat; it is an attribute of the entire class. TellWeight() is an instance method. The name and weight of each cat is per instance (i.e., each Cat has its own name and weight).

The Main() method accesses the shared HowManyCats() method directly, through the class:

```
    Cat.HowManyCats()
```

Main() then creates an instance of Cat and accesses the instance method TellWeight( ) through an instance (frisky) of Cat:

```
    Dim frisky As New Cat("Frisky", 5)
    frisky.TellWeight()
```

Each time a new Cat is created, HowManyCats() reports the increase.

You access the instance method through the object, but you can access the shared method either through an object or through the class name:

```
    whiskers.TellWeight()
    whiskers.HowManyCats()
    Cat.HowManyCats()
```

Destroying Objects

Unlike many other programming languages (C, C++, Pascal, etc.), VB.NET provides garbage collection. Your objects are automatically destroyed when you are done with them. You do not need to worry about cleaning up after your objects unless you use unmanaged resources. An unmanaged resource is an operating system feature outside of the .NET Framework, such as a file handle or a database connection. If you do control an unmanaged resource, you will need to explicitly free that resource when you are done with it. Implicit control over this resource is provided with a Finalize() method, which will be called by the garbage collector when your object is destroyed:

```
Protected Overrides Sub Finalize()
   ' release non-managed resources
   MyBase.Finalize()
End Sub
```

The `Protected` keyword is described in the "Access Modifiers" section earlier in this chapter. For a discussion of the `Overrides` keyword, see Chapter 13.

It is not legal to call Finalize() explicitly. Finalize() will be called by the garbage collector. If you do handle precious unmanaged resources (such as file handles) that you want to close and dispose of as quickly as possible, you ought to implement the IDisposable interface. (You will learn more about interfaces in Chapter 13.) The IDisposable interface requires that you create a method named Dispose() that will be called by your clients.

If you provide a Dispose() method, you should stop the garbage collector from calling your object's destructor. To stop the garbage collector, you call the shared method GC.SuppressFinalize(), passing in the `Me` reference for your object. Your Finalize() method can then call your Dispose() method. Thus, you might write:

```
Public Class Testing
   Implements IDisposable
   Dim is_disposed As Boolean = False

   Protected Sub Dispose(ByVal disposing As Boolean)
      If Not is_disposed Then
         If disposing Then
            Console.WriteLine("Not in destructor, OK to reference other objects")
         End If
         ' perform cleanup for this object
         Console.WriteLine("Disposing...")
      End If
      Me.is_disposed = True
   End Sub

   Public Sub Dispose() Implements IDisposable.Dispose
      Dispose(True)
      'tell the GC not to finalize
```

```
        GC.SuppressFinalize(Me)
    End Sub

    Protected Overrides Sub Finalize()
        Dispose(False)
        Console.WriteLine("In destructor.")
    End Sub

End Class
```

CHAPTER 9

Inside Methods

In Chapter 8, you saw that classes consist of fields and methods. Fields hold the state of the object, and methods define the object's behavior.

In this chapter, you'll explore how methods work in more detail. You've already seen how to create methods. In this chapter, you'll learn about method overloading, a technique that allows you to create more than one method with the same name. This allows your clients to invoke the method with different parameter types.

This chapter also introduces properties. Properties look to clients of your class like member variables, but properties are implemented as methods. This allows you to maintain good data hiding, while providing your clients with convenient access to the state of your class.

Chapter 8 described the difference between value types (i.e., primitives like Integer, Long, etc.,) and reference types (i.e., classes). This chapter explores the implications of passing value types to methods and shows how you can pass value types *by reference*, allowing the called method to act on the original object in the calling method.

Overloading Methods

Often you'll want to have more than one method with the same name. The most common example of this is to have more than one constructor. Having more than one constructor with the same name allows you to create the object with different parameters. For example, if you were creating a Time object, you might have circumstances where you want to create the Time object by passing in the date, hours, minutes, and seconds. Other times, you might want to create a Time object by passing in an existing Time object. Still other times, you might want to pass in just a date, without hours and minutes. Overloading the constructor allows you to provide these various options.

Chapter 8 explained that your constructor is automatically invoked when your object is created. Let's return to the Time class created in that chapter. It is possible to create a Time object by passing in a DateTime object to the constructor.

It would be convenient also to allow the client to create a new Time object by passing in year, month, date, hour, minute, and second values. Some clients might prefer one or the other constructor; you can provide both and the client can decide which better fits the situation.

In order to overload your constructor, you must make sure that each constructor has a unique *signature*. The signature of a method is composed of its name and its parameter list. Two methods differ in their signatures if they have different names or different parameter lists. Parameter lists can differ by having different numbers or types of parameters.

```
Public Sub MyMethod(p1 as Integer)
Public Sub MyMethod(p1 as Integer, p2 as Integer) 'different number
Public Sub MyMethod(p1 as Integer, s1 as String) 'different types
Public Sub SomeMethod(p1 as Integer)              'different name
```

The previous four lines of code show how you might distinguish methods by signature.

The first three methods are all overloads of the myMethod() method. The first differs from the second and third in the number of parameters. The second closely resembles the third version, but the second parameter in each is a different type. In the second method, the second parameter (p2) is an integer; in the third method, the second parameter (s1) is a string. These changes to the number or type of parameters are sufficient changes in the signature to allow the compiler to distinguish the methods.

The fourth method differs from the other three methods by having a different name. This is not method overloading, just different methods, but it illustrates that two methods can have the same number and type of parameters if they have different names. Thus, the fourth and first have the same parameter list, but their names are different.

A class can have any number of methods, as long as each one's signature differs from that of all the others. Example 9-1 illustrates a Time class with two constructors, one that takes a DateTime object, and the other that takes six integers.

Example 9-1. Overloading a method

```
Option Strict On
Imports System
Public Class Time
    ' private member variables
    Private Year As Integer
    Private Month As Integer
    Private Date As Integer
```

Example 9-1. Overloading a method (continued)

```
    Private Hour As Integer
    Private Minute As Integer
    Private Second As Integer

    ' public accessor methods
    Public Sub DisplayCurrentTime()
        System.Console.WriteLine( _
        "{0}/{1}/{2} {3}:{4}:{5}", _
        Month, Date, Year, Hour, Minute, Second)
    End Sub 'DisplayCurrentTime

    ' constructors
    Public Sub New(ByVal dt As System.DateTime)
        Year = dt.Year
        Month = dt.Month
        Date = dt.Date
        Hour = dt.Hour
        Minute = dt.Minute
        Second = dt.Second
    End Sub 'New

    Public Sub New( _
    ByVal Year As Integer, _
    ByVal Month As Integer, _
    ByVal Date As Integer, _
    ByVal Hour As Integer, _
    ByVal Minute As Integer, _
    ByVal Second As Integer)
        Me.Year = Year
        Me.Month = Month
        Me.Date = Date
        Me.Hour = Hour
        Me.Minute = Minute
        Me.Second = Second
    End Sub 'New
End Class 'Time

Module Module1

    Sub Main()
        Dim currentTime as System.DateTime = System.DateTime.Now
        Dim time1 As New Time(currentTime)
        time1.DisplayCurrentTime()
        Dim time2 As New Time(2005, 11, 18, 11, 3, 30)
        time2.DisplayCurrentTime()
    End Sub

End Module
```

Output:
5/1/2002 8:53:05
11/18/2005 11:3:30

The Time class in Example 9-1 has two constructors. If a function's signature consisted only of the function name, the compiler would not know which constructors to call when constructing the new Time objects time1 and time2. However, because the signature includes the function parameters and their types, the compiler is able to match the constructor call for time1 with the constructor whose signature requires a DateTime object.

```
Dim currentTime As New System.DateTime()
Dim time1 As New Time(currentTime)
time1.DisplayCurrentTime()
```

Likewise, the compiler is able to associate the time2 constructor call with the constructor method whose signature specifies six integer arguments.

```
Dim time2 As New Time(2005, 11, 18, 11, 3, 30)
time2.DisplayCurrentTime()
```

 When you overload a method, you must change the signature (i.e., the name, number, or type of the parameters). You are free, as well, to change the return type, but this is optional. Changing only the return type does not overload the method, and creating two methods with the same signature but differing return types will generate a compile error.

Encapsulating Data with Properties

It is generally desirable to designate the member variables of a class as private (using the Private keyword). This means that only member methods of that class can access their value. You make member variables private to support *data hiding*, which is part of the encapsulation of a class.

Object-oriented programmers are told that member variables should be private. That is fine, but how do you provide access to this data to your clients? The answer for VB.NET programmers is properties.

Properties allow clients to access class state as if they were accessing member fields directly, while actually implementing that access through a class method.

This is ideal. The client wants direct access to the state of the object. The class designer, however, wants to hide the internal state of the class in class fields, and provide indirect access through a method. The property provides both: the illusion of direct access for the client, the reality of indirect access for the class developer.

By decoupling the class state from the method that accesses that state, the designer is free to change the internal state of the object as needed. When the Time class is first created, the Hour value might be stored as a member variable. When the class is redesigned, the Hour value might be computed, or retrieved from a database. If the client had direct access to the original Hour member variable, the change to computing the value would break the client. By decoupling and forcing the client to go through a property, the Time class can change how it manages its internal state without breaking client code.

In short, properties provide the data hiding required by good object-oriented design. Example 9-2 creates a property called Hour, which is then discussed in the paragraphs that follow.

 It is a convention in VB.NET to give your private member variables names with a prefix to distinguish them from the property name. For example, you might prefix every member variable with the letter m (for member), thus mMinute and mHour. You are then free to use the unprefixed version (Hour and Minute) for the property. By convention, properties are named with Pascal case (first letters are uppercase).

Example 9-2. Properties

```
Option Strict On
Imports System
Public Class Time
    ' private member variables
    Private mYear As Integer
    Private mMonth As Integer
    Private mDate As Integer
    Private mHour As Integer
    Private mMinute As Integer
    Private mSecond As Integer

    Property Hour() As Integer
        Get
            Return mHour
        End Get
        Set(ByVal Value As Integer)
            mHour = Value
        End Set
    End Property

    ' public accessor methods
    Public Sub DisplayCurrentTime()
        Console.WriteLine( _
        "{0}/{1}/{2} {3}:{4}:{5}", _
        mMonth, mDate, mYear, mHour, mMinute, mSecond)
    End Sub 'DisplayCurrentTime

    ' constructors
    Public Sub New(ByVal dt As System.DateTime)
        mYear = dt.Year
        mMonth = dt.Month
        mDate = dt.Date
        mHour = dt.Hour
        mMinute = dt.Minute
        mSecond = dt.Second
    End Sub 'New
    Public Sub New( _
```

Example 9-2. Properties (continued)

```
    ByVal mYear As Integer, _
    ByVal mMonth As Integer, _
    ByVal mDate As Integer, _
    ByVal mHour As Integer, _
    ByVal mMinute As Integer, _
    ByVal mSecond As Integer)
        Me.mYear = mYear
        Me.mMonth = mMonth
        Me.mDate = mDate
        Me.mHour = mHour
        Me.mMinute = mMinute
        Me.mSecond = mSecond
    End Sub 'New

End Class 'Time

Module Module1

    Sub Main()
        Dim currentTime As System.DateTime = System.DateTime.Now
        Dim time1 As New Time(currentTime)
        time1.DisplayCurrentTime()

        'extract the hour to a local variable
        Dim theHour As Integer = time1.Hour

        'display the local variable
        Console.WriteLine("Retrieved the hour: {0}", _
         theHour)

        'add one to the local variable
        theHour += 1

        'write the time back to the object
        time1.Hour = theHour

        'display the result
        Console.WriteLine("Updated the hour: {0}", _
         time1.Hour)

    End Sub

End Module
```

Output:
```
5/1/2002 8:56:59
Retrieved the hour: 8
Updated the hour: 9
```

You create a property with this syntax:

```
    Property Identifier() As Type
      Get
```

```
        statements
    End Get

    Set(ByVal Value As Type)
        statements
    End Set
End Property
```

If you create the property in VS.NET however, the editor will provide extensive help with the syntax. For example, once you type:

```
Property Minute As Integer
```

the IDE will reformat your property as follows:

```
Property Minute() As Integer
    Get

    End Get
    Set(ByVal Value As Integer)

    End Set
End Property
```

In Example 9-2, Hour is a property. Its declaration creates two accessors: Get and Set.

```
Property Hour() As Integer
    Get
        Return mHour
    End Get
    Set(ByVal Value As Integer)
mHour = Value
    End Set
End Property
```

Each accessor has an *accessor-body* that does the work of retrieving and setting the property value. The property value might be stored in a database (in which case the accessor would do whatever work is needed to interact with the database), or it might just be stored in a private member variable (in this case, mHour):

```
Private mHour As Integer
```

The Get Accessor

The body of the Get accessor is similar to a class method that returns an object of the type of the property. In Example 9-2, the accessor for the Hour property is similar to a method that returns an integer. It returns the value of the private member variable mHour in which the value of the property has been stored:

```
Get
    Return mHour
End Get
```

In this example, the value of mHour is returned, but you could just as easily retrieve an integer value from a database or compute it on the fly.

Whenever you reference the property (other than to assign to it), the Get accessor is invoked to read the value of the property. For example, in the following code the value of the Time object's Hour property is assigned to a local variable. What actually happens is that the Get accessor is called, which returns the value of the Hour member variable, and that value is assigned to the local variable named theHour.

```
Dim time1 As New Time(currentTime)
Dim theHour As Integer = time1.Hour
```

The Set Accessor

The Set accessor sets the value of a property. Set has an implicit parameter, Value, that represents the assigned value. That is, when you write:

```
Minute = 5
```

the compiler passes the value you are assigning (5) to the Set statement as the Value parameter. You can then set the member variable to that value using the keyword:

```
mMinute = Value
```

The advantage of this approach is that the client can interact with the properties directly, without sacrificing the data hiding and encapsulation sacrosanct in good object-oriented design.

ReadOnly and WriteOnly Properties

At times you may want to create a property that allows you to retrieve a value but not to set it. You can mark your property ReadOnly, as in the following:

```
ReadOnly Property Hour() As Integer
```

Doing so allows you (and forces you) to leave out the Set statement in your property. If you do add a Set statement, the compiler will complain with the message:

```
Properties declared 'ReadOnly' cannot have a 'Set'
```

If you leave out the Set statement and then try to assign to the property, the compiler will complain with the message:

```
Property 'Hour' is 'ReadOnly'
```

In short, marking the property ReadOnly enlists the compiler in enforcing that you cannot use that property to set a value.

Similarly, you can mark a property WriteOnly:

```
WriteOnly Property Hour() As Integer
```

Doing so will cause the compiler to enforce that your property must have a Set and must not have a Get statement. If you leave out the Get or Set without marking the property WriteOnly or ReadOnly, respectively, you will receive a compile error.

You are not permitted to combine ReadOnly with WriteOnly, but this is not much of a burden.

Passing by Value and by Reference

Visual Basic .NET differentiates between *value types* and *reference types*. All the intrinsic types (Integer, Long, etc.), as well as structs (described in Chapter 12) are value types. Classes and interfaces (described in Chapters 8 and 13, respectively) are reference types.

Passing Arguments by Value

In many of the method calls shown in the previous chapters, the parameters were marked with the keyword ByVal. This indicates that the arguments are passed to the method by value; that is, a copy of the argument is passed to the method. Examine the code in Example 9-3. Try to guess what the output will be before reading further.

Example 9-3. Using the ByVal parameter

```
Option Strict On
Imports System
Public Class Tester
   Public Sub Run()
      ' declare a variable and initialize to 5
      Dim theVariable As Integer = 5

      ' display its value
      Console.WriteLine("In Run. theVariable: {0}", _
      theVariable)

      ' call a method and pass in the variable
      Doubler(theVariable)

      ' return and display the value again
      Console.WriteLine("Back in Run. theVariable: {0}", _
      theVariable)

   End Sub

   Public Sub Doubler(ByVal param As Integer)
      ' display the value that was passed in
      Console.WriteLine("In Method1. Received param: {0}", _
      param)

      'Double the value
      param *= 2
```

Example 9-3. Using the ByVal parameter (continued)

```
        ' Display the doubled value before returning
        Console.WriteLine( _
        "Updated param. Returning new value: {0}", _
        param)

    End Sub

End Class 'Tester

Module Module1

    Sub Main()
        Dim t As New Tester()
        t.Run()
    End Sub

End Module
```

In Example 9-3, the Main() method does nothing but instantiate a Tester object and call Run(). In Run(), you create a local variable, theVariable, and initialize its value to 5, which you then display:

```
Dim theVariable As Integer = 5
Console.WriteLine("In Run. theVariable: {0}", _
theVariable)
```

You pass theVariable to the Doubler() method, which displays the value, doubles it, and then redisplays it before returning:

```
Public Sub Doubler(ByVal param As Integer)
    Console.WriteLine("In Method1. Received param: {0}", _
    param)
    param *= 2
    Console.WriteLine( _
    "Updated param. Returning new value: {0}", _
    param)
End Sub
```

When you return from the call to Doubler(), you display the value of theVariable again. What is the value that is now displayed?

```
Console.WriteLine("Back in Run. theVariable: {0}", _
theVariable)
```

As shown in the output, the value of the variable that was passed in to Doubler() is, in fact, doubled in the Doubler() method but is *unchanged* in the calling method (Run):

```
In Run. theVariable: 5
In Method1. Received param: 5
Updated param. Returning new value: 10
Back in Run. theVariable: 5
```

The value of the parameter was passed by value, and thus a copy was made in the Doubler() method. This copy was doubled, but the original value was unaffected.

Passing Arguments by Reference

Visual Basic .NET also supports passing arguments by reference using the ByRef keyword. You can test this by making one tiny change to Example 9-3, changing the parameter of Doubler() from ByVal to ByRef:

```
Public Sub Doubler(ByRef param As Integer)
```

The rest of the program remains completely unchanged. Run the program again and compare the new output with the original:

```
In Run. theVariable: 5
In Method1. Received param: 5
Updated param. Returning new value: 10
Back in Run. theVariable: 10
```

The value of the argument to the method is now passed by reference. That is, rather than a copy being made, a reference to the object itself is passed, as illustrated in Figure 9-1. The object referred to by param is now the variable declared in Run(). Thus, when you change it in Doubler(), the change is reflected back in the Run() method.

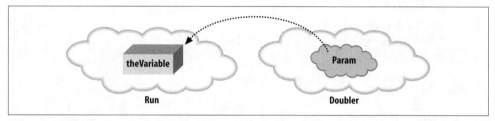

Figure 9-1. Passing arguments by reference

Passing Reference Types by Value

In Chapter 8, you saw how you can create a copy of a reference to an object and then have the two references refer to the same object. Similarly, when you pass a reference as a parameter, a copy of the parameter is made, but that is a copy of a reference, and the two references refer to the same object. You can see the effect by modifying Example 9-3 to pass an object, rather than an Integer, by value. The complete listing is shown in Example 9-4. An analysis follows the output.

Example 9-4. Passing a reference as a parameter

```
Option Strict On
Imports System
Public Class Cat
```

Example 9-4. Passing a reference as a parameter (continued)

```
    Private mWeight As Integer

    Public Sub New(ByVal weight As Integer)
        mWeight = weight
    End Sub

    Public Property Weight() As Integer
        Get
            Return mWeight
        End Get
        Set(ByVal Value As Integer)
            mWeight = Value
        End Set
    End Property

    Public Overrides Function ToString() As String
        Return mWeight.ToString()
    End Function

End Class

Public Class Tester
    Public Sub Run()
        ' declare a Cat and initialize to 5
        Dim theVariable As New Cat(5)

        ' display its value
        Console.WriteLine("In Run. theVariable: {0}", _
        theVariable)

        ' call a method and pass in the variable
        Doubler(theVariable)

        ' return and display the value again
        Console.WriteLine("Back in Run. theVariable: {0}", _
        theVariable)

    End Sub

    Public Sub Doubler(ByVal param As Cat)
        ' display the value that was passed in
        Console.WriteLine("In Method1. Received param: {0}", _
        param)

        'Double the value
        param.Weight = param.Weight * 2

        ' Display the doubled value before returning
        Console.WriteLine( _
        "Updated param. Returning new value: {0}", _
        param)
```

Example 9-4. Passing a reference as a parameter (continued)

```
    End Sub

End Class 'Tester

Module Module1

    Sub Main()
        Dim t As New Tester()
        t.Run()
    End Sub

End Module
```

Output:
```
In Run. theVariable: 5
In Method1. Received param: 5
Updated param. Returning new value: 10
Back in Run. theVariable: 10
```

Example 9-4 begins by defining a very simple Cat class:

```
    Public Class Cat
```

The class has a single private member variable, mWeight, and a property (Weight) to get and set the value of that variable:

```
    Private mWeight As Integer
    Public Property Weight() As Integer
        Get
            Return mWeight
        End Get
        Set(ByVal Value As Integer)
            mWeight = Value
        End Set
    End Property
```

The constructor allows you to initialize a Cat object by passing in an integer value for its weight:

```
    Public Sub New(ByVal weight As Integer)
        mWeight = weight
    End Sub
```

Finally, you override the ToString() method so that when you display the Cat object, its weight is displayed:

```
    Public Overrides Function ToString() As String
        Return mWeight.ToString()
    End Function
```

Overriding methods is explained in detail in Chapter 13. For now, you can use this method as shown to allow you to pass the Cat object to WriteLine() and have the weight displayed.

Example 9-4 changes Example 9-3 as little as possible. The Run() method still creates a local object named theVariable, but this time it is a Cat rather than an Integer:

```
Dim theVariable As New Cat(5)
```

The value of theVariable is displayed and then passed to the Doubler() method:

```
Console.WriteLine("In Run. theVariable: {0}", _
theVariable)
Doubler(theVariable)
```

In Example 9-4, the Doubler() method is changed to make the parameter be a Cat rather than an Integer. Note that the parameter is marked ByVal. The Cat reference will be passed by value, and a copy of the reference will be made:

```
Public Sub Doubler(ByVal param As Cat)
```

Within Doubler(), the value of the parameter is displayed, doubled, and then displayed again:

```
Console.WriteLine("In Method1. Received param: {0}
param)

param.Weight = param.Weight * 2

Console.WriteLine( _
"Updated param. Returning new value: {0}", _
param)
```

Back in Run(), the value of theVariable is displayed:

```
Console.WriteLine("Back in Run. theVariable: {0}", _
theVariable)
```

This is *identical* to Example 9-3 in which the integer value of theVariable was unchanged after returning from Doubler(). This time, however, the value is changed, even though the object was passed by value. The difference is that integers are value types, and classes are reference types.

CHAPTER 10

Basic Debugging

The debugger is your friend. There is simply no more powerful tool than a debugger for learning VB.NET and for writing quality VB.NET programs. The debugger will help you understand what is really going on when your program is running. It is the x-ray of software development, allowing you to see inside programs and diagnose potential problems.

Without a debugger you are guessing. With a debugger you are seeing. It is as simple as that. Whatever time you invest in learning to use your debugger is time well spent.

The debugger is also a powerful tool for understanding code written by others. By putting someone else's code into the debugger and stepping through it, you can see exactly how the methods work and what data they are manipulating.

This book assumes you are working with Visual Studio .NET. The debugger we'll investigate is the debugger integrated within VS.NET, which is a very powerful symbolic debugger.

The VS.NET debugger provides a number of windows for watching and interacting with your program while it executes. Getting comfortable with the debugger can make the difference between quickly finding bugs and struggling for hours or days.

Setting a Breakpoint

To get started with the debugger, return to Example 9-1. To see how this code actually works, you'll put a *breakpoint* on the first line of Main(). A breakpoint is an instruction to the debugger to stop running. You set a breakpoint and then run the program. The debugger will run the program up until the breakpoint. Then you will have the opportunity to examine the value of your variables at this point in the execution. Examining your program as it runs can help you untangle otherwise impenetrable problems.

It is common to set multiple breakpoints. This allows you to zip through your program, examining the state of your object at selected locations.

You can set a breakpoint in many different ways. The easiest is to click in the far-left margin. This causes a red dot to appear in the margin next to the relevant line of code, which is also highlighted in red, as shown (in black and white) in Figure 10-1. Notice that as you hover over the breakpoint, it tells you the line on which the breakpoint appears.

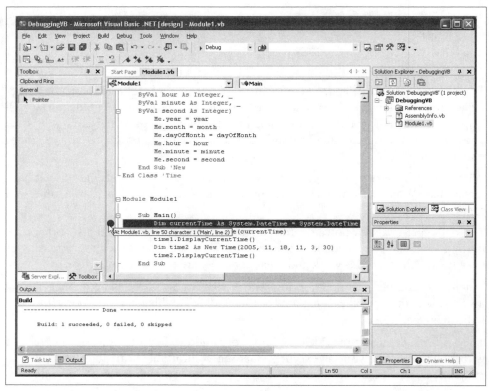

Figure 10-1. Setting a breakpoint

You are now ready to run the program to the breakpoint. Again, there are a number of ways to do so. You can click on the Start button (see Figure 4-6); or you can choose the Start item from the Debug menu (or use the keyboard shortcut for the menu item, the F5 key). In any case, the program will start and will run to the breakpoint, as shown in Figure 10-2.

The next statement to be executed is highlighted (in this case, the initialization of the currentTime object). There are a number of other helpful windows open as well, which will be examined in detail.

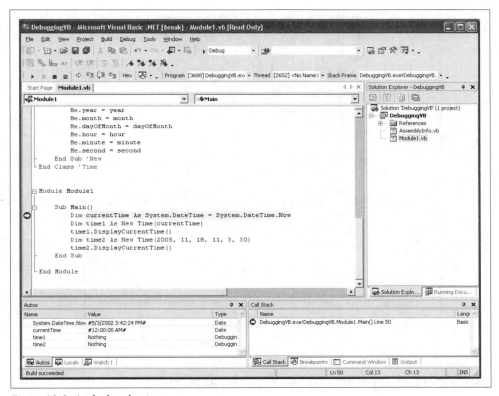

Figure 10-2. At the breakpoint

To step into the code, press the F11 function key twice. With the first keypress, the currentTime object is initialized. The second keypress moves you to the next line in the code, which initializes a second Time object called time1. (This line is also called the Time constructor.)

> F11 and F10 are the step commands. The difference is that F10 will step over method calls, while F11 will step into them.
>
> The methods are executed with F10; you just don't see each step in the debugger. The highlighting jumps to the next statement past the method call.
>
> If you use F11 to step into a method you meant to step over, Shift-F11 will step you out. The method you stepped into will run to completion, and you'll break on the first line back in the calling method.

Press the key seven more times to initialize each of the member variables. You can see their values being set in the so-called Autos window, in the lower-left corner of the debugger, as shown in Figure 10-3.

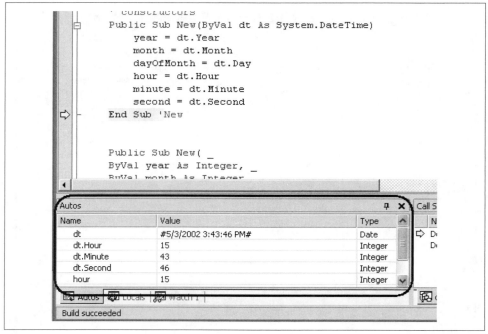

```
        " constructors
⊟       Public Sub New(ByVal dt As System.DateTime)
            year = dt.Year
            month = dt.Month
            dayOfMonth = dt.Day
            hour = dt.Hour
            minute = dt.Minute
            second = dt.Second
⇨       End Sub 'New


        Public Sub New( _
        ByVal year As Integer, _
        ByVal month As Integer
◄
```

Autos			╓ ✕	Call S
Name	Value	Type		N
dt	#5/3/2002 3:43:46 PM#	Date	⇨	D₁
dt.Hour	15	Integer		D₁
dt.Minute	43	Integer		
dt.Second	46	Integer		
hour	15	Integer		

Autos | Locals | Watch 1

Build succeeded

Figure 10-3. The Autos window close up

Using the Debug Menu to Set Your Breakpoint

Rather than clicking in the margin to set your breakpoint, you can use the New Breakpoint item on the Debug menu (or use the keyboard shortcut for the menu item, Control-B). This brings up the New Breakpoint dialog box, as shown in Figure 10-4.

The New Breakpoint dialog allows you far greater control over your breakpoint. You can set it to break only when a specific condition is hit (e.g., when counter > 10).

You can also set the *hit count* to designate that you want the debugger to break in only when the line has been hit a specified number of times (or a multiple of a specific number, etc.), as shown in Figure 10-5.

This can be very useful when you are in a loop (as described in Chapter 6). Rather than breaking each time through a loop of 100 iterations, you can choose the conditions under which to break.

You can also examine and manipulate all the breakpoints together in the Breakpoints window, as shown in Figure 10-6.

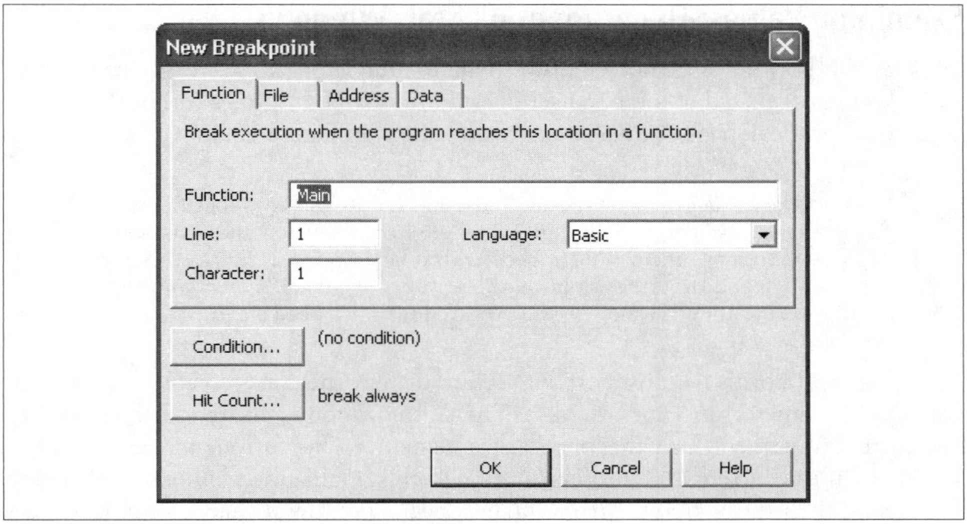

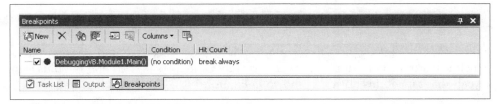

Figure 10-4. The New Breakpoint dialog

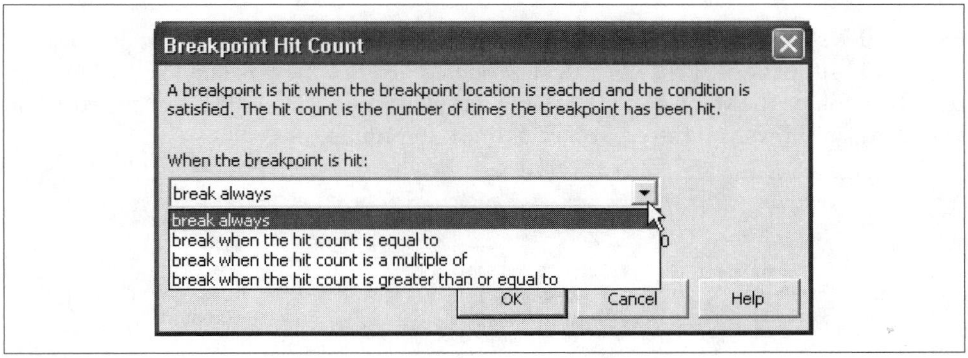

Figure 10-5. Breakpoint hit count

Figure 10-6. The Breakpoints window

Examining Values: The Autos and Locals Windows

Look at the bottom lefthand windows, where your variables are displayed. These variables are organized in a tabbed set of windows named Autos and Locals. You've already had a sneak peek at the Autos window, back in Figure 10-3.

 The debugger will stack the Autos and Locals windows together with tabs as shown in Figure 10-7. You are free to separate these windows or to move them to be tabbed with other windows. You can simply drag and drop the windows where you want them. When you drop one window on another, the two windows are tabbed together.

The Autos and Locals windows can be used to display the current value of each variable (and parameter) in your program. The Autos window shows variables used in the current statement and the previous statement. (The current statement is the statement at the current execution location, which is highlighted *automatically* in the debugger—thus the window's name.) The Locals window displays all objects currently in scope (that is, in the current method), also allowing you to see the object's member fields and variables.

Figure 10-7 shows the Locals tab selected to display the Locals window. The Locals window is showing you that the local variable currentTime has been set to the current date. (Since the value of currentTime has just been set, it will appear in red.) The window also shows you the two objects time1 and time2.

Locals			🔲 ✕
Name	Value	Type	
currentTime	#5/3/2002 3:48:55 PM#	Date	
⊞ time1	{DebuggingVB.Time}	Debuggin	
⊞ time2	{DebuggingVB.Time}	Debuggin	

📊 Autos   📊 Locals   📊 Watch 1

Figure 10-7. The Locals window on top

Notice the plus sign (+) next to the time1 object. This object is of type System.Time, which turns out to be a type with many member variables. Expanding the plus sign reveals the state of this object, as shown in Figure 10-8.

Explore the Locals and Autos windows as you step through the program. When you want to stop, choose the Stop debugging item from the Debug menu to stop processing and return to the editor.

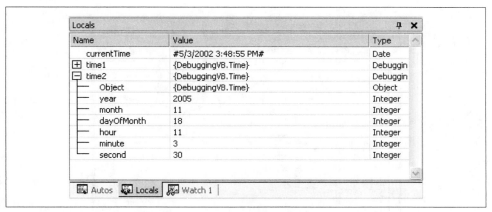

Figure 10-8. Expanding the object reveals its member variables

Set Your Watch

In a program with many local variables, it can be difficult to keep track of the particular variables you want to keep an eye on. You can track variables and objects in the Watch window. You can have up to four Watch windows at a time. Watch windows are like by-invitation versions of the Locals window; they will list the objects you ask the debugger to keep an eye on, and you can see their values change as you step through the program, as illustrated in Figure 10-9.

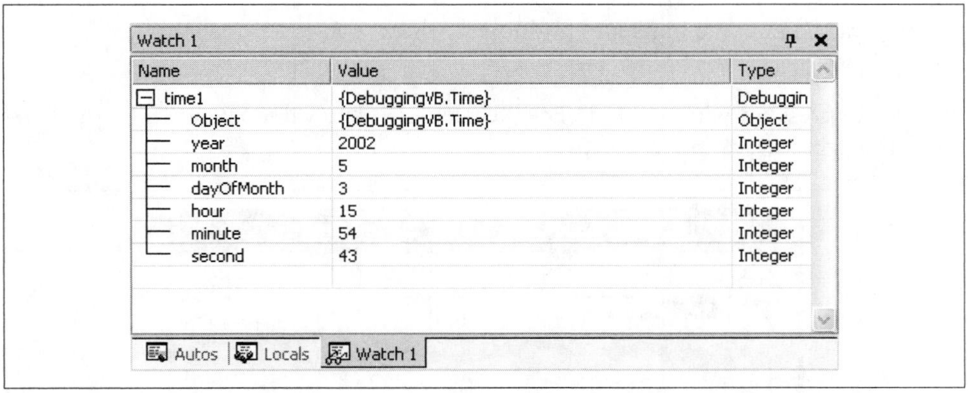

Figure 10-9. A Watch window

The Watch windows are usually tabbed with the Locals window. You might create more than one Watch window to organize the variables you keep an eye on.

You can add a watch by right-clicking on a variable and choosing Add Watch. You might instead choose Add QuickWatch, which opens a dialog box with watch information about a single object, as shown in Figure 10-10.

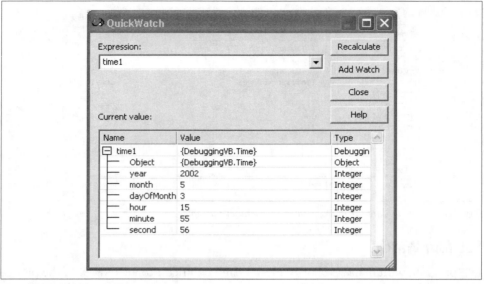

Figure 10-10. QuickWatch

From within the QuickWatch window, you can enter any expression and evaluate it. For example, suppose you had integer variables named varOne and varTwo:

```
Dim varOne As Integer = 5
Dim varTwo As Integer = 7
```

If you want to know the impact of multiplying them, you can just enter:

```
varOne * varTwo
```

into the Expression window and click Recalculate. The value is shown in the Current value window, as in Figure 10-11.

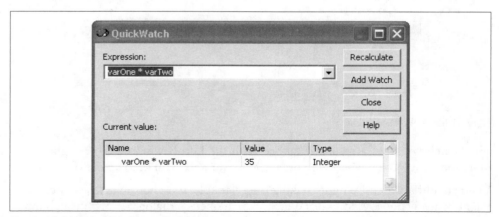

Figure 10-11. QuickWatch recalculation

The Call Stack

As you step in and out of methods, the Call Stack window will keep track of the order and hierarchy of method calls. If you look back at Figure 10-2, you'll see the Call Stack window in the lower righthand corner of the application. Figure 10-12 shows a close-up picture of the Call Stack window. You can see that the Time constructor was called by the Run() method, while the Run() method was in turn called by Main().

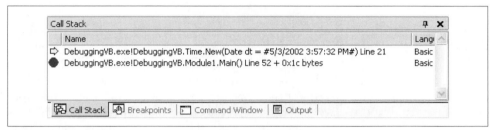

Figure 10-12. The call stack

In this case, if you double-click on the second line in the Call Stack window, the debugger will show you the line in Run() that called the Time constructor, as shown in Figure 10-13.

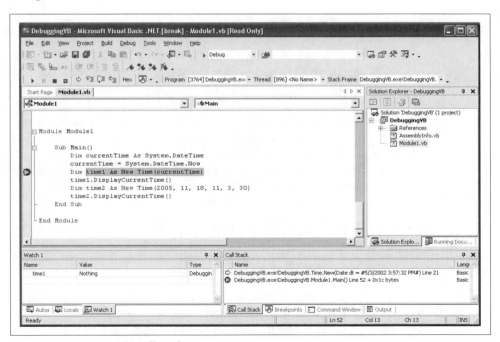

Figure 10-13. Tracing the call stack

CHAPTER 11

Inheritance and Polymorphism

In Chapter 8, you learned how to create new types by declaring classes, and in Chapter 3, you saw a discussion of the principle object relationships of association, aggregation, and specialization. This chapter focuses on *specialization*, which is implemented in VB.NET through *inheritance*. This chapter also explains how instances of more specialized classes can be treated as if they were instances of more general classes, a process known as *polymorphism*. This chapter ends with a consideration of *not inheritable classes*, which cannot be specialized, and a discussion of the root of all classes, the Object class.

Specialization and Generalization

Classes and their instances (objects) do not exist in a vacuum but rather in a network of interdependencies and relationships, just as we, as social animals, live in a world of relationships and categories. One of the most important relationships among objects in the real world is *specialization*, which can be described as an *is-a* relationship. When we say that a Dog *is-a* mammal, we mean that the dog is a specialized kind of mammal. It has all the characteristics of any mammal (it bears live young, nurses with milk, has hair), but it specializes these characteristics to the familiar characteristics of *canine domesticus*. A Cat is also a mammal. As such we expect it to share certain characteristics with the dog that are generalized in Mammal, but to differ in those characteristics that are specialized in Cat.

The specialization and generalization relationships are both reciprocal and hierarchical. They are reciprocal because specialization is the obverse side of the generalization coin. Thus, Dog and Cat specialize Mammal, and Mammal generalizes from Dog and Cat.

These relationships are hierarchical because they create a relationship tree, with specialized types branching off from more generalized types. As you move up the hierarchy you achieve greater *generalization*. You move up toward Mammal to generalize that Dogs and Cats and Horses all bear live young. As you move down the hierarchy, you specialize. Thus, the Cat specializes Mammal in having claws (a characteristic) and purring (a behavior).

Similarly, when you say that ListBox and Button *are* Windows, you indicate that you expect to find characteristics and behaviors of Windows in both of these types. In other words, Window generalizes the shared characteristics of both ListBox and Button, while each specializes its own particular characteristics and behaviors.

The Unified Modeling Language (UML) is a standardized "language" for describing an object-oriented system. In the UML, classes are represented as boxes. The name of the class appears at the top of the box, and (optionally) methods and members can be listed in the sections within the box.

In the UML, you model specialization relationships as shown in Figure 11-1. Note that the arrow points from the more specialized class up to the more general class. In the figure, the more specialized Button and ListBox classes point up to the more general Window class.

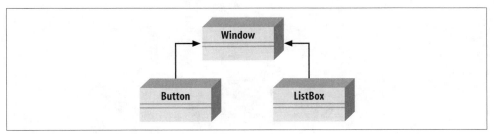

Figure 11-1. An is-a relationship

It is not uncommon for two classes share functionality. When this occurs, you can *factor out* these commonalities into a shared base class, which is more general than the more specialized classes. This provides you with greater reuse of common code, and with code that is easier to maintain.

For example, suppose you started out creating a series of objects as illustrated in Figure 11-2.

After working with RadioButtons, CheckBoxes, and Command buttons for a while, you realize that they share certain characteristics and behaviors that are more specialized than Window but more general than any of the three. You might factor these common traits and behaviors into a common base class, Button, and rearrange your inheritance hierarchy as shown in Figure 11-3. This is an example of how generalization is used in object-oriented development.

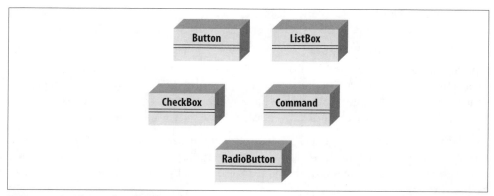

Figure 11-2. Objects deriving from Window

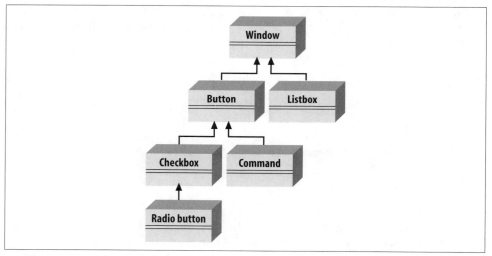

Figure 11-3. Factoring a Button class

The UML diagram in Figure 11-3 depicts the relationship among the factored classes and shows that both ListBox and Button derive from Window, and that Button is in turn specialized into CheckBox and Command. Finally, RadioButton derives from CheckBox. You can thus say that RadioButton is a CheckBox, which in turn is a Button, and that Buttons are Windows.

This is not the only, or even necessarily the best, organization for these objects, but it is a reasonable starting point for understanding how these types (classes) relate to one another.

Actually, although this might reflect how some widget hierarchies are organized, I am very skeptical of any system in which the model does not reflect how I perceive reality, and when I find myself saying that a RadioButton is a CheckBox, I have to think long and hard about whether that makes sense. I suppose a RadioButton *is* a kind of checkbox. It is a checkbox that supports the idiom of mutually exclusive choices. That said, it is a bit of a stretch and might be a sign of a shaky design.

Inheritance

In VB.NET, the specialization relationship is implemented using a principle called *inheritance*. This is not the only way to implement specialization, but it is the most common and most natural way to implement this relationship.

Saying that ListBox inherits from (or derives from) Window indicates that it specializes Window. Window is referred to as the *base* class, and ListBox is referred to as the *derived* class. That is, ListBox derives its characteristics and behaviors from Window and then specializes to its own particular needs.

Implementing Inheritance

In VB.NET, you create a derived class by adding the Inherits keyword after the name of the derived class, followed by the name of the base class:

```
Public Class ListBox
    Inherits Window
```

Or you might combine these two lines onto one as follows:

```
Public Class ListBox : Inherits Window
```

This code declares a new class, ListBox, that derives from Window. You can read the Inherits keyword as "derives from."

The derived class inherits all the members of the base class, both member variables and methods. These members can be treated just as if they were created in the derived class, as shown in Example 11-1.

Example 11-1. Deriving a new class

```
Option Strict On
Imports System
Public Class Window

    ' constructor takes two integers to
    ' fix location on the console
    Public Sub New(ByVal top As Integer, ByVal left As Integer)
        Me.top = top
        Me.left = left
```

Example 11-1. Deriving a new class (continued)

```
    End Sub 'New

    ' simulates drawing the window
    Public Sub DrawWindow()
        Console.WriteLine("Drawing Window at {0}, {1}", top, left)
    End Sub 'DrawWindow

    ' these members are private and thus invisible
    ' to derived class methods; we'll examine this
    ' later in the chapter
    Private top As Integer
    Private left As Integer
End Class 'Window

' ListBox derives from Window
Public Class ListBox
    Inherits Window

    ' constructor adds a parameter
    Public Sub New(ByVal top As Integer, ByVal left As Integer, ByVal theContents As
            String)
        MyBase.New(top, left) ' call base constructor
        mListBoxContents = theContents
    End Sub 'New

    ' a shadow version (note keyword) because in the
    ' derived method we change the behavior
    Public Shadows Sub DrawWindow()
        MyBase.DrawWindow() ' invoke the base method
        Console.WriteLine("Writing string to the listbox: {0}", mListBoxContents)
    End Sub 'DrawWindow
    Private mListBoxContents As String ' new member variable
End Class 'ListBox

Module Module1

    Sub Main()
        ' create a base instance
        Dim w As New Window(5, 10)
        w.DrawWindow()

        ' create a derived instance
        Dim lb As New ListBox(20, 30, "Hello world")
        lb.DrawWindow()
    End Sub

End Module
```

Output:
```
Drawing Window at 5, 10
Drawing Window at 20, 30
Writing string to the listbox: Hello world
```

Example 11-1 starts with the declaration of the base class Window. This class implements a constructor and a simple DrawWindow() method. There are two private member variables, top and left. The program is analyzed in detail in the following sections.

Calling Base Class Constructors

In Example 11-1, the new class ListBox derives from Window and has its own constructor, which takes three parameters (top, left, and theContents). The ListBox constructor invokes the constructor of its parent by calling MyBase.New and passing in the parameters (using the ByVal keyword, as described in Chapter 9):

```
Public Sub New( _
    ByVal top As Integer, _
    ByVal left As Integer, _
    ByVal theContents As String)
    MyBase.New(top, left) ' call base constructor
        mListBoxContents = theContents
End Sub 'New
```

Because classes cannot inherit constructors, a derived class must implement its own constructor and can make use of the constructor of its base class only by calling it explicitly.

If the base class has an accessible default constructor, the derived constructor is not required to invoke the base constructor explicitly; instead, the default constructor is called implicitly. However, if the base class does not have a default constructor, every derived constructor *must* explicitly invoke one of the base class constructors using the MyBase keyword. The keyword MyBase identifies the base class for the current object.

 As discussed in Chapter 8, if you do not declare a constructor of any kind, the compiler will create a default constructor for you. Whether you write it yourself or you use the one provided "by default" by the compiler, a default constructor is one that takes no parameters. Note, however, that once you do create a constructor of any kind (with or without parameters), the compiler does *not* create a default constructor for you.

Shadowing Base Methods

Also notice in Example 11-1 that ListBox implements a new version of DrawWindow():

```
Public Shadows Sub DrawWindow()
```

The keyword Shadows here indicates that the programmer is intentionally creating a new version of this method in the derived class.

In Example 11-1, the DrawWindow() method of ListBox hides and replaces the base class method. When you call DrawWindow() on an object of type ListBox, it is List-Box.DrawWindow() that will be invoked, not Window.DrawWindow(). Note, however, that ListBox.DrawWindow() can invoke the DrawWindow() method of its base class with the code:

```
MyBase.DrawWindow() 'invoke the base method
```

Controlling Access

The visibility of a class and its members can be restricted through the use of access modifiers, such as Public, Private, and Protected. (See Chapter 8 for a discussion of access modifiers.)

As you've seen, Public allows a member to be accessed by the member methods of other classes, while Private indicates that the member is visible only to member methods of its own class. The Protected keyword extends visibility to methods of derived classes.

Classes as well as their members can be designated with any of these accessibility levels. If a class member has a different access designation than the class, the more restricted access applies. Thus, if you define a class, someClass, as follows:

```
Public Class someClass
{
    '...
    Protected myValue As Integer
}
```

the accessibility for myValue is protected even though the class itself is public. A *public class* is one that is visible to any other class that wishes to interact with it.

Polymorphism

There are two powerful aspects to inheritance. One is code reuse. When you create a ListBox class, you're able to reuse some of the logic in the base (Window) class.

What is arguably more powerful, however, is the second aspect of inheritance: *polymorphism*. *Poly* means many and *morph* means form. Thus, polymorphism refers to being able to use many forms of a type without regard to the details.

When the phone company sends your phone a ring signal, it does not know what type of phone is on the other end of the line. You might have an old-fashioned Western Electric phone that energizes a motor to ring a bell, or you might have an electronic phone that plays digital music.

As far as the phone company is concerned, it knows only about the "base type" phone and expects that any "instance" of this type knows how to ring. When the phone company tells your phone to *ring*, it simply expects the phone to "do the right thing." Thus, the phone company treats your phone polymorphically.

Creating Polymorphic Types

Because a ListBox *is-a* Window and a Button *is-a* Window, you expect to be able to use either of these types in situations that call for a Window. For example, a form might want to keep a collection of all the instances of Window it manages so that when the form is opened, it can tell each of its Windows to draw itself. For this operation, the form does not want to know which elements are listboxes and which are buttons; it just wants to tick through its collection and tell each to "draw." In short, the form wants to treat all its Window objects polymorphically.

Creating Polymorphic Methods

To create a method that supports polymorphism, you need only mark it as virtual in its base class. For example, to indicate that the method DrawWindow() of class Window in Example 11-1 is polymorphic, simply add the keyword Overridable to its declaration, as follows:

```
Public Overridable Sub DrawWindow()
```

Now each derived class is free to implement its own version of DrawWindow() and the method will be invoked polymorphically. To do so, you simply override the base class virtual method by using the keyword Overrides in the derived class method definition, and then add the new code for that overridden method.

In the following excerpt from Example 11-2 (which appears later in this section), ListBox derives from Window and implements its own version of DrawWindow():

```
Public Overrides Sub DrawWindow()
    MyBase.DrawWindow() ' invoke the base method
    Console.WriteLine( _
      "Writing string to the listbox: {0}", listBoxContents)
End Sub 'DrawWindow
```

The keyword Overrides tells the compiler that this class has intentionally overridden how DrawWindow() works. Similarly, you'll override this method in another class, Button, also derived from Window.

In the body of Example 11-2, you'll create three objects: a Window, a ListBox, and a Button. You'll then call DrawWindow() on each:

```
Dim win As New Window(1, 2)
Dim lb As New ListBox(3, 4, "Stand alone list box")
Dim b As New Button(5, 6)
win.DrawWindow()
lb.DrawWindow()
b.DrawWindow()
```

This works much as you might expect. The correct DrawWindow() method is called for each. So far, nothing polymorphic has been done.

The real magic starts when you create an array of Window objects.

 Example 11-2 uses an array, which is a collection of objects, all of the same type. You create an array by indicating the type of objects to hold and then allocating space for a given number of those objects. For example, the following code declares winArray to be an array of three Window objects:

```
Dim winArray(3) As Window
```

You access the members of the array with parentheses. The first element is accessed with winArray(0), the second with winArray(1), and so forth. Arrays are explained in detail in Chapter 14.

Because a ListBox *is-a* Window, you are free to place a ListBox into an array of Windows. You can also place a Button into an array of Window objects because a Button is also a Window:

```
Dim winArray(3) As Window
winArray(0) = New Window(1, 2)
winArray(1) = New ListBox(3, 4, "List box in array")
winArray(2) = New Button(5, 6)
```

The first line of code declares an array named winArray that will hold three Window objects. The next three lines add new Window objects to the array. The first adds a Window. The second adds a ListBox (which is a Window because ListBox derives from Window), and the third adds a Button (Button also derives from Window).

What happens when you call DrawWindow() on each of these objects?

```
Dim offSet As Integer
For offSet = 0 To 2
    winArray(offSet).DrawWindow()
Next offSet
```

This code calls DrawWindow() on each element in the array in turn. The value offSet is initialized to zero and is incremented each time through the loop. The value of offSet is used as an index into the array.

All the compiler knows is that it has three Window objects and that you've called DrawWindow() on each. If you had not marked DrawWindow() as virtual, Window's original DrawWindow() method would be called three times.

However, because you did mark DrawWindow() as virtual, and because the derived classes override that method, when you call DrawWindow() on the array, the right thing happens for each object in the array. Specifically, the compiler determines the runtime type of the actual objects (a Window, a ListBox, and a Button) and calls the right method on each. This is the essence of polymorphism.

The runtime type of an object is the actual (derived) type. At compile time you do not have to decide what kind of objects will be added to your collection, so long as they all derive from the declared type (in this case Window). At runtime the actual type is discovered and the right method is called. This allows you to pick the actual type of objects to add to the collection while the program is running.

The complete code for this example is shown in Example 11-2.

Example 11-2. Virtual methods

```
Option Strict On
Imports System
Public Class Window

    ' constructor takes two integers to
    ' fix location on the console
    Public Sub New(ByVal top As Integer, ByVal left As Integer)
        Me.top = top
        Me.left = left
    End Sub 'New

    ' simulates drawing the window
    Public Overridable Sub DrawWindow()
        Console.WriteLine("Window: drawing Window at {0}, {1}", top, left)
    End Sub 'DrawWindow

    ' these members are protected and thus visible
    ' to derived class methods. We'll examine this
    ' later in the chapter
    Protected top As Integer
    Protected left As Integer
End Class 'Window

' ListBox derives from Window
Public Class ListBox
    Inherits Window

    ' constructor adds a parameter
    Public Sub New(ByVal top As Integer, ByVal left As Integer, ByVal contents As String)
        MyBase.New(top, left) ' call base constructor

        listBoxContents = contents
    End Sub 'New

    ' an overridden version (note keyword) because in the
    ' derived method we change the behavior
    Public Overrides Sub DrawWindow()
        MyBase.DrawWindow() ' invoke the base method
        Console.WriteLine( _
          "Writing string to the listbox: {0}", listBoxContents)
    End Sub 'DrawWindow
```

Example 11-2. Virtual methods (continued)

```
    Private listBoxContents As String ' new member variable
End Class 'ListBox

Public Class Button
    Inherits Window

    Public Sub New(ByVal top As Integer, ByVal left As Integer)
        MyBase.New(top, left)
    End Sub 'New

    ' an overridden version (note keyword) because in the
    ' derived method we change the behavior
    Public Overrides Sub DrawWindow()
        Console.WriteLine( _
            "Drawing a button at {0}, {1}" + ControlChars.Lf, top, Left)
    End Sub 'DrawWindow
End Class 'Button

Public Class Tester

    Shared Sub Main()
        Dim win As New Window(1, 2)
        Dim lb As New ListBox(3, 4, "Stand alone list box")
        Dim b As New Button(5, 6)
        win.DrawWindow()
        lb.DrawWindow()
        b.DrawWindow()
        Dim winArray(3) As Window
        winArray(0) = New Window(1, 2)
        winArray(1) = New ListBox(3, 4, "List box in array")
        winArray(2) = New Button(5, 6)

        Dim i As Integer
        For i = 0 To 2
            winArray(i).DrawWindow()
        Next i
    End Sub 'Main
End Class 'Tester
```

Output:
```
Window: drawing Window at 1, 2
Window: drawing Window at 3, 4
Writing string to the listbox: Stand alone list box
Drawing a button at 5, 6

Window: drawing Window at 1, 2
Window: drawing Window at 3, 4
Writing string to the listbox: List box in array
Drawing a button at 5, 6
```

Note that throughout this example, the overridden methods are marked with the keyword Overrides:

```
Public Overrides Sub DrawWindow()
```

The compiler now knows to use the overridden method when treating these objects polymorphically. The compiler is responsible for tracking the real type of the object and for handling the "late binding" so that it is ListBox.DrawWindow() that is called when the Window reference really points to a ListBox object.

Versioning with Overridable and Overrides

In VB.NET, the programmer's decision to override a virtual method is made explicit with the Overrides keyword. This helps you release new versions of your code; changes to the base class will not break existing code in the derived classes. The requirement to use the Overrides keyword helps prevent that problem.

Here's how: assume for a moment that the Window base class of the previous example was written by Company A. Suppose also that the ListBox and RadioButton classes were written by programmers from Company B using a purchased copy of the Company A Window class as a base. The programmers in Company B have little or no control over the design of the Window class, including future changes that Company A might choose to make.

Now suppose that one of the programmers for Company B decides to add a Sort() method to ListBox:

```
Public Class ListBox
  Inherits Window
   Public Overridable Sub Sort()
     '...
   End Sub
```

This presents no problems until Company A, the author of Window, releases Version 2 of its Window class, and it turns out that the programmers in Company A have also added a Sort() method to their public class Window:

```
Public Class Window
   Public Overridable Sub Sort()
     '...
   End Sub
```

In other object-oriented languages (such as C++), the new overridable Sort() method in Window would now act as a base method for the overridable Sort() method in ListBox. The compiler would call the Sort() method in ListBox when you intend to call the Sort() in Window. In Java, if the Sort() in Window had a different return type, the class loader would consider the Sort() in ListBox to be an invalid override and would fail to load.

VB.NET prevents this confusion. In VB.NET, an overridable function is always considered to be the root of dispatch; that is, once VB.NET finds an overridable method, it looks no further up the inheritance hierarchy. If a new overridable Sort() function is introduced into Window, the runtime behavior of ListBox is unchanged.

When ListBox is compiled again, however, the compiler generates a warning:

```
Module1.vb(31) : warning BC40005: sub 'Sort' shadows an
overridable method in a base class. To override the
base method, this method must be declared 'Overrides'.
```

To remove the warning, the programmer must indicate what he intends. He can mark the ListBox Sort() method Shadows, to indicate that it is *not* an override of the method in Window:

```
Public Class ListBox

    Inherits Window
    Public Shadows Sub Sort()
        '...
    End Sub 'Sort
```

This action removes the warning. If, on the other hand, the programmer does want to override the method in Window, he need only use the Overrides keyword to make that intention explicit:

```
Public Class ListBox

    Inherits Window
    Public Overrides Sub Sort()
        '...
    End Sub 'Sort
```

Abstract Classes

Each type of Window has a different shape and appearance. Drop-down listboxes look very different from buttons. Clearly, every subclass of Window *should* implement its own DrawWindow() method—but so far, nothing in the Window class enforces that they must do so. To require subclasses to implement a method of their base, you need to designate that method as *abstract*.

An abstract method has no implementation. It creates a method name and signature that must be implemented in all derived classes. Furthermore, making one or more methods of any class abstract has the side effect of making the class abstract.

Abstract classes establish a base for derived classes, but it is not legal to instantiate an object of an abstract class. Once you declare a method to be abstract, you prohibit the creation of any instances of that class.

Thus, if you were to designate DrawWindow() as an abstract method in the Window class, the Window class would thus become abstract. Then you could derive

The Idea Behind Abstraction

Abstract (`MustInherit`) classes should not just be an implementation trick; they should represent the idea of an abstraction that establishes a "contract" for all derived classes. In other words, abstract classes mandate the public methods of the classes that will implement the abstraction.

The idea of an abstract Window class ought to lay out the common characteristics and behaviors of all windows, even though you never intend to instantiate the abstraction Window itself.

The idea of an abstract class is implied in the word "abstract." It serves to implement the abstraction "Window" that will be manifest in the various concrete instances of Window, such as browser window, frame, button, listbox, drop-down, and so forth. The abstract class establishes what a Window is, even though we never intend to create a "Window" per se. An alternative to using `MustInherit` is to define an interface, as described in Chapter 13.

from Window, but you could not create any Window objects/instances. If the Window class is an abstraction, there is no such thing as a simple Window object; only objects derived from Window.

Making Window.DrawWindow() abstract means that each class derived from Window would have to implement its own DrawWindow() method. If the derived class failed to implement the abstract method, that derived class would also be abstract, and again no instances would be possible.

Designating a method as abstract is accomplished by placing the `MustOverride` keyword at the beginning of the method definition, as follows:

```
MustOverride Public Sub DrawWindow()
```

If one or more methods of the derived class are abstract (`MustOverride`), the base class definition must be marked `MustInherit`, as in the following:

```
MustInherit Public Class Window
```

Example 11-3 illustrates the creation of an abstract Window class and an abstract DrawWindow() method.

Example 11-3. An abstract class and method

```
Option Strict On
Imports System
MustInherit Public Class Window

    ' constructor takes two integers to
    ' fix location on the console
    Public Sub New(top As Integer, left As Integer)
        Me.top = top
```

Example 11-3. An abstract class and method (continued)

```
        Me.left = left
    End Sub 'New


    ' simulates drawing the window
    ' notice: no implementation
    Public MustOverride Sub DrawWindow()

    Protected top As Integer
    Protected left As Integer
End Class 'Window

' ListBox derives from Window
Public Class ListBox
    Inherits Window

    ' constructor adds a parameter
    Public Sub New(top As Integer, left As Integer, contents As String)
        MyBase.New(top, left) ' call base constructor

        listBoxContents = contents
    End Sub 'New


    ' an overridden version implementing the
    ' abstract method
    Public Overrides Sub DrawWindow()

        Console.WriteLine("Writing string to the listbox: {0}", listBoxContents)
    End Sub 'DrawWindow

    Private listBoxContents As String ' new member variable
End Class 'ListBox

Public Class Button
    Inherits Window

    Public Sub New(top As Integer, left As Integer)
        MyBase.New(top, left)
    End Sub 'New


    ' implement the abstract method
    Public Overrides Sub DrawWindow()
        Console.WriteLine("Drawing a button at {0}, {1}" + ControlChars.Lf, top, left)
    End Sub 'DrawWindow
End Class 'Button

Public Class Tester

    Shared Sub Main()
        Dim winArray(3) As Window
```

Example 11-3. An abstract class and method (continued)

```
    winArray(0) = New ListBox(1, 2, "First List Box")
    winArray(1) = New ListBox(3, 4, "Second List Box")
    winArray(2) = New Button(5, 6)

    Dim i As Integer
    For i = 0 To 2
        winArray(i).DrawWindow()
    Next i
End Sub 'Main

End Class 'Tester
```

Output:
```
Writing string to the listbox: First List Box
Writing string to the listbox: Second List Box
Drawing a button at 5, 6
```

In Example 11-3, the Window class has been declared `MustInherit` and therefore cannot be instantiated. If you replace the first array member:

```
    winArray(0) = New ListBox(1, 2, "First List Box")
```

with this code:

```
    winArray(0) = New Window(1, 2)
```

the program will generate the following error:

```
C:\...Module1.vb(63): 'New' cannot be used on class 'DebuggingVB.Window' because it
contains a 'MustOverride' member that has not been overridden.
```

You can instantiate the ListBox and Button objects because these classes override the `MustOverride` method, thus making the classes *concrete* (i.e., not abstract).

NotInheritable Classes

The opposite side of the design coin from abstract is *not inheritable*. Although an abstract class is intended to be derived from and to provide a template for its subclasses to follow, a not-inheritable class does not allow classes to derive from it at all. The `NotInheritable` keyword placed before the class declaration precludes derivation. Classes are most often marked not-inheritable to prevent accidental inheritance.

If the declaration of Window in Example 11-3 is changed from `MustInherit` to `NotInheritable` (eliminating the `MustOverride` keyword from the DrawWindow() declaration as well), the program will fail to compile. If you try to build this project, the compiler will return the following error message:

```
C:\...Module1.vb(13): 'NotInheritable' classes cannot have members declared
'MustOverride'.
```

Microsoft recommends using NotInheritable "when it will not be necessary to create derived classes"[*] and also when your class consists of nothing but shared methods and properties.

The Root of All Classes: Object

All VB.NET classes, of any type, are treated as if they ultimately derive from a single class, Object. Object is the base class for all other classes.

A base class is the immediate "parent" of a derived class. A derived class can be the base to further derived classes, creating an inheritance "tree" or hierarchy. A root class is the topmost class in an inheritance hierarchy. In VB.NET, the root class is Object. The nomenclature is a bit confusing until you imagine an upside-down tree, with the root on top and the derived classes below. Thus, the base class is considered to be "above" the derived class.

Object provides a number of methods that subclasses can and do override. These include Equals(), which determines if two objects are the same, GetType(), which returns the type of the object and ToString(), which returns a string to represent the current object. Specifically, ToString() returns a string with the name of the class to which the object belongs. Table 11-1 summarizes the methods of Object.

Table 11-1. The Object class

Method	What It Does
Equals()	Evaluates whether two objects are equivalent.
GetHashCode()	Allows objects to provide their own hash function for use in collections (see Chapter 15).
GetType()	Provides access to the type object.
ToString()	Provides a string representation of the object.
Finalize()	Cleans up nonmemory resources; implemented by a destructor.
MemberwiseClone()	Creates copies of the object; should never be implemented by your type.
ReferenceEquals()	Evaluates whether two objects refer to the same instance.

In Example 11-4, the Dog class overrides the ToString() method inherited from Object, to return the weight of the Dog. This example also takes advantage of the startling fact that intrinsic types (Integer, Long, etc.) can also be treated as if they derive from Object, and thus you can call ToString() on an integer variable! Calling ToString() on an intrinsic type returns a string representation of the variable's value.

[*] Visual Studio .NET Combined Collection: Base Class Usage Guidelines.

Example 11-4. Overriding ToString

```
Option Strict On
Imports System
Public Class Dog
    Private weight As Integer

    ' constructor
    Public Sub New(ByVal weight As Integer)
        Me.weight = weight
    End Sub 'New

    ' override Object.ToString
    Public Overrides Function ToString() As String
        Return weight.ToString()
    End Function 'ToString
End Class 'Dog

Public Class Tester

    Shared Sub Main()
        Dim i As Integer = 5
        Console.WriteLine("The value of i is: {0}", i.ToString())

        Dim milo As New Dog(62)
        Console.WriteLine("My dog Milo weighs {0} pounds", milo.ToString())
    End Sub 'Main
End Class 'Tester
```

Output:
```
The value of i is: 5
My dog Milo weighs 62 pounds
```

The documentation for Object.ToString() reveals its signature:

```
Overridable Public Function ToString() As String
```

It is an overridable public method that returns a string and that takes no parameters. All the built-in types, such as Integer, derive from Object and so can invoke Object's methods.

The Console class's Write() and WriteLine() methods call ToString() for you on objects that you pass in for display.

Example 11-4 overrides the Overridable ToString() function for Dog, so that calling ToString() on a Dog object will return a reasonable value. If you comment out the overridden function, the base method will be invoked. The base class default behavior is to return a string with the name of the class itself. Thus, the output would be changed to the meaningless:

```
My dog Milo weighs Dog pounds
```

Classes do not need to declare explicitly that they derive from Object; the inheritance is implicit.

Boxing and Unboxing Types

Boxing and *unboxing* are the processes that enable value types (e.g., integers) to be treated as reference types (objects). The value is "boxed" inside an Object and subsequently "unboxed" back to a value type. It is this process that allowed us to call the ToString() method on the integer in Example 11-4. (You will see additional uses for boxing and unboxing in Chapter 15.)

Boxing Is Implicit

Boxing is an implicit conversion of a value type to the type Object. Boxing a value allocates an instance of Object and copies the value into the new object instance, as shown in Figure 11-4.

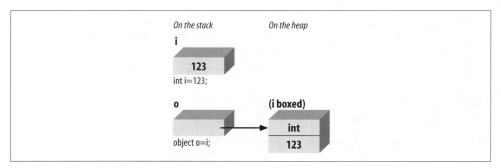

Figure 11-4. Boxing value types

Boxing is implicit when you provide a value type where a reference is expected. The compiler notices that you've provided a value type and silently boxes it within an object. You can, of course, explicitly cast the value type to a reference type, as in the following:

```
Dim myIntegerValue As Integer = 5
Dim myObject as Object = myIntegerValue ' explicitly cast to object
myObject.ToString()
```

This is not necessary, however, as the compiler will box the value for you, silently and with no action on your part:

```
Dim myIntegerValue As Integer = 5
myIntegerValue.ToString() ' boxed for you
```

Unboxing Must Be Explicit

To return the boxed object back to a value type, you must explicitly unbox it if Option Strict is On (as it should be). You will typically unbox by using the DirectCast() function or the CType() function. Figure 11-5 illustrates unboxing.

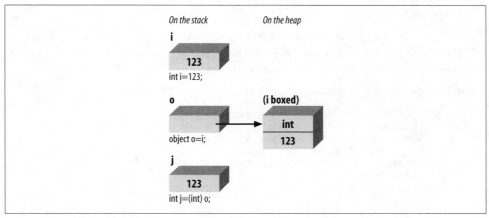

Figure 11-5. Unboxing

Boxing and unboxing are illustrated in Example 11-5.

Example 11-5. Boxing and unboxing

```
Option Strict On
Imports System

Public Class UnboxingTest
    Public Shared Sub Main()

        Dim myIntegerVariable As Integer = 123

        ' Boxing
        Dim myObjectVariable As Object = myIntegerVariable
        Console.WriteLine("myObjectVariable: {0}", _
            myObjectVariable.ToString())
        ' unboxing (must be explicit)
        Dim anotherIntegerVariable As Integer = _
            DirectCast(myObjectVariable, Integer)
        Console.WriteLine("anotherIntegerVariable: {0}", _
            anotherIntegerVariable)
    End Sub
End Class
```

Output:
```
myObjectVariable: 123
anotherIntegerVariable: 123
```

Example 11-5 creates an integer myIntegerVariable and implicitly boxes it when it is assigned to the object myObjectVariable; then, to exercise the newly boxed object, its value is displayed by calling toString().

The object is then explicitly unboxed and assigned to a new integer variable, anotherIntegerVariable, whose value is displayed to show that the value has been preserved.

Typically, you will wrap an unbox operation in a Try block, as explained in Chapter 16. If the object being unboxed is null or is a reference to an object of a different type, an InvalidCastException error occurs.

As an alternative, you can use the TypeOf() function, as follows:

```
' unboxing (must be explicit)
If TypeOf (myObjectVariable) Is Integer Then
    Dim anotherIntegerVariable As Integer = _
        DirectCast(myObjectVariable, Integer)
    Console.WriteLine("anotherIntegerVariable: {0}", _
        anotherIntegerVariable)
End If
```

CHAPTER 12

Structures

So far, the only user-defined type you've seen is the class. The class, as you know, defines a new type. Instances of a class are called objects. Classes are reference types; when you create a new instance of a class you get back a reference to the newly created object on the heap. (Creating classes is discussed in Chapter 8.)

A second type of user-defined type is a *structure*. Structures are designed to be lightweight alternatives to classes. In this case, the term lightweight means that structures use fewer resources (i.e., less memory) than classes, but they offer less functionality.

Structures are similar to classes in that they can contain constructors, properties, methods, fields, operators, nested types, and indexers. (See Chapter 14 for more on indexers.) There are, however, significant differences between classes and structures.

For example, structures don't support inheritance or destructors (in a sense, de-structure-ors). More important, while a class is a reference type, a structure is a value type.

The consensus view is that you ought to use structures only for types that are small, simple, and similar in their behavior and characteristics to built-in types. For example, if you were creating a class to represent a point on the screen (x,y coordinates), you might consider using a structure rather than a class.

In this chapter, you will learn how to define and work with structures and how to use constructors (or con-structure-ors, to be precise) to initialize their values.

 It is entirely possible to create robust commercial applications without structures. You can skip this chapter and come back to it when you actually need structures.

Defining a Structure

The syntax for declaring a structure is almost identical to that for a class:

```
[attributes] [access-modifiers] Structure identifier
[Implements interface-list]

    structure-members
End Structure
```

Attributes are not discussed in this book. *Access modifiers* (Public, Private, etc.) work just as they do with classes. (See Chapter 8 for a discussion of access modifiers.) The keyword Structure is followed by an *identifier* (the name of the structure). The optional *interface-list* is explained in Chapter 14. Within the body of the structure, you define fields and methods, also called the structure members, just as you do in a class.

Example 12-1 defines a structure named Location to hold the x,y coordinates of an object displayed on the screen. To create this application, open a console application in Visual Studio .NET and name it StructureDemonstration.

Example 12-1. Creating a structure for x,y coordinate location

```
Option Strict On
Imports System
Namespace StructureDemonstration

    ' declare a structure named Location
    Public Structure Location
        ' the Structure has private data
        Private myXVal As Integer
        Private myYVal As Integer

        ' constructor

        Public Sub New( _
          ByVal xCoordinate As Integer, ByVal yCoordinate As Integer)
            myXVal = xCoordinate
            myYVal = yCoordinate
        End Sub 'New

        ' property
        Public Property XVal() As Integer
            Get
                Return myXVal
            End Get
            Set(ByVal Value As Integer)
                myXVal = Value
            End Set
        End Property

        Public Property YVal() As Integer
```

```
            Get
                Return myYVal
            End Get
            Set(ByVal Value As Integer)
                myYVal = Value
            End Set
        End Property

        ' Display the structure as a String
        Public Overrides Function ToString() As String
            Return [String].Format("{0}, {1}", xVal, yVal)
        End Function 'ToString
    End Structure 'Location

    Class Tester
        Public Sub Run()
            ' create an instance of the structure
            Dim loc1 As New Location(200, 300)

            ' display the values in the structure
            Console.WriteLine("Loc1 location: {0}", loc1)

            ' invoke the default constructor
            Dim loc2 As New Location()
            Console.WriteLine("Loc2 location: {0}", loc2)

            ' pass the structure to a method
            myFunc(loc1)

            ' redisplay the values in the structure
            Console.WriteLine("Loc1 location: {0}", loc1)
        End Sub 'Run

        ' method takes a structure as a parameter
        Public Sub myFunc(ByVal loc As Location)
            ' modify the values through the properties
            loc.XVal = 50
            loc.YVal = 100
            Console.WriteLine("Loc1 location: {0}", loc)
        End Sub 'myFunc

        Shared Sub Main()
            Dim t As New Tester()
            t.Run()
        End Sub 'Main

    End Class 'Tester
End Namespace 'StructureDemonstration
```

Output:
```
Loc1 location: 200, 300
Loc2 location: 0, 0
```

Example 12-1. Creating a structure for x,y coordinate location (continued)

```
Loc1 location: 50, 100
Loc1 location: 200, 300
```

The Location structure is defined as public, much as you might define a class.

```
Public Structure Location
    ' the Structure has private data
    Private myXVal As Integer
    Private myYVal As Integer
```

Like with a class, you can define a constructor and properties for the structure. For example, you might create integer member fields myXVal and myYVal, and then provide public properties for them named XVal and YVal (see Chapter 9):

```
Public Sub New( _
  ByVal xCoordinate As Integer, ByVal yCoordinate As Integer)
    myXVal = xCoordinate
    myYVal = yCoordinate
End Sub 'New
Public Property XVal() As Integer
    Get
        Return myXVal
    End Get
    Set(ByVal Value As Integer)
        myXVal = Value
    End Set
End Property

Public Property YVal() As Integer
    Get
        Return myYVal
    End Get
    Set(ByVal Value As Integer)
        myYVal = Value
    End Set
End Property
```

Note that there is one significant difference in the way you create constructors and properties for structures and the way you do it for classes: in a structure, you are not permitted to create a custom default constructor. That is, you cannot write a constructor with no parameters. Thus the following code would not compile:

```
' won't compile - no custom default
' constructors for structures
Public Sub New()
    xVal = 5
    yVal = 10
End Sub 'New
```

Instead, the compiler creates a default constructor for you (whether or not you create other constructors), and that default constructor initializes all the member values to their default values (e.g., integers are initialized to zero).

The Run() method creates an instance of the Location structure named loc1, passing in the initial x,y coordinates of 200,300.

```
Dim loc1 As New Location(200, 300)
```

Loc1 is then passed to WriteLine() to display the x,y values:

```
Console.WriteLine("Loc1 location: {0}", loc)
```

As always, when you pass an object (in this case loc1) to Console.WriteLine(), WriteLine() automatically invokes the virtual method ToString() on the object. Thus, Location.ToString() is invoked, which displays the x and y coordinates of the loc1 object:

```
Loc1 location: 200, 300
```

Before modifying the values in loc1, the example creates a second instance of the Location structure, named loc2, and displays its values.

```
Dim loc2 As New Location()
Console.WriteLine("Loc2 location: {0}", loc2)
```

The creation of loc2 invokes the default constructor (note that no parameters are passed in). The output shows that the compiler-provided default constructor initialized the member variables to default values.

```
Loc2 location: 0, 0
```

Notice that you have not provided a default constructor; instead one has been provided for you by the compiler.

You next pass your first structure, loc1, (whose values are 200,300) to a method, myFunc(). In that method, the parameter is a Location object named loc. Within the myFunc() method, the XVal property is used to set the x coordinate to 50, and the YVal property is used to set the y coordinate to 100; then the new value is displayed using WriteLine():

```
Public Sub myFunc(ByVal loc As Location)
    ' modify the values through the properties
    loc.XVal = 50
    loc.YVal = 100
    Console.WriteLine("Loc1 location: {0}", loc)
End Sub 'myFunc
```

As expected, the results show the modification:

```
Loc1 location: 50, 100
```

When you return to the calling method (Run()), the values of loc1 are displayed, and they are unchanged from before the call to myFunc():

```
Loc1 location: 200, 300
```

When you passed loc1 to myFunc(), the structure was passed by value (structures, like the intrinsic types, are value types). A copy was made, and it was on that copy that you changed the values to 50 and 100. The original Location structure (loc1) was unaffected by the changes made within myFunc().

No Inheritance

Unlike classes, structures do not support inheritance Structs implicitly derive from Object (as do all types in VB.NET, including the built-in types) but cannot inherit from any other class or structure. Structs are also implicitly *not-inheritable* (that is, no class or structure can derive from a structure). See Chapter 11 for a discussion of inheritance and not-inheritable classes.

No Initialization

You cannot initialize fields in a structure. Thus, it is illegal to write:

```
Private xVal As Integer = 50
Private yVal As Integer = 100
```

though this kind of initialization is perfectly legal in a class. You must instead set the value of your member fields in the body of the constructor. As noted earlier, the default constructor (provided by the compiler) will set all the member variables to their default value.

Public Member Data?

Structs are designed to be simple and lightweight. While private member data promotes data hiding and encapsulation, some programmers feel it is overkill for structures. They make the member data public, thus simplifying the implementation of the structure. Other programmers feel that properties provide a clean and simple interface, and that good programming practice demands data hiding even with simple lightweight objects. Which you choose is a matter of design philosophy; the language will support either approach.

CHAPTER 13

Interfaces

At times a designer does not want to create a new type. Rather, the designer wants to describe a set of behaviors that any number of types might implement. For example, a designer might want to describe what it means to be storable (i.e., capable of being written to disk or to a database) or printable.

Such a description is called an interface. An *interface* is a contract: the designer of the interface says "if you want to provide this capability, you must implement these methods." The *implementer* of the interface agrees to the contract and implements the required methods.

When a class implements an interface, it tells any potential client "I guarantee I'll support the methods, properties, events, and indexers of the named interface." The interface details the return type from each method and the parameters to the methods.

See Chapter 9 for information about methods and properties; see Chapter 18 for information about events; and see Chapter 14 for coverage of indexers.

When specifying interfaces, it is easy to get confused about who is responsible for what. There are three concepts to keep clear:

The interface
> This is the contract. By convention, interface names begin with a capital I; thus, your interface might have a name like IPrintable. The IPrintable interface might describe a Print() method.

The implementing class
> This is the class that agrees to the contract described by the interface. For example, Document might be a class that implements IPrintable and thus implements the Print() method.

The client class

This is a class that calls methods from the implementing class. For example, you might have an Editor class that calls the Document class's Print() method.

Interfaces Versus Abstract Base Classes

Programmers learning VB.NET often ask about the difference between an interface and an abstract (`MustInherit`) base class. The key difference is subtle: an abstract base class serves as the base class for a family of derived classes, while an interface is meant to be mixed in with other inheritance trees.

Inheriting from an abstract class implements the *is-a* relationship, introduced in Chapter 11. Implementing an interface defines a different relationship, one we've not seen until now: the *implements* relationship. These two relationships are subtly different. A car *is a* vehicle, but it might *implement* the CanBeBoughtWithABigLoan capability (as can a house, for example).

Interfaces are a critical addition to any framework, and they are used extensively throughout .NET. For example, the collection classes (array lists, stacks, and queues) are defined, in large measure, by the interfaces they implement. (The collection classes are explained in detail in Chapter 15).

In this chapter, you will learn how to create, implement, and use interfaces. You'll learn how one class can implement multiple interfaces. You will also learn how to make new interfaces by combining existing interfaces or by extending (deriving from) an existing interface. Finally, you will learn how to test whether a class has implemented an interface.

Defining an Interface

The syntax for defining an interface is very similar to the syntax for defining a class or a structure:

```
[attributes] [access-modifier] Interface identifier
[interface-bases]
interface-body
End Interface
```

The optional *attributes* are not discussed in this book. *Access modifiers* (`Public`, `Private`, etc.) work just as they do with classes. (See Chapter 8 for more about access modifiers.) The `Interface` keyword is followed by an *identifier* (the interface name). It is common (but not required) to begin the name of your interface with a capital I. Thus, IStorable, ICloneable, IAndThou, etc. The optional list of *interface-bases* is discussed in the section titled "Extending Interfaces," later in this chapter.

The body of the interface is terminated with the keywords `End Interface`.

Suppose you want to create an interface to define the contract for data being stored to a database or file. Your interface will define the methods and properties a class will need to implement in order to be stored. You decide to call this interface IStorable.

In this interface, you might specify two methods, Read() and Write(), and a property, Status, which appear in the interface body:

```
Interface IStorable
    Sub Read()
    Sub Write(object)
    Property Status() As Integer
End Interface
```

Note that when declaring the methods of the interface, you provide a prototype:

```
Sub Read()
```

but no implementation and no `End Function`, `End Sub`, or `End Property` statement. Notice also that the IStorable method declarations do not include access modifiers (e.g., `Public`, `Private`, `Protected`, `Friend`). In fact, providing an access modifier generates a compile error. Interface methods are implicitly public because an interface is a contract meant to be used by other classes.

Implementing an Interface

Suppose you are the author of a Document class, which specifies that Document objects can be stored in a database. You decide to have Document implement the IStorable interface. It isn't required that you do so, but by implementing the IStorable interface you signal to potential clients that the Document class can be used just like any other IStorable object. This will, for example, allow your clients to add your Document objects to a collection of IStorable objects, and to otherwise interact with your Document in this very general and well-understood way.

To implement the IStorable interface, you must do two things:

1. Declare that a particular class implements the interface, using the `Implements` keyword. The following code declares that the Document class implements IStorable:

   ```
   Public Class Document
   Implements IStorable
   ```

2. Implement each of the interface methods, events, properties, and so forth, and explicitly mark each member as implementing the corresponding interface member. The following code would implement the IStorable interface's Read() method:

   ```
   Public Sub Read() Implements IStorable.Read
       Console.WriteLine("Implementing the Read Method for IStorable")
   End Sub 'Read
   ```

Visual Studio .NET will assist you in this effort through IntelliSense. When you enter the keyword `Implements`, IntelliSense prompts you with the various interfaces, as shown in Figure 13-1.

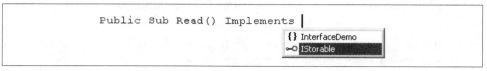

Figure 13-1. IntelliSense helps with Implements

Once you enter the name of the interface, IntelliSense can help you identify which member you are implementing, as shown in Figure 13-2.

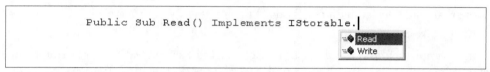

Figure 13-2. Choosing a method from an interface

Your definition of this class might look like this:

```
Public Class Document
    Implements IStorable

    Public Sub Read() Implements IStorable.Read
    '...
    End Sub 'Read

    Public Sub Write(ByVal o As Object) Implements IStorable.Write
        '...
    End Sub 'Write

    Public Property Status() As Integer Implements IStorable.Status
    '...
    End Property
End Class 'Document
```

It is now your responsibility, as the author of the Document class, to provide a meaningful implementation of the IStorable methods and property. Having designated Document as implementing IStorable, you must implement all the IStorable members, or you will generate an error when you compile. Defining and implementing the IStorable interface is illustrated in Example 13-1.

Example 13-1. Document class implementing IStorable

```
Option Strict On
Imports System
Namespace InterfaceDemo
    ' define the interface
    Interface IStorable
```

Example 13-1. Document class implementing IStorable (continued)

```
    Sub Read()
    Sub Write(ByVal obj As Object)
    Property Status() As Integer
End Interface 'IStorable

' create a class that implements the IStorable interface
Public Class Document
    Implements IStorable

    Public Sub New(ByVal s As String)
        Console.WriteLine("Creating document with: {0}", s)
    End Sub 'New

    ' implement the Read method
    Public Sub Read() Implements IStorable.Read
        Console.WriteLine("Implementing the Read Method for IStorable")
    End Sub 'Read

    ' implement the Write method
    Public Sub Write(ByVal o As Object) Implements IStorable.Write
        Console.WriteLine( _
            "Implementing the Write Method for IStorable")
    End Sub 'Write

    ' implement the property
    Public Property Status() As Integer Implements IStorable.Status
        Get
            Return myStatus
        End Get
        Set(ByVal Value As Integer)
            myStatus = Value
        End Set
    End Property

    ' store the value for the property
    Private myStatus As Integer = 0
End Class 'Document

Class Tester

    Public Sub Run()
        Dim doc As New Document("Test Document")
        doc.Status = -1
        doc.Read()
        Console.WriteLine("Document Status: {0}", doc.Status)
    End Sub 'Run

    Public Shared Sub Main()
        Dim t As New Tester()
        t.Run()
    End Sub 'Main
End Class 'Tester
```

Example 13-1. Document class implementing IStorable (continued)

```
End Namespace 'InterfaceDemo
```

Output:
```
Creating document with: Test Document
Implementing the Read Method for IStorable
Document Status: -1
```

Example 13-1 defines a simple interface, IStorable, with two methods, Read() and Write(), and a property, Status, of type integer:

```
' define the interface
    Interface IStorable
        Sub Read()
        Sub Write(ByVal obj As Object)
        Property Status() As Integer
    End Interface 'IStorable
```

Notice that the IStorable method declarations for Read() and Write() do not include access modifiers, as was explained earlier, because interface methods need to be public so that they can be used by other classes.

Once you've defined the IStorable interface, you can define classes that implement the interface. Keep in mind that you cannot create an instance of an interface; instead you instantiate a class that implements the interface.

The class implementing the interface must fulfill the contract exactly and completely. Thus, your Document class must provide both a Read() and a Write() method and the Status property.

```
' create a class which implements the IStorable interface
    Public Class Document
        Implements IStorable
        Public Sub New(ByVal s As String)
            Console.WriteLine("Creating document with: {0}", s)
        End Sub 'New

        ' implement the Read method
        Public Sub Read() Implements IStorable.Read
            Console.WriteLine("Implementing the Read Method for IStorable")
        End Sub 'Read

        ' implement the Write method
        Public Sub Write(ByVal o As Object) Implements IStorable.Write
            Console.WriteLine( _
                "Implementing the Write Method for IStorable")
        End Sub 'Write

        ' implement the property
        Public Property Status() As Integer Implements IStorable.Status
            Get
                Return myStatus
            End Get
```

```
            Set(ByVal Value As Integer)
                myStatus = Value
            End Set
        End Property

        ' store the value for the property
        Private myStatus As Integer = 0
    End Class 'Document
```

How your Document class fulfills the requirements of the interface, however, is entirely up to you. Although IStorable dictates that Document must have a Status property, it does not know or care whether Document stores the actual status as a member variable or looks it up in a database. Example 13-1 implements the Status property by returning (or setting) the value of a private member variable, status.

Implementing More Than One Interface

Classes can derive from only one class (and if you don't explicitly derive from a class, then you implicitly derive from Object). Classes can implement any number of interfaces. When you design your class, you can choose not to implement any interfaces, you can implement a single interface, or you can implement two or more interfaces. For example, in addition to IStorable, you might have a second interface, ICompressible, for files that can be compressed to save disk space. If your Document class can be stored and it also can be compressed, you might choose to have Document implement both the IStorable and ICompressible interfaces.

 Both IStorable and ICompressible are interfaces created for this book and are not part of the standard .NET Framework.

Example 13-2 shows the complete listing of the new ICompressible interface and demonstrates how you modify the Document class to implement the two interfaces.

Example 13-2. IStorable and ICompressible, implemented by Document

```
Option Strict On
Imports System
Namespace InterfaceDemo

    Interface IStorable
        Sub Read()
        Sub Write(ByVal obj As Object)
        Property Status() As Integer
    End Interface 'IStorable

    ' here's the new interface
    Interface ICompressible
        Sub Compress()
```

```vb
      Sub Decompress()
    End Interface 'ICompressible

' Document implements both interfaces
    Public Class Document
        Implements ICompressible, IStorable

        ' the document constructor
        Public Sub New(ByVal s As String)
            Console.WriteLine("Creating document with: {0}", s)
        End Sub 'New

        ' implement IStorable
        Public Sub Read() Implements IStorable.Read
            Console.WriteLine("Implementing the Read Method for IStorable")
        End Sub 'Read

        Public Sub Write(ByVal o As Object) Implements IStorable.Write
            Console.WriteLine( _
                "Implementing the Write Method for IStorable")
        End Sub 'Write

    Public Property Status() As Integer Implements IStorable.Status
            Get
                Return myStatus
            End Get
            Set(ByVal Value As Integer)
                myStatus = Value
            End Set
        End Property

        ' implement ICompressible
        Public Sub Compress() Implements ICompressible.Compress
            Console.WriteLine("Implementing Compress")
        End Sub 'Compress

        Public Sub Decompress() Implements ICompressible.Decompress
            Console.WriteLine("Implementing Decompress")
        End Sub 'Decompress

        ' hold the data for IStorable's Status property
        Private myStatus As Integer = 0
    End Class 'Document

    Class Tester

        Public Sub Run()
            Dim doc As New Document("Test Document")
            doc.Status = -1
            doc.Read()
            doc.Compress()
            Console.WriteLine("Document Status: {0}", doc.Status)
```

```
        End Sub 'Run

        Shared Sub Main()
            Dim t As New Tester()
            t.Run()
        End Sub 'Main
    End Class 'Tester
End Namespace 'InterfaceDemo
```

Output:
```
Creating document with: Test Document
Implementing the Read Method for IStorable
Implementing Compress
Document Status: -1
```

As Example 13-2 shows, you declare the fact that your Document class will implement two interfaces by changing the declaration (in the list of interface bases) to indicate that both interfaces are implemented, separating the two interfaces with commas:

```
Public Class Document
    Implements ICompressible, IStorable
```

After you've done this, the Document class must also implement the methods specified by the ICompressible interface. ICompressible has only two methods, Compress() and Uncompress(), which are specified as:

```
Interface ICompressible
        Sub Compress()
        Sub Decompress()
    End Interface 'ICompressible
```

In this simplified example, Document implements these two methods as follows, printing notification messages to the console:

```
Public Sub Compress() Implements ICompressible.Compress
        Console.WriteLine("Implementing Compress")
    End Sub 'Compress

    Public Sub Decompress() Implements ICompressible.Decompress
        Console.WriteLine("Implementing Decompress")
    End Sub 'Decompress
```

Casting to an Interface

You can access the members (i.e., methods and properties) of an interface through the object of any class that implements the interface. Thus, you can access the methods and properties of IStorable through the Document object, as if they were members of the Document class:

```
Dim doc As New Document("Test Document")
doc.Status = -1
doc.Read()
```

Alternatively, you can create an instance of the interface and then use that interface to access the methods:

```
Dim isDoc As IStorable = doc
isDoc.status = 0
isDoc.Read()
```

In Chapter 15, you'll learn that at times you may create collections of objects that implement a given interface (e.g., a collection of storable objects). You can manipulate them without knowing their real type—so long as they implement IStorable. For instance, you won't know that you have a Document object; rather you'll know only that the object in question implements IStorable. You can create a variable of type IStorable and cast your Document to that type. You can then access the IStorable methods through the IStorable variable.

When you cast you say to the compiler, "trust me, I know this object is really of this type." In this case you are saying "trust me, I know this document really implements IStorable, so you can treat it as an IStorable."

As stated earlier, you cannot instantiate an interface directly—that is, you cannot write:

```
IStorable isDoc As New IStorable()
```

You can, however, create an instance of the implementing class and then create an instance of the interface:

```
Dim isDoc As IStorable = doc
```

(isDoc is a reference to an IStorable object.) This is considered a widening conversion (from Document to the IStorable interface), and so the compiler makes it work with no need for an explicit cast.

In general, it is a better design decision to access the interface methods through an interface reference. Thus, it was better to use isDoc.Read(), than doc.Read(), in the previous example. Access through an interface allows you to treat the interface polymorphically. In other words, you can have two or more classes implement the interface, and then by accessing these classes only through the interface, you can ignore their real runtime type and treat them simply as instances of the interface. You'll see the power of this technique in Chapter 15.

There may be instances in which you do not know in advance (at compile time) that an object supports a particular interface. For instance, given a collection of objects, you might not know whether each object in the collection implements IStorable, ICompressible, or both.

You can find out what interfaces are implemented by a particular object by casting blindly and then catching the exceptions that arise when you've tried to cast the object to an interface it hasn't implemented. The code to cast Document to ICompressible might be:

```
Dim icDoc As ICompressible = doc
icDoc.Compress()
```

If it turns out that Document implements only the IStorable interface but not the ICompressible interface:

```
Public Class Document
    Implements IStorable
```

the cast to ICompressible will fail if Option Strict is On. If you turn Option Strict Off, the code will compile, but at runtime, because of the illegal cast, the program will throw an exception:

```
System.InvalidCastException: Specified cast is not valid.
```

 Exceptions are used to report errors and are covered in detail in Chapter 17.

You could then catch the exception and take corrective action, but this approach is ugly and evil, and you should not do things this way. This is like testing whether a gun is loaded by firing it; it's dangerous and it annoys the neighbors.

Rather than firing blindly, you would like to be able to ask the object if it implements an interface, in order to then invoke the appropriate methods. VB.NET provides the is operator to help you ask the object if it implements an interface.

The Is Operator

The Is operator lets you query whether an object implements an interface. You use the Is operator with the TypeOf keyword, as follows:

```
TypeOf expression Is type
```

The Is operator evaluates true if the expression (which must be a reference type, e.g., an instance of a class) can be safely cast to type (e.g., an interface) without throwing an exception.

Example 13-3 illustrates the use of the Is operator to test whether a Document object implements the IStorable and ICompressible interfaces.

Example 13-3. The Is operator

```
Option Strict On
Imports System
Namespace InterfaceDemo

    Interface IStorable
        Sub Read()
```

Example 13-3. The Is operator (continued)

```
    Sub Write(ByVal obj As Object)

    Property Status() As Integer
End Interface 'IStorable

' here's the new interface
Interface ICompressible
    Sub Compress()
    Sub Decompress()
End Interface 'ICompressible

' Document implements both interfaces
Public Class Document
    Implements IStorable

    ' the document constructor
    Public Sub New(ByVal s As String)
        Console.WriteLine("Creating document with: {0}", s)
    End Sub 'New

    ' implement IStorable
    Public Sub Read() Implements IStorable.Read
        Console.WriteLine("Implementing the Read Method for IStorable")
    End Sub 'Read

    Public Sub Write(ByVal o As Object) Implements IStorable.Write
        Console.WriteLine( _
            "Implementing the Write Method for IStorable")
    End Sub 'Write

    Public Property Status() As Integer Implements IStorable.Status
        Get
            Return Status
        End Get
        Set(ByVal Value As Integer)
            Status = Value
        End Set
    End Property
    ' hold the data for IStorable's Status property
    Private myStatus As Integer = 0
End Class 'Document

Class Tester
    Public Sub Run()
        Dim doc As New Document("Test Document")

        ' only cast if it is safe
        If TypeOf doc Is IStorable Then
            Dim isDoc As IStorable = doc
            isDoc.Read()
        Else
            Console.WriteLine("Could not cast to IStorable")
```

Example 13-3. The Is operator (continued)

```
            End If

            ' this test will fail
            If TypeOf doc Is ICompressible Then
                Dim icDoc As ICompressible = doc
                icDoc.Compress()
            Else
                Console.WriteLine("Could not cast to ICompressible")
            End If
        End Sub 'Run

        Shared Sub Main()
            Dim t As New Tester()
            t.Run()
        End Sub 'Main

    End Class 'Tester
End Namespace 'InterfaceDemo
```

Output:
```
Creating document with: Test Document
Implementing the Read Method for IStorable
Could not cast to ICompressible
```

In Example 13-3, the Document class implements only IStorable:

```
Public Class Document
    Implements IStorable
```

In the Run() method of the Tester class, you create an instance of Document:

```
Dim doc As New Document("Test Document")
```

and you test whether that instance is an IStorable (that is, does it implement the IStorable interface?):

```
If TypeOf doc Is IStorable Then
```

If so, you create an instance of the IStorable interface and call an interface method (isDoc.Read):

```
Dim isDoc As IStorable = doc
isDoc.Read()
```

You then repeat the test with ICompressible, and if the test fails, you print an error message:

```
If TypeOf doc Is ICompressible Then
    Dim icDoc As ICompressible = CType(doc, ICompressible)
    icDoc.Compress()
Else
    Console.WriteLine("Could not cast to ICompressible")
End If
```

The output shows that the first test (IStorable) succeeds (as expected) and the second test, of ICompressible fails, also as expected.

```
Implementing the Read Method for IStorable
Could not cast to ICompressible
```

Extending Interfaces

It is possible to extend an existing interface to add new methods or members, or to modify how existing members work. For example, you might extend ICompressible with a new interface, ICompressible2, which extends the original interface with methods to keep track of the bytes saved.

The following code creates a new interface named ILoggedCompressible that is identical to ICompressible except that it adds the method LogSavedBytes():

```
Interface ICompressible2
    Inherits ICompressible
    Sub LogSavedBytes()
End Interface 'ICompressible2
```

 Notice that your new interface (ICompressible2) inherits from the base interface (ICompressible). Classes can inherit only from a single class, but interfaces can inherit from more than one interface, as shown later in this chapter.

Classes are now free to implement either ICompressible or ICompressible2, depending on whether they need the additional functionality. If a class does implement ICompressible2, it must implement all the methods of both ICompressible2 and also ICompressible. Objects of that type can be cast either to ICompressible2 or to ICompressible.

In Example 13-4, you'll extend ICompressible to create ICompressible2. You'll then cast the Document first to be of type IStorable, then to be of type ICompressible2. Finally, you'll cast the Document object to ICompressible. This last cast is safe because any object that implements ICompressible2 must also have implemented ICompressible (the former is a superset of the latter). This is the same logic that says you can cast any object of a derived type to an object of a base type (that is, if Student derives from Human, then all Students are Human, even though not all Humans are Students).

Example 13-4. Extending interfaces

```
Option Strict On
Imports System
Namespace InterfaceDemo

    Interface IStorable
```

Example 13-4. Extending interfaces (continued)

```
        Sub Read()
        Sub Write(ByVal obj As Object)
        Property Status() As Integer
    End Interface 'IStorable

    ' the Compressible interface is now the
    ' base for ICompressible2
    Interface ICompressible
        Sub Compress()
        Sub Decompress()
    End Interface 'ICompressible

    ' extend ICompressible to log the bytes saved
    Interface ICompressible2
        Inherits ICompressible
    Sub LogSavedBytes()
End Interface 'ICompressible2

    ' Document implements both interfaces
Public Class Document
        Implements ICompressible2, IStorable
        ' the document constructor
    Public Sub New(s As String)
        Console.WriteLine("Creating document with: {0}", s)
    End Sub 'New

  ' implement IStorable
        Public Sub Read() Implements IStorable.Read
        Console.WriteLine("Implementing the Read Method for IStorable")
        End Sub 'Read

        Public Sub Write(ByVal o As Object) Implements IStorable.Write
            Console.WriteLine( _
                "Implementing the Write Method for IStorable")
        End Sub 'Write

        Public Property Status() As Integer Implements IStorable.Status
            Get
                Return myStatus
            End Get
            Set(ByVal Value As Integer)
                myStatus = Value
            End Set
        End Property

        ' implement ICompressible
        Public Sub Compress() Implements ICompressible.Compress
            Console.WriteLine("Implementing Compress")
        End Sub 'Compress

        Public Sub Decompress() Implements ICompressible.Decompress
            Console.WriteLine("Implementing Decompress")
```

Example 13-4. Extending interfaces (continued)

```
        End Sub 'Decompress

        ' implement ICompressible2
        Public Sub LogSavedBytes() Implements ICompressible2.LogSavedBytes
            Console.WriteLine("Implementing LogSavedBytes")
        End Sub 'LogSavedBytes

        ' hold the data for IStorable's Status property
        Private myStatus As Integer = 0
    End Class 'Document

    Class Tester

        Public Sub Run()
            Dim doc As New Document("Test Document")

            If TypeOf doc Is IStorable Then
                Dim isDoc As IStorable = doc
                isDoc.Read()
            Else
                Console.WriteLine("Could not cast to IStorable")
            End If

            If TypeOf doc Is ICompressible2 Then
                Dim ilDoc As ICompressible2 = doc
                Console.Write("Calling both ICompressible and ")
                Console.WriteLine("ICompressible2 methods...")
                ilDoc.Compress()
                ilDoc.LogSavedBytes()
            Else
                Console.WriteLine("Could not cast to ICompressible2")
            End If

            If TypeOf doc Is ICompressible Then
                Dim icDoc As ICompressible = doc '
                Console.WriteLine( _
                    "Treating the object as Compressible... ")
                icDoc.Compress()
            Else
                Console.WriteLine("Could not cast to ICompressible")
            End If
        End Sub 'Run

        Shared Sub Main()
            Dim t As New Tester()
            t.Run()
        End Sub 'Main
    End Class 'Tester
End Namespace 'InterfaceDemo
```

Output:
```
Creating document with: Test Document
```

Example 13-4. Extending interfaces (continued)

```
Implementing the Read Method for IStorable

Calling both ICompressible and ICompressible2 methods...
Implementing Compress
Implementing LogSavedBytes

Treating the object as Compressible...
Implementing Compress
```

Example 13-4 starts by creating the ICompressible2 interface:

```
Interface ICompressible2
    Inherits ICompressible
    Sub LogSavedBytes()
End Interface 'ICompressible2
```

Notice that the syntax for extending an interface is the same as that for deriving from a class. This extended interface explicitly defines only one method, LogSavedBytes(); but of course any class implementing this interface must also implement the base interface (ICompressible) and all its members.

You define the Document class to implement both IStorable and ICompressible2:

```
Public Class Document
    Implements ICompressible2, IStorable
```

You are now free to cast the Document object to IStorable, ICompressible2, or to ICompressible:

```
If TypeOf doc Is IStorable Then
    Dim ilDoc As IStorable = doc

If TypeOf doc Is ICompressible Then
    Dim icDoc As ICompressible = doc

If TypeOf doc Is ICompressible2 Then
    Dim ic2Doc As ICompressible2 = doc
```

If you take a look back at the output, you'll see that all three of these casts succeed.

Combining Interfaces

You can also create new interfaces by combining existing interfaces and optionally adding new methods or properties. For example, you might decide to combine the definitions of IStorable and ICompressible2 into a new interface called IStorable-Compressible. This interface would combine the methods of each of the other two interfaces but would also add a new method, LogOriginalSize(), to store the original size of the pre-compressed item:

```
Interface IStorableCompressible
Inherits IStorable, ICompressible2
```

```
            Sub LogOriginalSize()
    End Interface
```

Having created this interface, you can now modify Document to implement IStor-ableCompressible:

```
Public Class Document
    Implements IStorableCompressible
```

You are now free to cast the Document object to any of the four interfaces you've created so far:

```
If TypeOf doc Is IStorable Then
    Dim isDoc As IStorable = doc

If TypeOf doc Is ICompressible Then
    Dim icDoc As ICompressible = doc

If TypeOf doc Is ICompressible2 Then
    Dim ic2Doc As ICompressible2 = doc

If TypeOf doc is IStorableCompressible Then
    Dim iscDoc as IStorableCompressible = doc
```

When you cast to the new, combined interface, you can invoke any of the methods of any of the interfaces it extends or combines. The following code invokes four methods on iscDoc (the IStorableCompressible object). Only one of these methods is defined in IStorableCompressible, but all four are methods defined by interfaces that IStorableCompressible extends or combines.

```
isDoc.Read()
icDoc.Compress()
ic2Doc.LogSavedBytes()
iscDoc.LogOriginalSize()
```

Overriding Interface Implementations

An implementing class is free to mark any or all of the methods that implement the interface as overridable. Derived classes can then override or provide new implementations. For example, a Document class might implement the IStorable interface and mark the Read() and Write() methods as overridable. The Document might Read() and Write() its contents to a File type. The developer might later derive new types from Document, such as perhaps a Note or EmailMessage type. While the Document class implements Read() and Write to save to a File, the Note class might implement Read() and Write() to read from and write to a database.

Example 13-5 strips down the complexity of the previous examples and illustrates overriding an interface implementation. In this example, you'll derive a new class named Note from the Document class.

Document implements the IStorable-required Read() method as an overridable method, and Note overrides that implementation.

 Notice that Document does not mark Write() as overridable. You'll see the implications of this decision in the analysis section that follows the output.

The complete listing is shown in Example 13-5 and analyzed in detail following.

Example 13-5. Overriding an interface implementation

```
Option Strict On

Imports System
Imports Microsoft.VisualBasic

Namespace OverridingInterfaces
    Interface IStorable
        Sub Read()
        Sub Write()
    End Interface

    ' Simplify Document to implement only IStorable
    Public Class Document : Implements IStorable

        ' the document constructor
        Public Sub New(ByVal s As String)
            Console.WriteLine("Creating document with: {0}", s)
        End Sub

        ' Make read virtual
        Public Overridable Sub Read() Implements IStorable.Read
            Console.WriteLine("Document Virtual Read Method for IStorable")
        End Sub

        ' NB: Not virtual!
        Public Sub Write() Implements IStorable.Write
            Console.WriteLine("Document Write Method for IStorable")
        End Sub
    End Class

    ' Derive from Document
    Public Class Note : Inherits Document

        Public Sub New(ByVal s As String)
            MyBase.New(s)
            Console.WriteLine("Creating note with: {0}", s)
        End Sub

        ' override the Read method
        Public Overrides Sub Read()
```

Example 13-5. Overriding an interface implementation (continued)

```
            Console.WriteLine("Overriding the Read method for Note!")
        End Sub

        ' implement my own Write method
        Public Shadows Sub Write()
            Console.WriteLine("Implementing the Write method for Note!")
        End Sub
    End Class

    Class Tester
        Public Sub Run()
            ' Create a Document object
            Dim theNote As Document = New Note("Test Note")

            ' cast the Document to IStorable
            If TypeOf theNote Is IStorable Then
                Dim isNote As IStorable = theNote
                isNote.Read()
                isNote.Write()
            End If

            Console.WriteLine(vbCrLf)

            ' direct call to the methods
            theNote.Read()
            theNote.Write()

            Console.WriteLine(vbCrLf)

            ' create a note object
            Dim note2 As New Note("Second Test")

            ' Cast the note to IStorable
            If TypeOf note2 Is IStorable Then
                Dim isNote2 As IStorable = note2
                isNote2.Read()
                isNote2.Write()
            End If
            Console.WriteLine(vbCrLf)

            ' directly call the methods
            note2.Read()
            note2.Write()
        End Sub

        Public Shared Sub Main()
            Dim t As New Tester()
            t.Run()
        End Sub
    End Class
End Namespace
```

Example 13-5. Overriding an interface implementation (continued)

Output:
```
Creating document with: Test Note
Creating note with: Test Note
Overriding the Read method for Note!
Document Write Method for IStorable

Overriding the Read method for Note!
Document Write Method for IStorable

Creating document with: Second Test
Creating note with: Second Test
Overriding the Read method for Note!
Document Write Method for IStorable

Overriding the Read method for Note!
Implementing the Write method for Note!
```

In Example 13-5, the IStorable interface is simplified for clarity's sake:

```
Interface IStorable
    Sub Read()
    Sub Write()
End Interface
```

The Document class implements the IStorable interface:

```
Public Class Document : Implements IStorable
```

The designer of Document has opted to make the Read() method overridable but not to make the Write() method overridable:

```
Public Overridable Sub Read() Implements IStorable.Read
Public Sub Write() Implements IStorable.Write
```

 In a real-world application, you would almost certainly mark both as overridable, but I've differentiated them to demonstrate that the developer is free to pick and choose which methods can be overridden.

The new class, Note, derives from Document:

```
Public Class Note : Inherits Document
```

It is not necessary for Note to override Read() (it may shadow it instead), but it is free to do so and has done so here:

```
Public Overrides Sub Read()
```

To illustrate the implications of marking an implementing method as overridable, the Run() method calls the the Read() and Write() methods in four ways:

• Through the base class reference to a derived object
• Through an interface created from the base class reference to the derived object

- Through a derived object
- Through an interface created from the derived object

As you'll see, the base class reference and the derived class reference act just as they always have: overridable methods are implemented polymorphically and nonoverridable methods are not. The interfaces created from these references work just like the references themselves: overridable implementations of the interface methods are polymorphic, and nonoverridable methods are not.

The one surprising aspect is this: when you call the nonpolymorphic Write() method on the IStorable interface cast from the derived Note, you actually get the Document's Write() method. This is because Write() is implemented in the base class and is not overridable.

To accomplish the first two calls, a Document (base class) reference is created, and the address of a new Note (derived) object created on the heap is assigned to the Document reference:

```
Dim theNote As Document = New Note("Test Note")
```

An interface reference is created and the Note is cast to the IStorable interface:

```
If TypeOf theNote Is IStorable Then
    Dim isNote As IStorable = theNote
```

You then invoke the Read() and Write() methods through that interface. The output reveals that the Read() method is responded to polymorphically and the Write() method is not, just as you would expect:

```
Overriding the Read method for Note!
Document Write Method for IStorable
```

The Read() and Write() methods are then called directly on the derived object itself:

```
theNote.Read()
theNote.Write()
```

and once again you see the polymorphic implementation has worked:

```
Overriding the Read method for Note!
Document Write Method for IStorable
```

In both cases, the Read() method of Note was called, but the Write() method of Document was called.

To prove to yourself that this is a result of the overriding method, you next create a second Note object, this time assigning its address to a reference to a Note. This will be used to illustrate the final cases (i.e., a call through a derived object and a call through an interface created from the derived object):

```
Dim note2 As New Note("Second Test")
```

Once again, when you cast to a reference, the overridden Read() method is called. When, however, methods are called directly on the Note object:

```
note2.Read()
note2.Write()
```

the output reflects that you've called a Note and not an overridden Document:

```
Overriding the Read method for Note!
Implementing the Write method for Note!
```

CHAPTER 14

Arrays

Most of the examples in previous chapters have dealt with one object at a time. In many applications, however, you will want to work with a *collection* of objects all at the same time. The simplest collection in VB.NET is the *array*, which this chapter covers in detail. More complicated collection classes, such as Stack and Queue, are covered in the next chapter.

In this chapter, you will learn to work with three types of arrays: one-dimensional arrays, multidimensional rectangular arrays, and multidimensional jagged arrays.

To picture a one-dimensional array, imagine a series of mailboxes, all lined up one after the other. Each mailbox can hold exactly one object (one letter, one box, etc.). It turns out that all the mailboxes must hold the same kind of object; you declare the type of object the mailboxes will hold when you declare the array.

A multidimensional array allows you to create rows of mailboxes, one above the other. If all the rows are the same length, you have a rectangular array. If each row of mailboxes is a different length, you have a jagged array.

You can think of a multidimensional array as being like a grid of rows and columns in which each slot (mailbox) contains information. For example, each column might contain information pertinent to an employee. Each row would contain all the information for a single employee.

Most often you will deal with one-dimensional arrays, and if you do create multidimensional arrays, they will be two-dimensional—but larger multidimensional arrays (3-D, 4-D, etc.) are also possible.

A jagged array is a type of two-dimensional array in which each row can have a different number of columns. A jagged array is less of a grid, and more of an array of arrays—that is, an array in which the elements are arrays. This allows you to group a few arrays of varying sizes into a single array. For example, you might have an array of ten buttons, and a second array of five listboxes, and a third array of seven checkboxes. You can group all three into a jagged array of controls.

The current chapter also introduces the concept of indexers, a feature of VB.NET that makes it possible to create your own classes that can be treated like arrays.

Arrays

An *array* is an indexed collection of objects, all of the same type (e.g., all integers, all strings, etc.). When you declare an array, you are actually creating an instance of the Array class in the System namespace (System.Array). The System.Array class is discussed in detail later in this chapter.

Declaring Arrays

In order to declare an array, you must use a constructor, but you are free to use it in a variety of ways. For example, you can use either an implicit or an explicit constructor, as in the following:

```
Dim myIntArray() As Integer  ' implicit constructor
Dim myIntArray As Integer = New Integer() {} ' explicit constructor
```

which you use is a matter of personal style.

In all of these examples, the parentheses tell the VB.NET compiler that you are declaring an array, and the type specifies the type of the elements it will contain. In all of the arrays we have declared so far, myIntArray is an array of Integers.

It is important to distinguish between the array itself (which is a collection of elements) and the component elements within the array. myIntArray is the array; its elements are the integers it holds.

While VB.NET arrays are reference types, created on the heap, the elements of an array are allocated based on their type. Thus, myIntArray is a reference type allocated on the heap; and the integer elements in myIntArray are value types, allocated on the stack. (While you can *box* a value type so that it can be treated like a reference type, as explained in Chapter 11, it is not necessary or desirable to box the integers in an array.) By contrast, an array that contains reference types, such as Employee or Button, will contain nothing but references to the elements, which are themselves created on the heap.

The Size of the Array

Arrays are zero-based,[*] which means that the index of the first element is always zero, as in myArray(0). The second element is element 1. Index 3 indicates the ele-

---

[*] It is possible to create arrays that are not zero-based, but only with multidimensional arrays, and it is rarely a good idea. To do so you must use the CreateInstance() method of the Array class, and the resulting arrays are not compliant with the Common Language Specification.

ment that is offset from the beginning of the array by 3 elements—that is, the fourth element in the array. You access element 3 by writing:

```
myArray(3) ' return the 4th element (at offset 3)
```

You declare the initial size of the array (that is, how many elements it will hold) by specifying the upper bounds of the array. The following declarations both specify an array with seven elements; the first uses an implicit constructor for this purpose, the second an explicit constructor:

```
Dim myIntArray(6) As Integer  ' implicit constructor, 7 members
Dim myIntArray As Integer = New Integer(6) {}' explicit, 7 members
```

Note that these arrays have seven elements (not six) because with an upper bound of 6, the element indices are 0,1,2,3,4,5,6 for a total of 7 elements.

The ReDim Keyword

You can change the size of an array at any time using the ReDim keyword. Changing the size is commonly referred to as redimensioning the array.*

There are two ways to redimension an array. If you use the Preserve keyword, the data in the array is preserved; otherwise, all the data in the array is lost when it is resized using ReDim.

You can resize an array named myArray from its current size to 50 by writing:

```
ReDim myArray(50)
```

You can make the same change to myArray, but preserve the existing data in the array by writing:

```
ReDim Preserve myArray(50)
```

At times, you will not want to resize an array to a particular size but rather to expand the array by a particular increment. For example, if you are adding items to an array, and you find you're about to run out of room, you might add 50 to the current size of the array. You can use the UBound property of the array which returns the current upper bound of the array. The following line resizes myArray to 50 elements larger than its current size:

```
ReDim Preserve myArray(myArray(UBound) + 50)
```

---

* Redimensioning is a terribly misleading term. It suggests you are changing the dimensions of the array (which is described later in this chapter); in fact you are changing the array's size. Redimensioning should more properly be called resizing the array, but the terminology was established early in the history of Visual Basic, and it's too late now; we're stuck with the term redimensioning.

Understanding Default Values

When you create an array of value types, each element initially contains the default value for the type stored in the array. (See Table 8-2.) The following declaration creates an array (myIntArray) of six integers, each of whose value is initialized to 0, the default value for Integer types:

```
'six Integers with default values
Dim myIntArray As Integer = New Integer(6) {}
```

With an array of reference types, the elements are *not* initialized to their default values. Instead, they are initialized to Nothing. If you attempt to access any of the elements in an array of reference types before you have specifically initialized them, you will generate an exception (exceptions are covered in Chapter 17).

Assume you have created a Button class. You declare an array of Button objects (thus reference types) with the following statement:

```
Button() myButtonArray
```

and you instantiate the actual array, to hold three Buttons, like this:

```
myButtonArray = New Button(3) {}
```

Note that you can combine the two steps and write:

```
Button myButtonArray = New Button(3) {}
```

In either case, unlike with the earlier integer example, this statement does *not* create an array with references to four Button objects. Since Button objects are reference types, this creates the array myButtonArray with four null references. To use this array, you must first construct and assign a Button object for each reference in the array. This is called *populating* the array. You can construct the objects in a loop that adds them one by one to the array. Example 14-1 illustrates creating an array of value types (integers) and of reference types (Employee objects).

Example 14-1. Creating an array

```
Option Strict On
Imports System

' a simple class to store in the array
Public Class Employee
    Private empID As Integer
    ' constructor
    Public Sub New(ByVal empID As Integer)
        Me.empID = empID
    End Sub
End Class

Class Tester
    Public Sub Run()
        Dim intArray As Integer()
        Dim empArray As Employee()
```

Example 14-1. Creating an array (continued)

```
        intArray = New Integer(5) {}
        empArray = New Employee(3) {}
        ' populate the array
        Dim i As Integer
        ' for indices 0 through 3
        For i = 0 To empArray.Length - 1
            empArray(i) = New Employee(i + 5)
            i = i + 1
        Next
    End Sub

    Shared Sub Main()
        Dim t As New Tester()
        t.Run()
    End Sub
End Class
```

Example 14-1 begins by creating a simple Employee class to add to the array. When Run() begins, two arrays are declared, one of type Integer, the other of type Employee:

```
Dim intArray As Integer()
Dim empArray As Employee()
```

The Integer array is populated with Integers set to zero. The Employee array is initialized with null references.

empArray does not have Employee objects whose member fields are set to null; it does not have Employee objects at all. What is in the cubby holes of the array is just nulls. Nothing. Nada. When you create the Employee objects, you can then store them in the array.

You must populate the Employee array before you can refer to its elements:

```
For i = 0 To empArray.Length - 1
    empArray(i) = New Employee(i + 5)
    i = i + 1
Next
```

The exercise has no output. You've added the elements to the array, but how do you use them? How do you refer to them?

Accessing Array Elements

You access a particular element within an array using parentheses and a numeric value known as an *index*, or *offset*. You access element 3 by writing:

```
myArray(3) ' return the 4th element (at offset 3)
```

Because arrays are objects, they have properties. One of the more useful properties of the Array class is Length, which tells you how many objects are in an array. Array objects can be indexed from 0 to Length-1. That is, if five elements are in an array, their indices are 0,1,2,3,4.

In Example 14-2, you create an array of Employees and an array of integers, populate the Employee array, and then you print the values in each array.

Example 14-2. Accessing two simple arrays

```
Option Strict On
Imports System
Namespace ArrayDemo

    ' a simple class to store in the array
    Public Class Employee
        Private empID As Integer

        ' constructor
        Public Sub New(ByVal empID As Integer)
            Me.empID = empID
        End Sub 'New

        Public Overrides Function ToString() As String
            Return empID.ToString()
        End Function 'ToString
    End Class 'Employee

    Class Tester

        Public Sub Run()
            Dim intArray() As Integer
            Dim empArray() As Employee
            intArray = New Integer(5) {}
            empArray = New Employee(3) {}

            ' populate the array
            Dim i As Integer
            For i = 0 To empArray.Length - 1
                empArray(i) = New Employee(i + 5)
            Next i

            Console.WriteLine("The Integer array...")
            For i = 0 To intArray.Length - 1
                Console.WriteLine(intArray(i).ToString())
            Next i
            Console.WriteLine(ControlChars.Lf + "The employee array...")
            For i = 0 To empArray.Length - 1
                Console.WriteLine(empArray(i).ToString())
            Next i
        End Sub 'Run

        Shared Sub Main()
```

Example 14-2. Accessing two simple arrays (continued)

```
            Dim t As New Tester()
            t.Run()
        End Sub 'Main
    End Class 'Tester
End Namespace 'ArrayDemo
```

Output:
```
The Integer array...
0
0
0
0
0
The employee array...
5
6
7
```

Example 14-2 starts with the definition of an Employee class that implements a constructor that takes a single integer parameter. The ToString() method inherited from Object is overridden to print the value of the Employee object's employee ID.

The Run() method declares and then instantiates a pair of arrays. The Integer array is automatically filled with Integers whose value is set to zero. The Employee array contents must be constructed by hand (or will contain values set to Nothing).

To populate the array by hand, you construct each Employee object in turn, adding them to the Array as they are created:

```
Dim i As Integer
For i = 0 To empArray.Length - 1
    empArray(i) = New Employee(i + 5)
Next i
```

In this For loop, each Employee is created with a value equal to five more than its index in the array. These are arbitrary values used here to illustrate how to add Employee objects to the array.

Finally, the contents of the arrays are printed to ensure that they are filled as intended. The five Integers print their value first, followed by the three Employee objects.

If you comment out the code in which the Employee objects are created, you'll generate an exception when you try to display the contents of the Employee array. This demonstrates that arrays of reference types are initialized with Nothing references.

```
Unhandled Exception: System.NullReferenceException: Object
reference not set to an instance of an object. at
InterfaceDemo.ArrayDemo.Tester.Run() in C:\...\InterfaceDemo\
Module1.vb:line 40 at InterfaceDemo.ArrayDemo.Tester.Main()
in C:\...InterfaceDemo\Module1.vb:line 47
```

The For Each Statement

The For Each looping statement allows you to iterate through all the items in an array (or other collection), examining each item in turn. The syntax for the For Each statement is:

```
For Each identifier In collection
    statement
Next
```

The For Each statement creates a new object that will hold a reference to each of the objects in the collection, in turn, as you loop through the collection. For example, you might write:

```
Dim intValue As Integer
For Each intValue In intArray
```

Each time through the loop, the next member of intArray will be assigned to the integer variable intValue. You can then use that object to display the value, as in:

```
Console.WriteLine(intValue.ToString())
```

Similarly, you might iterate through the Employee array:

```
Dim e As Employee
For Each e In empArray
    Console.WriteLine(e)
Next
```

In the case shown here, e is an object of type Employee. For each turn through the loop, e will refer to the next Employee in the array.

Example 14-3 rewrites the Run() method of Example 14-2 to use a For Each loop but is otherwise unchanged.

Example 14-3. Using a For Each loop

```
Option Strict On
Imports System
Public Sub Run()
    Dim intArray() As Integer
    Dim empArray() As Employee
    intArray = New Integer(5) {}
    empArray = New Employee(3) {}

    ' populate the array
    Dim i As Integer
    For i = 0 To empArray.Length - 1
        empArray(i) = New Employee(i + 5)
    Next i

    Console.WriteLine("The Integer array...")
    Dim intValue As Integer
    For Each intValue In intArray
        Console.WriteLine(intValue.ToString())
```

Example 14-3. Using a For Each loop (continued)

```
    Next

Console.WriteLine("The employee array...")
    Dim e As Employee
    For Each e In empArray
        Console.WriteLine(e)
    Next
End Sub 'Run
```

Output:
```
The Integer array...
0
0
0
0
0
The employee array...
5
6
7
```

The output for Example 14-3 is identical to Example 14-2. However, rather than creating a For statement that measures the size of the array and uses a temporary counting variable as an index into the array:

```
For i = 0 To empArray.Length - 1
    Console.WriteLine(empArray(i).ToString())
Next i
```

you now iterate over the array with the For Each loop, which automatically extracts the next item from within the array and assigns it to a temporary object you've created in the head of the statement. In the following case, the temporary object is of type Employee (it is a reference to an Employee object) and is named e:

```
Dim e As Employee
For Each e In empArray
    Console.WriteLine(e)
Next
```

Since the object extracted from the array is of the appropriate type (i.e., e is a reference to an Employee), you can call any public method of Employee.

Initializing Array Elements

Rather than assigning elements to the array as we have done so far, it is possible to initialize the contents of an array at the time it is instantiated. You do so by providing a list of values delimited by curly braces ({}). VB.NET provides two different syntaxes to accomplish the same task:

```
Dim myIntArray1() As Integer = { 2, 4, 5, 8, 10}
Dim myIntArray2() As Integer  = New Integer(4) { 2, 4, 6, 8, 10 }
```

There is no practical difference between these two statements, and most programmers will use the shorter syntax because we are, by nature, lazy. We are so lazy, we'll work all day to save a few minutes doing a task—which isn't so crazy if we're going to do that task hundreds of times! Example 14-4 again rewrites the Run() method of Example 14-2, this time demonstrating initialization of both arrays.

Example 14-4. Initializing array elements

```
Option Strict On
Imports System
Public Sub Run()
    Dim intArray As Integer() = {2, 4, 6, 8, 10}
    Dim empArray As Employee() = _
      {New Employee(5), New Employee(7), New Employee(9)}

    Console.WriteLine("The Integer array...")
    Dim theInt As Integer
    For Each theInt In intArray
        Console.WriteLine(theInt.ToString())
    Next theInt

    Console.WriteLine("The employee array...")
    Dim e As Employee
    For Each e In empArray
        Console.WriteLine(e.ToString())
    Next e
End Sub 'Run
```

Output:

```
The Integer array...
2
4
6
8
10

The employee array...
5
7
9
```

The ParamArray Keyword

What do you do if you need to pass parameters to a method but you don't know how many parameters you'll want to pass? It is possible that the decision on how many parameters you'll pass in won't be made until runtime.

VB.NET provides the ParamArray keyword to allow you to pass in a variable number of parameters. As far as the client (the calling method) is concerned, you pass in a variable number of parameters. As far as the implementing method is concerned, it has been passed an array, and so it can just iterate through the array to find each parameter!

For example, you can create a method called DisplayVals() that takes integers as parameters and displays them to the console:

```
Public Sub DisplayVals(ByVal ParamArray intVals() As Integer)
    Dim i As Integer
    For Each i In intVals
        Console.WriteLine("DisplayVals {0}", i)
    Next i
End Sub 'DisplayVals
```

The ParamArray keyword indicates that you can pass in any number of integers, and the method will treat them as if you had passed in an array of integers. Thus you can call this method from Run() with:

```
DisplayVals(5, 6, 7, 8)
```

And the DisplayVals() method will treat this *exactly* as if you had written:

```
Dim explicitArray() As Integer = {5, 6, 7, 8}
DisplayVals(explicitArray)
```

And in fact, you are free to create such an array and send it in as the parameter, as demonstrated in Example 14-5.

Example 14-5. The ParamArray keyword

```
Option Strict On
Imports System
Namespace ArrayDemo

    Class Tester

        Public Sub Run()
            Dim a As Integer = 5
            Dim b As Integer = 6
            Dim c As Integer = 7
            Console.WriteLine("Calling with three Integers")
            DisplayVals(a, b, c)

            Console.WriteLine("Calling with four Integers")
            DisplayVals(5, 6, 7, 8)

            Console.WriteLine("calling with an array of four Integers")
            Dim explicitArray() As Integer = {5, 6, 7, 8}
            DisplayVals(explicitArray)
        End Sub 'Run

        ' takes a variable number of Integers
        Public Sub DisplayVals(ByVal ParamArray intVals() As Integer)
            Dim i As Integer
            For Each i In intVals
                Console.WriteLine("DisplayVals {0}", i)
```

Example 14-5. The ParamArray keyword (continued)

```
            Next i
        End Sub 'DisplayVals

        Shared Sub Main()
            Dim t As New Tester()
            t.Run()
        End Sub 'Main
    End Class 'Tester
End Namespace 'ArrayDemo
```

Output:
```
Calling with three Integers
DisplayVals 5
DisplayVals 6
DisplayVals 7

Calling with four Integers
DisplayVals 5
DisplayVals 6
DisplayVals 7
DisplayVals 8

calling with an array of four Integers
DisplayVals 5
DisplayVals 6
DisplayVals 7
DisplayVals 8
```

In Example 14-5, the first time you call DisplayVals() you pass in three integer variables:

```
Dim a As Integer = 5
Dim b As Integer = 6
Dim c As Integer = 7
DisplayVals(a, b, c)
```

The second time you call DisplayVals() you use four literal constants:

```
DisplayVals(5,6,7,8)
```

In both cases, DisplayVals() treats the parameters as if they were declared in an array. In the final invocation, you explicitly create an array and pass that as the parameter to the method:

```
Dim explicitArray() As Integer = {5, 6, 7, 8
DisplayVals(explicitArray)
```

Multidimensional Arrays

Arrays can be thought of as long rows of slots into which values can be placed. Once you have a picture of a row of slots, imagine ten rows, one on top of another. This is the classic two-dimensional array of rows and columns. The rows run across the array, and the columns run up and down the array, as illustrated in Figure 14-1.

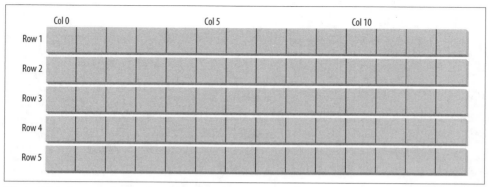

Figure 14-1. Rows and columns create a multidimensional array

A third dimension is possible but somewhat harder to picture. Imagine making your arrays three-dimensional, with new rows stacked atop the old two-dimensional array. OK, now imagine four dimensions. Now imagine ten.

Those of you who are not string-theory physicists have probably given up, as have I. Multidimensional arrays are useful, however, even if you can't quite picture what they would look like. You might, for example, use a four-dimensional array to track movement in three dimensions (x,y,z) over time.

VB.NET supports two types of multidimensional arrays: rectangular and jagged. In a rectangular array, every row is the same length. In a jagged array, however, each row can be a different length. In fact, you can think of each row in a jagged array as an array unto itself. Thus, a jagged array is actually an array of arrays.

Rectangular Arrays

A *rectangular array* is an array of two (or more) dimensions. In the classic two-dimensional array, the first dimension is the number of rows, and the second dimension is the number of columns.

To declare and instantiate a two-dimensional rectangular array named rectangularArray that contains two rows and three columns of integers, you could use either of the following syntax lines:

```
Dim rectangularArray (,) As Integer
Dim rectangularArray As Integer(,)
```

Either line will create an empty two-dimensional array.

In Example 14-6, you create a two-dimensional array of integers, and you populate the array using two For loops. The outer For loop iterates once for each row, the inner For loop iterates once for each column in each row:

```
Dim i As Integer
For i = 0 To rows - 1
    Dim j As Integer
    For j = 0 To columns - 1
        rectangularArray(i, j) = i + j
    Next j
Next i
```

You then use a second set of For loops to display the contents of the array:

```
For i = 0 To rows - 1
    Dim j As Integer
    For j = 0 To columns - 1
        Console.WriteLine( _
          "rectangularArray[{0},{1}] = {2}", _
          i, j, rectangularArray(i, j))
    Next j
Next i
```

 Note that for the second loop, you do not redeclare the variable i, because it was declared earlier. You *do*, however, redeclare j, because the first instance of j was declared within the scope of the earlier for loop, and so is not visible here.

The complete listing is shown in Example 14-6, followed by the output.

Example 14-6. Rectangular array

```
Option Strict On
Imports System
Namespace ArrayDemo

    Class Tester

        Public Sub Run()
            Const rowsUB As Integer = 4
            Const columnsUB As Integer = 3

            ' declare a 4x3 Integer array
            Dim rectangularArray(rowsUB, columnsUB) As Integer

            ' populate the array
            Dim i As Integer
            For i = 0 To rowsUB - 1
                Dim j As Integer
                For j = 0 To columnsUB - 1
                    rectangularArray(i, j) = i + j
                Next j
            Next i
```

Example 14-6. Rectangular array (continued)

```
        ' report the contents of the array
        For i = 0 To rowsUB - 1
            Dim j As Integer
            For j = 0 To columnsUB - 1
                Console.WriteLine( _
                    "rectangularArray[{0},{1}] = {2}", _
                    i, j, rectangularArray(i, j))
            Next j
        Next i
    End Sub 'Run

    Shared Sub Main()
        Dim t As New Tester()
        t.Run()
    End Sub 'Main
    End Class 'Tester
End Namespace 'ArrayDemo
```

Output:
```
rectangularArray[0,0] = 0
rectangularArray[0,1] = 1
rectangularArray[0,2] = 2
rectangularArray[1,0] = 1
rectangularArray[1,1] = 2
rectangularArray[1,2] = 3
rectangularArray[2,0] = 2
rectangularArray[2,1] = 3
rectangularArray[2,2] = 4
rectangularArray[3,0] = 3
rectangularArray[3,1] = 4
rectangularArray[3,2] = 5
```

In Example 14-6, you declare a pair of constant values to be used to specify the upper bound of the rows (rowsUB) and the upper bound of the columns (columnsUB) in the two-dimensional array:

```
Const rowsUB As Integer = 4
Const columnsUB As Integer = 3
```

Creating these constants allows you to refer to these values by number throughout the program; if you decide later to change the value of either, you only have to make the change in one location in your code.

You use these upper bounds to declare the array:

```
Dim rectangularArray(rowsUB, columnsUB) As Integer
```

Notice the syntax. The parentheses indicate that the type is an array, and the comma indicates the array has two dimensions; two commas indicate three dimensions, and so on.

Just as you can initialize a one-dimensional array using bracketed lists of values, you can initialize a two-dimensional array using similar syntax:

```
Dim rectangularArray(,) As Integer = _
    { {2, 1},{2, 2}, {3, 1}, {3, 2} }
```

The outer braces mark the entire array initialization; the inner braces mark each of the elements in the second dimension. Since this is a 4x3 array (four rows by three columns), you have four sets of 3 initialized values (12 in all). Example 14-7 rewrites the Run() method from Example 14-6 to use initialization.

Example 14-7. Initializing a two-dimensional array

```
        Public Sub Run()
            Const rowsUB As Integer = 4
            Const columnsUB As Integer = 3

            ' define and initialize the array
            Dim rectangularArray As Integer(,) = _
            {{0, 1, 2}, {3, 4, 5}, {6, 7, 8}, {9, 10, 11}}

            ' report the contents of the array
            Dim i As Integer
            For i = 0 To rowsUB - 1
                Dim j As Integer
                For j = 0 To columnsUB - 1
                    Console.WriteLine( _
                      "rectangularArray[{0},{1}] = {2}", _
                      i, j, rectangularArray(i, j))
                Next j
            Next i
        End Sub 'Run
```

Output:
```
rectangularArray[0,0] = 0
rectangularArray[0,1] = 1
rectangularArray[0,2] = 2
rectangularArray[1,0] = 3
rectangularArray[1,1] = 4
rectangularArray[1,2] = 5
rectangularArray[2,0] = 6
rectangularArray[2,1] = 7
rectangularArray[2,2] = 8
rectangularArray[3,0] = 9
rectangularArray[3,1] = 10
rectangularArray[3,2] = 11
```

As the output illustrates, the VB.NET compiler understands the syntax of your initialization; the objects are accessed with the appropriate offsets.

You might guess that this is a 12-element array, and that you can just as easily access an element at rectangularArray(0,3) as at rectangularArray(1,0), but if you try, you will run right into an exception:

```
Unhandled Exception: System.IndexOutOfRangeException:
Index was outside the bounds of the array.
    at DebuggingVB.ArrayDemo.Tester.Run() in ...Module1.vb:line 13
    at DebuggingVB.ArrayDemo.Tester.Main() in ...Module1.vb:line 29
```

The specification rectangularArray(0,3) addresses the array element at row 1 in column 4 (offset 0,3). Since the array has been defined as having four rows and *three* columns, this position does not exist in the array. VB.NET arrays are smart and they keep track of their bounds. When you define a 4x3 array, you must treat it as such, and not as a 3x4 or a 12x1 array.

Had you written the initialization as:

```
Dim rectangularArray As Integer(,) = _
{ {0,1,2,3}, {4,5,6,7}, {8,9,10,11} }
```

you would instead have implied a 3x4 array, and rectangularArray(0,3) would be valid.

Jagged Arrays

A *jagged array* is an array of arrays. Specifically, a jagged array is a type of multi-dimensional array in which each row can be a different size from all the other rows. Thus, a graphical representation of the array has a "jagged" appearance, as in Figure 14-2.

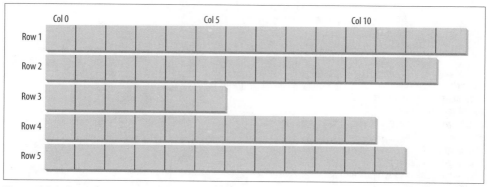

Figure 14-2. Jagged array

You can think of each row in a jagged array as an array unto itself—a one-dimensional array. Thus, technically speaking, a jagged array is an array of arrays. When you create a jagged array, you declare the number of rows in your array. Each row will hold a one-dimensional array, and each row can be of any length. To declare a jagged array, you use the following syntax, where the number of pairs of parentheses indicates the number of dimensions of the array:

```
Dim identifier()() As type
```

For example, you declare a two-dimensional jagged array of integers named myJaggedArray as follows:

```
Dim myJaggedArray()() As Integer
```

You address the elements in the array as follows. The array name followed by the offset into the array of arrays (the row), followed by the offset into the chosen array (the column within the chosen row). That is, to access the fifth element of the third array, you write:

```
myJaggedArray(2)(4)
```

Remember that all arrays are zero-based. The third element is at offset 2, and the fifth element is at offset 4.

Example 14-8 creates a jagged array named myJaggedArray, initializes its elements, and then prints their content. To save space, the program takes advantage of the fact that integer array elements are automatically initialized to zero, and it initializes the values of only some of the elements.

Example 14-8. Jagged array

```
Option Strict On
Imports System
Namespace JaggedArray
    Public Class Tester
        Public Sub Run()
            Const rowsUB As Integer = 3   ' upper bounds
            Const rowZero As Integer = 5
            Const rowOne As Integer = 2
            Const rowTwo As Integer = 3
            Const rowThree As Integer = 5

            Dim i As Integer

            ' declare the jagged array as 4 rows high
            Dim jaggedArray(rowsUB)() As Integer

            ' declare the rows of various lengths
            ReDim jaggedArray(0)(rowZero)
            ReDim jaggedArray(1)(rowOne)
            ReDim jaggedArray(2)(rowTwo)
            ReDim jaggedArray(3)(rowThree)

            ' Fill some (but not all) elements of the rows
            jaggedArray(0)(3) = 15
            jaggedArray(1)(1) = 12
            jaggedArray(2)(1) = 9
            jaggedArray(2)(2) = 99
            jaggedArray(3)(0) = 10
            jaggedArray(3)(1) = 11
            jaggedArray(3)(2) = 12
            jaggedArray(3)(3) = 13
            jaggedArray(3)(4) = 14
```

Example 14-8. Jagged array (continued)

```
            For i = 0 To rowZero
                Console.WriteLine("jaggedArray(0)({0}) = {1}", _
                    i, jaggedArray(0)(i))
            Next

            For i = 0 To rowOne
                Console.WriteLine("jaggedArray(1)({0}) = {1}", _
                    i, jaggedArray(1)(i))
            Next

            For i = 0 To rowTwo
                Console.WriteLine("jaggedArray(2)({0}) = {1}", _
                    i, jaggedArray(2)(i))
            Next

            For i = 0 To rowThree
                Console.WriteLine("jaggedArray(3)({0}) = {1}", _
                    i, jaggedArray(3)(i))
            Next
        End Sub

        Public Shared Sub Main()
            Dim t As Tester = New Tester()
            t.Run()
        End Sub
    End Class
End Namespace
```

Output:
```
jaggedArray(0)(0) = 0
jaggedArray(0)(1) = 0
jaggedArray(0)(2) = 0
jaggedArray(0)(3) = 15
jaggedArray(0)(4) = 0
jaggedArray(0)(5) = 0
jaggedArray(1)(0) = 0
jaggedArray(1)(1) = 12
jaggedArray(1)(2) = 0
jaggedArray(2)(0) = 0
jaggedArray(2)(1) = 9
jaggedArray(2)(2) = 99
jaggedArray(2)(3) = 0
jaggedArray(3)(0) = 10
jaggedArray(3)(1) = 11
jaggedArray(3)(2) = 12
jaggedArray(3)(3) = 13
jaggedArray(3)(4) = 14
jaggedArray(3)(5) = 0
```

Example 14-8 creates a jagged array with four rows:

```
    Dim jaggedArray(rowsUB)() As Integer
```

Notice that the size of the second dimension is not specified. The columns in a jagged array vary by row; thus they are set by creating a new array for each row. Each of these arrays can have a different size:

```
ReDim jaggedArray(0)(rowZero)
ReDim jaggedArray(1)(rowOne)
ReDim jaggedArray(2)(rowTwo)
ReDim jaggedArray(3)(rowThree)
```

If you look back at the values of the constants (rowZero through rowThree), you'll be able to figure out that there are 15 slots in this array.

Notice that you use the ReDim keyword (discussed earlier) to dimension the internal arrays. Here it is being used to resize the internal arrays from their initial size of zero to the size you designate.

Once an array size is specified for each row, you need only populate the various members of each array (row) and then print out their contents to ensure that all went as expected.

Notice that when you accessed the members of the rectangular array, you put the indexes all within one set of square brackets:

```
rectangularArray(i,j)
```

while with a jagged array you need a pair of brackets:

```
jaggedArray(3)(i)
```

You can keep this straight by thinking of the first as a single array of more than one dimension and the jagged array as an array of arrays.

System.Array

VB.NET implements arrays with the class System.Array. The Array class has a number of useful methods. Table 14-1 shows a few of the more important methods and properties of the System.Array class.

Table 14-1. Useful methods and properties of System.Array

Method or Property	Description
Clear()	Public shared method that sets a range of elements in the array to zero or to a null reference
Copy()	Overloaded public shared method that copies a section of one array to another array
IndexOf()	Overloaded public shared method that returns the index (offset) of the first instance of a value in a one-dimensional array
LastIndexOf()	Overloaded public shared method that returns the index of the last instance of a value in a one-dimensional array
Reverse()	Overloaded public shared method that reverses the order of the elements in a one-dimensional array
Sort()	Overloaded public shared method that sorts the values in a one-dimensional array

Table 14-1. Useful methods and properties of System.Array (continued)

Method or Property	Description
IsFixedSize	Public property that returns a value indicating whether the array has a fixed size
Length	Public property that returns the length of the array
Rank	Public property that returns the number of dimensions of the array

The Array class's shared methods, Reverse() and Sort(), make manipulation of the objects within the array very easy. Note, however, that to reverse or sort the elements of the array, they must be of a type that implements the IComparable interface, described in Chapter 13. The .NET Framework includes the String class, which does implement this interface, so we'll demonstrate both Reverse() and Sort() with Strings. The complete listing is shown in Example 14-9, followed by the output and analysis.

Example 14-9. Sort() and Reverse() methods of Array

```
Option Strict On
Imports System
Namespace ReverseAndSort
    Class Tester

        Public Shared Sub DisplayArray(ByVal theArray() As Object)

            Dim obj As Object
            For Each obj In theArray
                Console.WriteLine("Value: {0}", obj)
            Next obj
            Console.WriteLine(ControlChars.Lf)
        End Sub 'DisplayArray

        Public Sub Run()
            Dim myArray As [String]() = {"Who", "is", "John", "Galt"}

            Console.WriteLine("Display myArray...")
            DisplayArray(myArray)

            Console.WriteLine("Reverse and display myArray...")
            Array.Reverse(myArray)
            DisplayArray(myArray)

            Dim myOtherArray As [String]() = _
               {"We", "Hold", "These", "Truths", "To", "Be", "Self", "Evident"}

            Console.WriteLine("Display myOtherArray...")
            DisplayArray(myOtherArray)

            Console.WriteLine("Sort and display myOtherArray...")
            Array.Sort(myOtherArray)
            DisplayArray(myOtherArray)
        End Sub 'Run
```

Example 14-9. Sort() and Reverse() methods of Array (continued)

```
        Public Shared Sub Main()
            Dim t As New Tester()
            t.Run()
        End Sub 'Main
    End Class 'Tester
End Namespace 'ReverseAndSort
```

Output:
```
Display myArray...
Value: Who
Value: is
Value: John
Value: Galt

Reverse and display myArray...
Value: Galt
Value: John
Value: is
Value: Who

Display myOtherArray...
Value: We
Value: Hold
Value: These
Value: Truths
Value: To
Value: Be
Value: Self
Value: Evident

Sort and display myOtherArray...
Value: Be
Value: Evident
Value: Hold
Value: Self
Value: These
Value: To
Value: Truths
Value: We
```

Example 14-9 begins by creating myArray, an array of strings, containing the words:

```
"Who", "is", "John", "Galt"
```

This array is displayed and then passed to the Array.Reverse() method, where it is displayed again to see that the array itself has been reversed:

```
Value: Galt
Value: John
Value: is
Value: Who
```

Similarly, the example creates a second array, myOtherArray, containing the words:

```
"We", "Hold", "These", "Truths",
"To", "Be", "Self", "Evident",
```

which is passed to the Array.Sort() method. Then Array.Sort() happily sorts them alphabetically:

```
Value: Be
Value: Evident
Value: Hold
Value: Self
Value: These
Value: To
Value: Truths
Value: We
```

The method to display the strings has been made somewhat generic by declaring the type passed in to be an array of objects:

```
Public Shared Sub DisplayArray(ByVal theArray() As Object)
```

The DisplayArray() method iterates through the array of objects, passing each to WriteLine(). Since WriteLine() calls ToString() on objects, and since every object (including String) supports ToString(), declaring the temporary variable obj to be of type Object works very well. Using objects has the advantage that you can reuse your DisplayArray() method with arrays of other types of objects, once you know how to implement the IComparable interface (shown in the next chapter).

Indexers and the Default Property

Some classes contain their own internal collection. For example, you might write your own School class that would contain, as a private member variable, a collection of the Students enrolled in the school. You might then want to access the School class as if it were an array of Students. To do so, you would use the *default* property, which will allow you to write:

```
Dim joe As Student = mySchool(5)
```

accessing the sixth element in mySchool's internal collection!

As another example, suppose you create a listbox control named myListBox that contains a list of strings stored in a one-dimensional array, a private member variable named myStrings. A listbox control contains member properties and methods in addition to its array of strings. However, it would be convenient to be able to access the listbox array with an index, just as if the listbox were an array. For example, such a property would permit statements like the following:

```
Dim theFirstString As String = myListBox(0)
```

You implement this with the default property. Each class can have one default property, designated with the Default keyword. It is common to use the property name Item for the default property, but that is not required.

You can retrieve the default property with or without the property name. The following two code lines both retrieve the default property (which in this case, *is* called Item); the first uses the name, the second doesn't:

```
Dim theFirstString As String = myListBox.Item(0)
Dim theFirstString As String = myListBox(0)
```

In either case, the default property is acting as an *indexer*, a property used to index into the class as if it were a collection.

Example 14-10 declares a listbox control class that contains a simple array (myStrings) and a default property (Item) that acts as an indexer for accessing its contents. To keep the example simple, you'll strip the listbox control down to the few features.

The listing ignores everything having to do with being a user control and focuses only on the list of strings the listbox maintains and methods for manipulating them. In a real application, of course, these are a small fraction of the total methods of a listbox, whose principal job is to display the strings and enable user choice.

Example 14-10. Indexer

```
Option Strict On
Imports System

Namespace Indexers
    ' a simplified ListBox control
    Public Class ListBoxTest
        Private strings(255) As String
        Private ctr As Integer = 0

        ' initialize the list box with strings
        Public Sub New(ByVal ParamArray initialStrings() As String)
            Dim s As String

            ' copy the strings passed in to the constructor
            For Each s In initialStrings
                strings(ctr) = s
                ctr += 1
            Next
        End Sub

        ' add a single string to the end of the list box
        Public Sub Add(ByVal theString As String)
            If ctr >= Strings.Length Then
                ' handle bad index
            Else
                Strings(ctr) = theString
```

Example 14-10. Indexer (continued)

```
                    ctr += 1
            End If
      End Sub


      ' allow array-like access
      Default Public Property Item(ByVal index As Integer) As String
          Get
              If index < 0 Or index >= strings.Length Then
                  ' handle bad index
              Else
                  Return strings(index)
              End If
          End Get
          Set(ByVal Value As String)
              If index >= ctr Then
                  ' handle error
              Else
                  strings(index) = Value
              End If
          End Set
      End Property


      ' publish how many strings you hold
      Public Function Count() As Integer
          Return ctr
      End Function
End Class

Public Class Tester
    Public Sub Run()
        ' create a new list box and initialize
        Dim lbt As New ListBoxTest("Hello", "World")
        Dim i As Integer

        Console.WriteLine("After creation...")
        For i = 0 To lbt.Count - 1
            Console.WriteLine("lbt({0}): {1}", i, lbt(i))
        Next

        ' add a few strings
        lbt.Add("Who")
        lbt.Add("Is")
        lbt.Add("John")
        lbt.Add("Galt")

        Console.WriteLine("After adding strings...")
        For i = 0 To lbt.Count - 1
            Console.WriteLine("lbt({0}): {1}", i, lbt(i))
        Next

        ' test the access
        Dim subst As String = "Universe"
```

Example 14-10. Indexer (continued)

```
            lbt(1) = subst

            ' access all the strings
            Console.WriteLine("After editing strings...")
            For i = 0 To lbt.Count - 1
                Console.WriteLine("lbt({0}): {1}", i, lbt(i))
            Next
        End Sub

        Public Shared Sub Main()
            Dim t As New Tester()
            t.Run()
        End Sub
    End Class
End Namespace
```

Output:
```
After creation...
lbt(0): Hello
lbt(1): World

After adding strings...
lbt(0): Hello
lbt(1): World
lbt(2): Who
lbt(3): Is
lbt(4): John
lbt(5): Galt

After editing strings...
lbt(0): Hello
lbt(1): Universe
lbt(2): Who
lbt(3): Is
lbt(4): John
lbt(5): Galt
```

Example 14-10 begins by creating two private member variables, strings and ctr:

```
    Private strings(255) As String
    Private ctr As Integer = 0
```

In this program, the listbox maintains a simple array of strings, named (appropriately) strings. The member variable ctr keeps track of how many strings are added to the array.

The constructor initializes the array with the strings passed in as parameters. Because you cannot know how many strings will be added, you use the keyword ParamArray, as described earlier in this chapter.

```
    Public Sub New(ByVal ParamArray initialStrings() As String)
        Dim s As String
```

```
        ' copy the strings passed in to the constructor
        For Each s In initialStrings
            strings(ctr) = s
            ctr += 1
        Next
    End Sub
```

Our focus is on the default property, Item, created using the following code:

```
Default Public Property Item(ByVal index As Integer) As String
```

In Example 14-10, the Get() method endeavors to implement rudimentary bounds checking, and assuming the index requested is acceptable, it returns the value requested:

```
Get
    If index < 0 Or index >= strings.Length Then
        ' handle bad index
    Else
        Return strings(index)
    End If
End Get
```

The Set() method checks to make sure that the index you are setting already has a value in the list box. If not, it treats the set as an error; note that new elements can only be added using Add with this approach. The Set() accessor takes advantage of the implicit parameter value that represents whatever is assigned to the property.

```
Set(ByVal Value As String)
    If index >= ctr Then
        ' handle error
    Else
        strings(index) = Value
    End If
End Set
```

Thus, if you write:

```
lbt(5) = "Hello World"
```

the compiler will call the default property Item's Set() method on your object and pass in the string "Hello World" as an implicit parameter-named value.

Default Properties and Assignment

In Example 14-10, you cannot assign to an index that does not have a value. Thus, if you write:

```
lbt(10) = "wow!"
```

you trigger the error handler in the Set() method, which would note that the index you've passed in (10) is larger than the counter (6).

Of course, you can use the Set() method for assignment; you simply have to handle the indexes you receive. To do so, you might change the Set() method to check the

Length property of the buffer rather than the current value of the counter (ctr). If a value was entered for an index that did not yet have a value, you would update ctr:

```
Set(ByVal Value As String)
    If index >= strings.Length Then
        ' handle error
    Else
        strings(index) = Value
        if ctr < index + 1 then
            ctr = index + 1
        end if
    End If
End Set
```

This allows you to create a "sparse" array in which you can assign to offset 10 without ever having assigned to offset 9. Thus, if you were to write:

```
lbt(10) = "wow!"
```

the output would be:

```
lbt(0): Hello
lbt(1): Universe
lbt(2): Who
lbt(3): Is
lbt(4): John
lbt(5): Galt
lbt(6):
lbt(7):
lbt(8):
lbt(9):
lbt(10): wow!
```

In the Run() method of Example 14-10, you create an instance of the ListBoxTest class named lbt and pass in two strings as parameters:

```
Dim lbt As New ListBoxTest("Hello", "World")
```

You then call Add() to add four more strings:

```
lbt.Add("Who")
lbt.Add("Is")
lbt.Add("John")
lbt.Add("Galt")
```

Finally, you modify the second value (at index 1):

```
Dim subst As String = "Universe"
lbt(1) = subst
```

At each step, you display each value in a loop:

```
For i = 0 To lbt.Count - 1
    Console.WriteLine("lbt({0}): {1}", i, lbt(i))
Next
```

Indexing on Other Values

VB.NET does not require that you always use an integer value as the index to a collection. When you create a custom collection class and create your indexer, you are free to overload the default property so that a given collection can be indexed—for example, by an integer value or by a string value, depending on the needs of the client.

In the case of your listbox, you might want to be able to index into the listbox based on a string. Example 14-11 illustrates a string index. Example 14-11 is identical to Example 14-10 except for the addition of an overloaded default property, which can match a string, and findString(), a helper method created to support that index. The indexer calls findString() to return a record based on the value of the string provided.

Notice that the overloaded indexer of Example 14-11 and the indexer from Example 14-10 are able to coexist. The complete listing is shown, followed by the output and then a detailed analysis.

Example 14-11. String indexer

```
Option Strict On
Imports System

Namespace Indexers
    ' a simplified ListBox control
    Public Class ListBoxTest
        Private strings(255) As String
        Private ctr As Integer = 0

        ' initialize the list box with strings
        Public Sub New(ByVal ParamArray initialStrings() As String)
            Dim s As String

            ' copy the strings passed in to the constructor
            For Each s In initialStrings
                strings(ctr) = s
                ctr += 1
            Next
        End Sub

        ' add a single string to the end of the list box
        Public Sub Add(ByVal theString As String)
            If ctr >= strings.Length Then
                ' handle bad index
            Else
                strings(ctr) = theString
                ctr += 1
            End If
        End Sub

        ' allow array-like access
        Default Public Property Item( _
```

Example 14-11. String indexer (continued)

```
            ByVal index As Integer) As String
            Get
                If index < 0 Or index >= strings.Length Then
                    ' handle bad index
                Else
                    Return strings(index)
                End If
            End Get
            Set(ByVal Value As String)
                If index >= ctr Then
                    ' handle error
                Else
                    strings(index) = Value
                End If
            End Set
        End Property


        ' index on string
        Default Public Property Item( _
            ByVal index As String) As String
            Get
                If index.Length = 0 Then
                    ' handle bad index
                Else
                    Return strings(findString(index))
                End If
            End Get
            Set(ByVal Value As String)
                strings(findString(index)) = Value
            End Set
        End Property


        ' helper method, given a string find
        ' first matching record that starts with the target
        Private Function findString( _
            ByVal searchString As String) As Integer
            Dim i As Integer
            For i = 0 To strings.Length - 1
                If strings(i).StartsWith(searchString) Then
                    Return i
                End If
            Next
            Return -1
        End Function


        ' publish how many strings you hold
        Public Function Count() As Integer
            Return ctr
        End Function
    End Class

Public Class Tester
```

Example 14-11. String indexer (continued)

```
    Public Sub Run()
        ' create a new list box and initialize
        Dim lbt As New ListBoxTest("Hello", "World")
        Dim i As Integer

        Console.WriteLine("After creation...")
        For i = 0 To lbt.Count - 1
            Console.WriteLine("lbt({0}): {1}", i, lbt(i))
        Next

        ' add a few strings
        lbt.Add("Who")
        lbt.Add("Is")
        lbt.Add("John")
        lbt.Add("Galt")

        Console.WriteLine(vbCrLf & "After adding strings...")
        For i = 0 To lbt.Count - 1
            Console.WriteLine("lbt({0}): {1}", i, lbt(i))
        Next

        ' test the access
        Dim subst As String = "Universe"
        lbt(1) = subst
        lbt("Hel") = "GoodBye"

        ' access all the strings
        Console.WriteLine(vbCrLf & "After editing strings...")
        For i = 0 To lbt.Count - 1
            Console.WriteLine("lbt({0}): {1}", i, lbt(i))
        Next
    End Sub

    Public Shared Sub Main()
        Dim t As New Tester()
        t.Run()
    End Sub
    End Class
End Namespace
```

Output:
```
lbt[0]: GoodBye
lbt[1]: Universe
lbt[2]: Who
lbt[3]: Is
lbt[4]: John
lbt[5]: Galt
```

In Example 14-11, the findString() method simply iterates through the strings held in myStrings until it finds a string that starts with the target string used in the index. If found, it returns the index of that string; otherwise it returns the value –1.

You can see in Main() that the user passes in a string segment to the index, just as was done with an integer:

```
lbt("Hel") = "GoodBye"
```

This calls the overloaded default property, which does some rudimentary error checking (in this case, making sure the string passed in has at least one letter) and then passes the value (Hel) to findString(). It gets back an index and uses that index to index into the strings array:

```
Return strings(findString(index))
```

The set accessor works in the same way:

```
strings(findString(index)) = Value
```

If the string does not match, a value of -1 is returned, which is then used as an index into myStrings. This action then generates an exception (System.NullReferenceException), as you can see by un-commenting the following line in Main():

```
lbt["xyz"] = "oops"
```

The proper handling of not finding a string is, as they say, left as an exercise for the reader. You might consider displaying an error message or otherwise allowing the user to recover from the error. Exceptions are discussed in Chapter 17.

CHAPTER 15

Collection Interfaces and Types

A collection is a container that holds a group of objects. Collections are used to hold all the strings in a listbox, to hold all the employees in a company, to hold all the controls on a page, and so forth. You've already seen the simplest collection, the array (see Chapter 14). An array is a collection that provides an indexed list of elements, all of the same type.

The .NET Framework provides a number of already built and tested collection classes, including the ArrayList, Collection, Queue, and Stack. This chapter will explain how to use these collections and will provide examples of their use.

The Collection Interfaces

Every collection has certain shared characteristics. These are captured by the *collection interfaces*. The .NET Framework provides standard interfaces for enumerating, comparing, and creating collections.

 Chapter 13 introduced interfaces, which create a contract that a class can fulfill. Implementing an interface allows clients of the class to know exactly what to expect from the class.

By implementing the collection interfaces, your custom class can provide the same semantics as the collection classes available through the .NET Framework. Table 15-1 lists the key collection interfaces and their uses.

Table 15-1. The collection interfaces

Interface	Purpose
IEnumerable	Designates a class that can be enumerated
IEnumerator	A class that iterates over a collection; supports the For Each loop
ICollection	Implemented by all collections

Table 15-1. The collection interfaces (continued)

Interface	Purpose
IComparer	Compares two objects; used for sorting
IList	Used by collections that can be indexed
IDictionary	For key/value-based collections
IDictionaryEnumerator	Allows enumeration with For Each of a collection that supports IDictionary

The current chapter will focus on the IEnumerable interface, using it to demonstrate how you can implement the collection interfaces in your own classes to allow clients to treat your custom classes as if they were collections. For example, you might create a custom class named ListBoxTest. Your ListBoxTest class will have a set of strings to be displayed. You can implement the collection interfaces in your ListBoxTest class to allow clients to treat your ListBoxTest as if it were a collection. This will allow clients to add to the ListBoxTest using the index operator (e.g., myListBox(5) = "New String"), to sort the ListBoxTest, to enumerate the elements of the ListBoxTest, and so forth.

The IEnumerable Interface

In the previous chapter, you developed a simple ListBoxTest class that provided an indexer for array-like semantics. That is, your ListBoxTest implemented its own indexer, so that you could treat the ListBoxTest object like it was an array.

```
myListBoxTest(5) = "Hello World"
dim theText as String = myListBoxTest(1)
```

Of course, ListBoxTest is not an array; it is just a custom class that can be treated like an array, because you gave it this indexer. You can make your ListBoxTest class even more like a real array by providing support for iterating over the contents of the array using the For Each statement.

The For Each statement will work with any class that implements the IEnumerable interface. Classes that implement the IEnumerable interface have a single method, GetEnumerator(), that returns an object that implements a second interface, IEnumerator.

 Note the subtle difference in the names of these two interfaces: IEnu**merable** vs. IEnume**rator**. The former designates a class that can be enumerated; the latter designates a class that does the actual enumeration.

The entire job of the IEnumerable interface is to define the GetEnumerator() method. The job of the GetEnumerator() method is to generate an enumerator—that is, an instance of a class that implements the IEnumerator interface.

By implementing the IEnumerable interface, your ListBoxTest class is saying "you can enumerate my members, just ask me for my enumerator." The client asks the ListBoxTest for its enumerator by calling the GetEnumerator() method. What it gets back is an instance of a class that knows how to iterate over a listbox. That class, ListBoxEnumerator, will implement the IEnumerator interface.

 When you iterate over an array, you visit each member in turn. Programmers talk about iterating over an array, iterating the array, iterating through the array, and enumerating the array. All of these terms mean the same thing.

This gets a bit confusing, so let's use an example. When you implement the IEnumerable interface for ListBoxTest, you are promising potential clients that ListBoxTest will support enumeration. That will allow clients of your ListBoxTest class to write code like this:

```
Dim s As String
For Each s In ListBoxText
    '...
Next
```

You implement IEnumerable by providing the GetEnumerator() method, which returns an implementation of the IEnumerator interface. In this case, you'll return an instance of the ListBoxEnumerator class, and ListBoxEnumerator will implement the IEnumerator interface:

```
Public Function GetEnumerator() As IEnumerator _
        Implements IEnumerable.GetEnumerator
            Return New ListBoxEnumerator(Me)
        End Function
```

The ListBoxEnumerator is a specialized instance of IEnumerator that knows how to enumerate the contents of your ListBoxTest class. Notice two things about this implementation. First, the constructor for ListBoxEnumerator takes a single argument, and you pass in the Me keyword. Doing so passes in a reference to the current ListBoxTest object, which is the object that will be enumerated. Second, notice that the ListBoxEnumerator is returned as an instance of IEnumerator. This implicit cast is safe because the ListBoxEnumerator class implements the IEnumerator interface.

 An alternative to creating a specialized class to implement IEnumerator is to have the enumerable class (ListBoxTest) implement IEnumerator itself. In that case, the IEnumerator returned by GetEnumerator() would be the ListBoxTest object, cast to IEnumerator.

Putting the enumeration responsibility into a dedicated class that implements IEnumerator (ListBoxEnumerator) is generally preferred to the alternative of letting the collection class (ListBoxTest) know how to enumerate itself. The specialized enumeration class encapsulates the responsibility of enumeration, and the collection class (ListBoxTest) is not cluttered with a lot of enumeration code.

Because ListBoxEnumerator is specialized to know only how to enumerate ListBox-Test objects (and not any other enumerable objects), you will make ListBoxEnumerator a private class, contained within the definition of ListBoxTest. (The collection class is often referred to as the container class because it contains the members of the collection.) The complete listing is shown in Example 15-1, followed by a detailed analysis.

Example 15-1. Enumeration

```
Option Strict On

Imports System
Imports System.Collections

Namespace Enumeration

    Public Class ListBoxTest : Implements IEnumerable
        Private strings() As String
        Private ctr As Integer = 0

        ' private nested implementation of ListBoxEnumerator
        Private Class ListBoxEnumerator
            Implements IEnumerator
            ' member fields of the nested ListBoxEnumerator class
            Private currentListBox As ListBoxTest
            Private index As Integer

            ' public within the private implementation
            ' thus, private within ListBoxTest
            Public Sub New(ByVal currentListBox As ListBoxTest)
                ' a particular ListBoxTest instance is
                ' passed in, hold a reference to it
                ' in the member variable currentListBox.
                Me.currentListBox = currentListBox
                index = -1
            End Sub

            ' Increment the index and make sure the
            ' value is valid
            Public Function MoveNext() As Boolean _
              Implements IEnumerator.MoveNext
                index += 1
                If index >= currentListBox.strings.Length Then
                    Return False
                Else
                    Return True
                End If
            End Function

            Public Sub Reset() _
              Implements IEnumerator.Reset
                index = -1
            End Sub
```

Example 15-1. Enumeration (continued)

```
        ' Current property defined as the
        ' last string added to the listbox
        Public ReadOnly Property Current() As Object _
        Implements IEnumerator.Current
            Get
                Return currentListBox(index)
            End Get
        End Property
    End Class   ' end nested class

    ' Enumerable classes can return an enumerator
    Public Function GetEnumerator() As IEnumerator _
    Implements IEnumerable.GetEnumerator
        Return New ListBoxEnumerator(Me)
    End Function

    ' initialize the list box with strings
    Public Sub New( _
      ByVal ParamArray initialStrings() As String)
        ' allocate space for the strings
        ReDim strings(7)

        ' copy the strings passed in to the constructor
        Dim s As String
        For Each s In initialStrings
            strings(ctr) = s
            ctr += 1
        Next
    End Sub

    ' add a single string to the end of the list box
    Public Sub Add(ByVal theString As String)
        strings(ctr) = theString
        ctr += 1
    End Sub

    ' allow array-like access
    Default Public Property Item( _
      ByVal index As Integer) As String
        Get
            If index < 0 Or index >= strings.Length Then
                ' handle bad index
                Exit Property
            End If
            Return strings(index)
        End Get
        Set(ByVal Value As String)
            strings(index) = Value
        End Set
    End Property

    ' publish how many strings you hold
```

Example 15-1. Enumeration (continued)

```
        Public Function GetNumEntries() As Integer
            Return ctr
        End Function

    End Class

    Public Class Tester
        Public Sub Run()
            ' create a new list box and initialize
            Dim currentListBox As New _
                ListBoxTest("Hello", "World")

            ' add a few strings
            currentListBox.Add("Who")
            currentListBox.Add("Is")
            currentListBox.Add("John")
            currentListBox.Add("Galt")

            ' test the access
            Dim subst As String = "Universe"
            currentListBox(1) = subst

            ' access all the strings
            Dim s As String
            For Each s In currentListBox
                Console.WriteLine("Value: {0}", s)
            Next
        End Sub

        Shared Sub Main()
            Dim t As New Tester()
            t.Run()
        End Sub
    End Class
End Namespace
```

Output:
```
Value: Hello
Value: Universe
Value: Who
Value: Is
Value: John
Value: Galt
Value:
Value:
```

The GetEnumerator() method of ListBoxTest passes a reference to the current object (ListBoxEnumerator) to the enumerator, using the Me keyword:

```
    Return New ListBoxEnumerator(Me)
```

The enumerator will enumerate the members of the ListBoxTest object passed in as a parameter.

The class to implement the Enumerator is implemented as ListBoxEnumerator. The most interesting aspect of this code is the definition of the ListBoxEnumerator class. Notice that this class is defined within the definition of ListBoxTest. It is a contained class. It is also marked private; the only method that will ever instantiate a ListBox-Enumerator object is the GetEnumerator() method of ListBoxTest:

```
' private nested implementation of ListBoxEnumerator
        Private Class ListBoxEnumerator
            Implements IEnumerator
```

ListBoxEnumerator is defined to implement the IEnumerator interface, which defines one property and two methods, as shown in Table 15-2.

Table 15-2. IEnumerator members

Property or Method	Description
Current	Property that returns the current element.
MoveNext()	Method that advances the enumerator to the next element.
Reset()	Method that sets the enumerator to its initial position, *before* the first element.

The ListBoxTest object to be enumerated is passed in as an argument to the ListBox-Enumerator constructor, where it is assigned to the member variable currentListBox. The constructor also sets the member variable index to -1, indicating that you have not yet begun to enumerate the object:

```
Public Sub New(ByVal currentListBox As ListBoxTest)
    Me.currentListBox = currentListBox
    index = -1
End Sub
```

 The number -1 is used as a signal to indicate that the enumerator is not yet pointing to any of the elements in the ListBoxTest object. You can't use the value 0, because 0 is a valid offset into the collection.

The MoveNext() method increments the index and then checks the length property of the strings array to ensure that you've not run past the end of the strings array. If you have run past the end, you return false; otherwise, you return true:

```
Public Function MoveNext() As Boolean _
    Implements IEnumerator.MoveNext
        index += 1
        If index >= currentListBox.strings.Length Then
            Return False
        Else
            Return True
        End If
End Function
```

The IEnumerator method Reset() does nothing but reset the index to -1. You can call Reset() any time you want to start over iterating the ListBoxTest object.

The Current property is implemented to return the string at the index. This is an arbitrary decision; in other classes, Current will have whatever meaning the designer decides is appropriate. However defined, every enumerator must be able to return the current member, as accessing the current member is what enumerators are for. The interface defines the Current property to return an object. Since strings are derived from object, there is an implicit cast of the string to the more general object type.

```
Public ReadOnly Property Current() As Object _
Implements IEnumerator.Current
    Get
        Return currentListBox(index)
    End Get
End Property
```

The call to For Each fetches the enumerator and uses it to enumerate over the array. Because For Each will display every string, whether or not you've added a meaningful value, in this example the strings array is initialized to hold only eight strings.

Now that you've seen how ListBoxTest implements IEnumerable, let's examine how the ListBoxTest object is used. The program begins by creating a new ListBoxTest object and passing two strings to the constructor.

```
Public Class Tester
    Public Sub Run()
        Dim currentListBox As New _
            ListBoxTest("Hello", "World")
```

When the ListBoxTest object (currentListBox) is created, an array of String objects is created with room for eight strings. The initial two strings passed in to the constructor are added to the array.

```
Public Sub New( _
  ByVal ParamArray initialStrings() As String)

    ReDim strings(7)

    Dim s As String
    For Each s In initialStrings
        strings(ctr) = s
        ctr += 1
    Next
End Sub
```

Back in Run(), four more strings are added using the Add() method, and the second string is updated with the word "Universe," just as in Example 14-11.

```
currentListBox.Add("Who")
currentListBox.Add("Is")
currentListBox.Add("John")
currentListBox.Add("Galt")
```

```
Dim subst As String = "Universe"
currentListBox(1) = subst
```

You iterate over the strings in currentListBox with a For Each loop, displaying each string in turn:

```
Dim s As String
For Each s In currentListBox
    Console.WriteLine("Value: {0}", s)
Next
```

The For Each loop checks that your class implements IEnumerable (and throws an exception if it does not) and invokes GetEnumerator():

```
Public Function GetEnumerator() As IEnumerator _
Implements IEnumerable.GetEnumerator
    Return New ListBoxEnumerator(Me)
End Function
```

GetEnumerator() calls the ListBoxEnumerator constructor, thus initializing the index to -1.

```
Public Sub New(ByVal currentListBox As ListBoxTest
    Me.currentListBox = currentListBox
    index = -1
End Sub
```

The first time through the loop, For Each automatically invokes MoveNext(), which immediately increments the index to 0 and returns true.

```
Public Function MoveNext() As Boolean _
  Implements IEnumerator.MoveNext
    index += 1
    If index >= currentListBox.strings.Length Then
        Return False
    Else
        Return True
    End If
End Function
```

The For Each loop then uses the Current property to get back the current string.

```
Public ReadOnly Property Current() As Object _
Implements IEnumerator.Current
    Get
        Return currentListBox(index)
    End Get
End Property
```

The Current property invokes the ListBoxTest's indexer, getting back the string stored at index 0. This string is assigned to the variable s defined in the For Each loop, and that string is displayed on the console. The For Each loop repeats these steps (call MoveNext(), access the Current property, display the string) until all the strings in the ListBoxTest object have been displayed.

Walking Through the For Each Loop in a Debugger

The calls to MoveNext() and Current are done for you by the For Each construct; you will not see these invoked directly, though you can step into the methods in the debugger as you iterate through the For Each loop. The debugger makes the relationships among the For Each construct, the ListBoxTest class, and its enumerator explicit. To examine these relationships, put a breakpoint at the For Each loop, as shown in Figure 15-1.

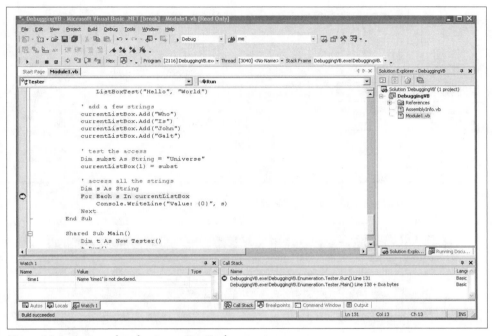

Figure 15-1. Setting a breakpoint on For Each

Run the application to the breakpoint by pressing the F5 key. Press F11 to step into the For Each loop, and you'll find that you are in the MoveNext() method of the ListBoxEnumerator. (There is no explicit call to this method, but the method is invoked by the For Each construct itself.) Notice the Locals window shows the Me reference and the index (currently -1), both circled and highlighted in Figure 15-2.

Now expand the Me reference in the Locals window. You'll see the CurrentListBox as a property. Expand that property and you'll see the strings as a property, as well as ctr, indicating that there are six strings so far, as shown in Figure 15-3.

Expand the strings member variable and you'll see the six strings, nicely tucked away in the strings array, in the order you added them. This is shown in Figure 15-4.

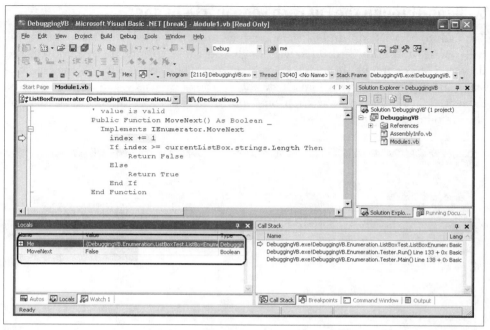

Figure 15-2. The Locals window in MoveNext()

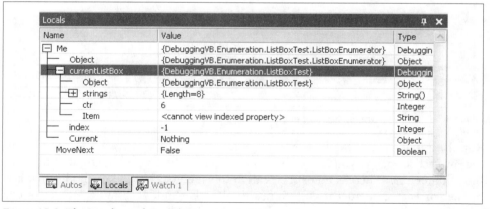

Figure 15-3. The Locals window with Me expanded

Press the F11 key once. This increments the index property from -1 to 0. You'll see the index property listed in red in the Locals window. (Each time a value changes, it is marked in red.)

The MoveNext() method tests whether the index (0) is greater than the Length property of the array (8). Since at this point it is not, MoveNext() returns true, indicating that you have not exceeded the bounds of the array but instead have moved to the next valid value in the collection.

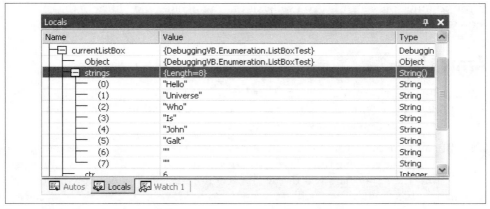

Figure 15-4. The strings expanded

Press F11 repeatedly, until you return to the For Each loop. Pressing F11 again moves the highlight to the string in the For Each statement, and one more press of F11 steps you into the Current property's accessor. Continue pressing F11, you'll step into the indexer of the ListBoxTest class, where the current index (0) is used as an index into the internal strings array, as shown in Figure 15-5.

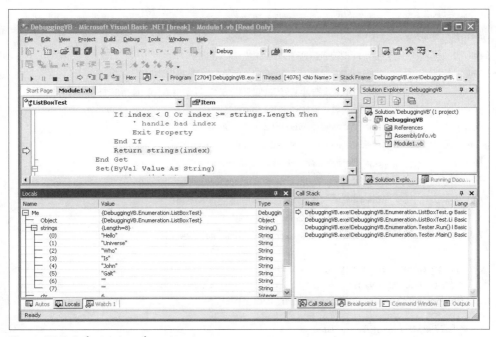

Figure 15-5. Indexing into the strings array

If you continue pressing F11, you will exit the enumerator and return to the For Each loop where the string (Hello) is displayed.

Array Lists

Imagine that your program asks the user for input or gathers input from a web site. As it finds objects (strings, books, values, etc.), you would like to add them to an array, but you have no idea how many objects you'll collect in any given session.

It is difficult to use an array for such a purpose because you must declare the size of an Array object at compile time. If you try to add more objects than you've allocated memory for, the Array class will throw an exception. If you do not know in advance how many objects your array will be required to hold, you run the risk of declaring either too small an array (and running out of room) or too large an array (and wasting memory).

The .NET Framework provides a class designed for just this situation. The ArrayList class is an array whose size is dynamically increased as required. The ArrayList class provides many useful methods and properties. A few of the most important are shown in Table 15-3.

Table 15-3. ArrayList members

Method or property	Purpose
Capacity	Property containing the number of elements the array can currently hold.
Count	Property that returns the number of elements currently in the array.
Item()	Method that gets or sets the element at the specified index; this is the indexer for the ArrayList class.
Add()	Method that adds an object to the ArrayList.
Clear()	Method that removes all elements from the ArrayList.
GetEnumerator()	Method that returns an enumerator to iterate an ArrayList.
Insert()	Method that inserts an element into ArrayList.
RemoveAt()	Method that removes the element at the specified index.
Reverse()	Method that reverses the order of elements in the ArrayList.
Sort()	Method that alphabetically sorts the ArrayList.
ToArray()	Method that copies the elements of the ArrayList to a new array.

When you create an ArrayList, you do not define how many objects it will contain. You add to the ArrayList using the Add() method, and the list takes care of its own internal bookkeeping, as illustrated in Example 15-2.

Example 15-2. Using an ArrayList

```
Option Strict On
Imports System
Namespace ArrayListDemo
```

Example 15-2. Using an ArrayList (continued)

```vb
' a class to hold in the array list
Public Class Employee
    Private myEmpID As Integer

    Public Sub New(ByVal empID As Integer)
        Me.myEmpID = empID
    End Sub 'New

    Public Overrides Function ToString() As String
        Return myEmpID.ToString()
    End Function 'ToString

    Public Property EmpID() As Integer
        Get
            Return myEmpID
        End Get
        Set(ByVal Value As Integer)
            myEmpID = Value
        End Set
    End Property
End Class 'Employee

Class Tester

    Public Sub Run()
        Dim empArray As New ArrayList()
        Dim intArray As New ArrayList()

        ' populate the arraylists
        Dim i As Integer
        For i = 0 To 4
            empArray.Add(New Employee(i + 100))
            intArray.Add((i * 5))
        Next i

        ' print each member of the array
        For Each i In intArray
            Console.Write("{0} ", i.ToString())
        Next i

        Console.WriteLine(ControlChars.Lf)
        ' print each employee
        Dim e As Employee
        For Each e In empArray
            Console.Write("{0} ", e.ToString())
        Next e

        Console.WriteLine(ControlChars.Lf)
        Console.WriteLine("empArray.Capacity: {0}", empArray.Capacity)
    End Sub 'Run

    Shared Sub Main()
```

Example 15-2. Using an ArrayList (continued)

```
        Dim t As New Tester()
        t.Run()
    End Sub 'Main
  End Class 'Tester
End Namespace 'ArrayListDemo
```

Output:
```
0 5 10 15 20
100 101 102 103 104
empArray.Capacity: 16
```

Suppose you're defining two ArrayList objects, empArray to hold Employee objects, and intArray to hold integers:

```
Dim empArray As New ArrayList()
Dim intArray As New ArrayList()
```

Each ArrayList object has a property, Capacity, which is the number of elements the ArrayList is capable of storing.

 The default capacity for the ArrayList class is 16. You are free to set a different starting capacity for your ArrayList, but typically there is no need for you ever to do so.

You add elements to the ArrayList with the Add() method:

```
empArray.Add(New Employee(i + 100))
intArray.Add((i * 5))
```

When you add the 17th element, the capacity is automatically doubled to 32. If you change the For loop to:

```
For i = 0 To 17
```

the output looks like this:

```
0 5 10 15 20 25 30 35 40 45 50 55 60 65 70 75 80 85
100 101 102 103 104 105 106 107 108 109 110 111 112 113 114 115 116 117
empArray.Capacity: 32
```

Similarly, if you added a 33rd element, the capacity would be doubled to 64. The 65th element increases the capacity to 128, the 129th element increases it to 256, and so forth.

The Collection Class

Visual Basic .NET offers a generic collection class named, aptly, Collection. In many ways, the Collection object serves as an object-oriented alternative to Array, much as ArrayList does.

These two constructs (ArrayList and Collection) are very similar. Both offer and Add() and Remove() methods as well as an Item property. The Collection class, however, overloads the Item property to take a string as a key into the collection. This allows the Collection class to act as a dictionary, associating keys with values. You can also use the Item property to access members of the collection by index value; however the Collection uses a one-based index (i.e., the first element is index 1 rather than 0).

Example 15-3 illustrates the use of a VB.NET Collection object.

Example 15-3. Using a Collection object

```
Option Strict On
Imports System
Namespace CollectionDemo
    ' a class to hold in the array list
    Public Class Employee
        Private myEmpID As Integer

        Public Sub New(ByVal empID As Integer)
            Me.myEmpID = empID
        End Sub 'New

        Public Overrides Function ToString() As String
            Return myEmpID.ToString()
        End Function 'ToString

        Public Property EmpID() As Integer
            Get
                Return myEmpID
            End Get
            Set(ByVal Value As Integer)
                myEmpID = Value
            End Set
        End Property
    End Class 'Employee

    Class Tester

        Public Sub Run()
            Dim intCollection As New Collection()
            Dim empCollection As New Collection()
            Dim empCollection2 As New Collection()

            ' populate the Collections
            Dim i As Integer
            For i = 0 To 4
                empCollection.Add(New Employee(i + 100))
                intCollection.Add((i * 5))
            Next i

            ' add key/value pairs
```

Example 15-3. Using a Collection object (continued)

```
            empCollection2.Add(New Employee(1789), "George Washington")
            empCollection2.Add(New Employee(1797), "John Adams")
            empCollection2.Add(New Employee(1801), "Thomas Jefferson")

            ' print each member of the array
            For Each i In intCollection
                Console.Write("{0} ", i.ToString())
            Next i

            Console.WriteLine()
            Console.WriteLine("Employee collection...")
            Dim e As Employee
            For Each e In empCollection
                Console.Write("{0} ", e.ToString())
            Next e

            Console.WriteLine()
            Console.WriteLine("Employee collection 2...")
            For Each e In empCollection2
                Console.Write("{0} ", e.ToString())
            Next e

            Console.WriteLine()

            ' retrieve an Employee by key
            Dim emp As Employee
            emp = empCollection2.Item("John Adams")
            Console.WriteLine( _
              "Key John Adams retrieved empID {0}", emp.ToString())

            ' note that indexing is 1-based (rather than zero based)
            emp = empCollection2.Item(1)
            Console.WriteLine( _
              "Index(1) retrieved empID {0}", emp.ToString())

        End Sub 'Run

        Shared Sub Main()
            Dim t As New Tester()
            t.Run()
        End Sub 'Main
    End Class 'Tester
End Namespace 'CollectionDemo
```

Output:
```
0 5 10 15 20
Employee collection...
100 101 102 103 104
Employee collection 2...
1789 1797 1801
Key John Adams retrieved empID 1797
Index(1) retrieved empID 1789
```

Example 15-3 creates three Collection objects (intCollection, empCollection, and empCollection2):

```
Dim intCollection As New Collection()
Dim empCollection As New Collection()
Dim empCollection2 As New Collection()
```

The first two objects are populated in For loops, just as the ArrayList was created in Example 15-2.

```
Dim i As Integer
For i = 0 To 4
    empCollection.Add(New Employee(i + 100))
    intCollection.Add((i * 5))
Next i
```

The third Collection object, empCollection2, is populated using key values. Each new Employee is associated with a string, representing the name of the Employee:

```
empCollection2.Add(New Employee(1789), "George Washington")
empCollection2.Add(New Employee(1797), "John Adams")
empCollection2.Add(New Employee(1801), "Thomas Jefferson")
```

You retrieve objects from the collection much as you did from the ArrayLists:

```
For Each i In intCollection
    Console.Write("{0} ", i.ToString())
Next i

Dim e As Employee
For Each e In empCollection
    Console.Write("{0} ", e.ToString())
Next e

For Each e In empCollection2
    Console.Write("{0} ", e.ToString())
Next e
```

You can, however, retrieve objects from the collection using either the key value or an index value (one-based):

```
Dim emp As Employee
emp = empCollection2.Item("John Adams")
Console.WriteLine("Key John Adams retrieved empID {0}", emp.ToString())

emp = empCollection2.Item(1)
Console.WriteLine("Index(1) retrieved empID {0}", emp.ToString())
```

Queues

A *queue* represents a first-in first-out (FIFO) collection. The classic analogy is a line (or queue if you are British) at a ticket window. The first person to get in the line ought to be the first person to come off the line to buy a ticket.

The Queue class is a good collection to use when you are managing a limited resource. For example, you might want to send messages to a resource that can handle only one message at a time. You would then create a message queue so that you can say to your clients: "Your message is important to us. Messages are handled in the order in which they are received."

The Queue class has a number of member methods and properties, the most important of which are shown in Table 15-4.

Table 15-4. Queue members

Method or property	Purpose
Count	Public property that gets the number of elements in the Queue
Clear( )	Method that removes all objects from the Queue
Contains( )	Method that determines if an element is in the Queue
CopyTo( )	Method that copies the Queue elements to an existing one-dimensional array
Dequeue( )	Method that removes and returns the object at the beginning of the Queue
Enqueue( )	Method that adds an object to the end of the Queue
GetEnumerator( )	Method that returns an enumerator for the Queue
Peek( )	Method that returns the object at the beginning of the Queue without removing it
ToArray( )	Method that copies the elements to a new array

Add elements to your queue with the Enqueue() method, and take them off the queue with Dequeue() or by using an enumerator. Example 15-4 shows how to use a Queue, followed by the output and a complete analysis.

Example 15-4. Implementing the Queue class

```
Option Strict On
Imports System
Namespace QueueDemo
    Class Tester
        Public Sub Run( )
            Dim intQueue As New Queue( )

            ' populate the array
            Dim i As Integer
            For i = 0 To 4
                intQueue.Enqueue((i * 5))
            Next i

            ' Display the Queue.
            Console.WriteLine("intQueue values:")
            DisplayValues(intQueue)

            ' Remove an element from the queue.
            Console.WriteLine("(Dequeue) {0}", intQueue.Dequeue( ))
```

Example 15-4. Implementing the Queue class (continued)

```
                ' Display the Queue.
                Console.WriteLine("intQueue values:")
                DisplayValues(intQueue)

                ' Remove another element from the queue.
                Console.WriteLine("(Dequeue) {0}", intQueue.Dequeue())

                ' Display the Queue.
                Console.WriteLine("intQueue values:")
                DisplayValues(intQueue)

                ' View the first element in the
                ' Queue but do not remove.
                Console.WriteLine("(Peek)   {0}", intQueue.Peek())

                ' Display the Queue.
                Console.WriteLine("intQueue values:")
                DisplayValues(intQueue)
        End Sub 'Run

        Public Shared Sub DisplayValues(ByVal myCollection As IEnumerable)
            Dim myEnumerator As IEnumerator = myCollection.GetEnumerator()
            While myEnumerator.MoveNext()
                Console.WriteLine("{0} ", myEnumerator.Current)
            End While
            Console.WriteLine()
        End Sub 'DisplayValues

        Shared Sub Main()
            Dim t As New Tester()
            t.Run()
        End Sub 'Main
    End Class 'Tester
End Namespace 'QueueDemo
```

Output:
```
intQueue values:
0
5
10
15
20

(Dequeue) 0
intQueue values:
5
10
15
20

(Dequeue) 5
intQueue values:
```

Example 15-4. Implementing the Queue class (continued)

```
10
15
20

(Peek)    10
intQueue values:
10
15
20
```

In Example 15-4, the ArrayList from Example 15-2 is replaced by a Queue. I've dispensed with the Employee class and enqueued integers to save room in the book, but of course you can enqueue user-defined objects as well.

The program begins by creating an instance of a Queue, called intQueue:

```
Dim intQueue As New Queue()
```

The queue is populated with integers:

```
For i = 0 To 4
    intQueue.Enqueue((i * 5))
Next i
```

The contents of the queue are then displayed using the DisplayValues() method. This method takes a collection that implements the IEnumerable interface (as does each of the collections provided by the .NET Framework) and asks that collection for its Enumerator. It then explicitly iterates over the collection, displaying each element in turn.

```
Public Shared Sub DisplayValues(ByVal myCollection As IEnumerable)
    Dim myEnumerator As IEnumerable = myCollection.GetEnumerator()
    While myEnumerator.MoveNext()
        Console.Write("{0} ", myEnumerator.Current)
    End While
    Console.WriteLine()
End Sub 'DisplayValues
```

 Every collection in the .NET Framework implements IEnumerable.

You can avoid all the details of the Enumerator by using the For Each loop instead:

```
Public Shared Sub DisplayValues( _
        ByVal myCollection As IEnumerable)
    Dim o As Object
    For Each o In myCollection
        Console.WriteLine(o)
    Next
End Sub 'DisplayValues
```

Either version of DisplayValues() will work equally well.

You can display the first value in the queue without removing it by calling the Peek() method:

```
Console.WriteLine("(Peek) {0}", intQueue.Peek())
```

Or, having displayed the values in the For Each loop, you can remove the current value by calling the Dequeue() method:

```
Console.WriteLine("(Dequeue) {0}", intQueue.Dequeue())
```

Stacks

A *stack* is a last-in first-out (LIFO) collection, like a stack of dishes at a buffet table or a stack of coins on your desk. You add a dish on top, and it is the first dish you take off the stack.

 The classic example of a stack is *the* stack, the portion of memory on which parameters and local variables are stored. See Chapter 8 for more about the stack.

The principal methods for adding to and removing from an instance of the Stack class are Push() and Pop(); Stack also offers a Peek() method, very much like Queue. The most important methods and properties for Stack are shown in Table 15-5.

Table 15-5. Stack members

Method or property	Purpose
Count	Public property that gets the number of elements in the Stack
Clear()	Method that removes all objects from the Stack
Contains()	Method that determines if an element is in the Stack
CopyTo()	Method that copies the Stack elements to an existing one-dimensional array
GetEnumerator()	Method that returns an enumerator for the Stack
Peek()	Method that returns the object at the top of the Stack without removing it
Pop()	Method that removes and returns the object at the top of the Stack
Push()	Method that inserts an object at the top of the Stack
ToArray()	Method that copies the elements to a new array

In Example 15-5, you rewrite Example 15-4 to use a Stack rather than a Queue. The logic is almost identical. The key difference is that a Stack is Last In First Out, while a Queue is First In First Out.

Example 15-5. Using a Stack

```
Option Strict On
Imports System
Namespace StackDemo
```

Example 15-5. Using a Stack (continued)

```
    Class Tester
        Public Sub Run()
            Dim intStack As New Stack()

            ' populate the stack
            Dim i As Integer
            For i = 0 To 7
                intStack.Push((i * 5))
            Next i

            ' Display the Stack.
            Console.WriteLine("intStack values:")
            DisplayValues(intStack)

            ' Remove an element from the stack.
            Console.WriteLine("(Pop){0}", intStack.Pop())

            ' Display the Stack.
            Console.WriteLine("intStack values:")
            DisplayValues(intStack)

            ' Remove another element from the stack.
            Console.WriteLine("(Pop){0}", intStack.Pop())

            ' Display the Stack.
            Console.WriteLine("intStack values:")
            DisplayValues(intStack)

            ' View the first element in the
            ' Stack but do not remove.
            Console.WriteLine("(Peek)   {0}", intStack.Peek())

            ' Display the Stack.
            Console.WriteLine("intStack values:")
            DisplayValues(intStack)
        End Sub 'Run

        Public Shared Sub DisplayValues(ByVal myCollection As IEnumerable)
            Dim o As Object
            For Each o In myCollection
                Console.WriteLine(o)
            Next o
        End Sub 'DisplayValues

        Shared Sub Main()
            Dim t As New Tester()
            t.Run()
        End Sub 'Main
    End Class 'Tester
End Namespace 'StackDemo
```

Output:
```
intStack values:
```

Example 15-5. Using a Stack (continued)

```
35
30
25
20
15
10
5
0
(Pop)35
intStack values:
30
25
20
15
10
5
0
(Pop)30
intStack values:
25
20
15
10
5
0
(Peek)    25
intStack values:
25
20
15
10
5
```

You start Example 15-5 by creating a Stack object called intStack:

```
Dim intStack As New Stack()
```

You populate the stack with integers by calling the Push() method, which pushes each integer object onto the stack (i.e., adds it to the top of the Stack):

```
For i = 0 To 7
    intStack.Push((i * 5))
Next i
```

You remove an object from the stack by popping it off the stack with the Pop() method:

```
Console.WriteLine("(Pop){0}", intStack.Pop())
```

Just as you could peek at the object at the beginning of the Queue without dequeing it, you can Peek() at the object on top of the stack without popping it:

```
Console.WriteLine("(Peek)    {0}", intStack.Peek())
```

Copying from a Collection Type to an Array

The ArrayList, Queue, and Stack types contain overloaded CopyTo() and ToArray() methods for copying their elements to an array. The CopyTo() method copies its elements to an existing one-dimensional array, overwriting the contents of the array beginning at the index you specify. The ToArray() method returns a new array with the contents of the type's elements.

For example, in the case of a Stack, ToArray() would return a new array containing the elements in the Stack. CopyTo() would copy the Stack over a preexisting array. Example 15-6 modifies Example 15-5 to demonstrate both methods. The listing is followed by a complete analysis.

Example 15-6. Copying from Stack to an array

```
Option Strict On

Namespace StackDemo
    Class Tester

        Public Sub Run()
            Dim intStack As New Stack()

            ' populate the array
            Dim i As Integer
            For i = 1 To 4
                intStack.Push((i * 5))
            Next i

            ' Display the Stack.
            Console.WriteLine("intStack values:")
            DisplayValues(intStack)

            Const arraySize As Integer = 10
            Dim testArray(arraySize) As Integer

            ' populate the array
            For i = 1 To arraySize - 1
                testArray(i) = i * 100
            Next i
            Console.WriteLine("Contents of the test array")
            DisplayValues(testArray)

            ' Copy the intStack into the new array, start offset 3
            intStack.CopyTo(testArray, 3)
            Console.WriteLine("TestArray after copy:  ")
            DisplayValues(testArray)

            ' Copy the entire source Stack
            ' to a new standard array.
            Dim myArray As Object() = intStack.ToArray()
```

Example 15-6. Copying from Stack to an array (continued)

```
            ' Display the values of the new standard array.
            Console.WriteLine("The new array:")
            DisplayValues(myArray)
        End Sub 'Run

        Public Shared Sub DisplayValues(ByVal myCollection As IEnumerable)
            Dim o As Object
            For Each o In myCollection
                Console.WriteLine(o)
            Next o
        End Sub 'DisplayValues

        Shared Sub Main()
            Dim t As New Tester()
            t.Run()
        End Sub 'Main
    End Class 'Tester
End Namespace 'StackDemo
```

Output:
```
intStack values:
20
15
10
5
Contents of the test array
0
100
200
300
400
500
600
700
800
900
0
TestArray after copy:
0
100
200
20
15
10
5
700
800
900
0
The new array:
20
15
```

Example 15-6. Copying from Stack to an array (continued)

```
10
5
```

You begin again by creating the Stack (intStack), populating it with integers, and displaying its contents using WriteLine():

```
Dim intStack As New Stack()

' populate the array
Dim i As Integer
For i = 1 To 4
    intStack.Push((i * 5))
Next i

' Display the Stack.
Console.WriteLine("intStack values:")
DisplayValues(intStack)
```

You next create an array, populate it, and display its values:

```
Const arraySize As Integer = 10
Dim testArray(arraySize) As Integer
' populate the array
For i = 1 To arraySize - 1
    testArray(i) = i * 100
Next i
Console.WriteLine("Contents of the test array")
DisplayValues(testArray)
```

You are ready to copy the stack over the array. You do so with the CopyTo() method, passing in the array name, and the offset at which to begin the copy:

```
intStack.CopyTo( testArray, 3 )
```

This copies the four values from the stack over the array, starting at offset 3 (the fourth element in the array).

```
0
100
200
20
15
10
5
700
800
900
```

Rather than copying to an existing array, you are free to copy to a new array. You do this with the ToArray() method, which generates a properly sized new array to hold the contents of the stack:

```
Dim myArray As Object() = intStack.ToArray()
```

CHAPTER 16

Strings

People once thought of computers as manipulating numeric values exclusively. Early computers were first used to calculate missile trajectories, and programming was taught in the math department of major universities.

Today, most programs are concerned more with strings of characters than with numbers. Typically these strings are used for word processing, document manipulation, and creation of web pages.

VB.NET provides built-in support for a fully functional String type. More importantly, VB.NET treats Strings as objects that encapsulate all the manipulation, sorting, and searching methods normally applied to strings of characters.

Complex string manipulation and pattern matching is aided by the use of *regular expressions*. VB.NET combines the power and complexity of regular expression syntax, originally found only in string manipulation languages such as awk and Perl, with a fully object-oriented design.

In this chapter, you will learn to work with the VB.NET String type and the .NET Framework System.String class that it aliases. You will see how to extract substrings, manipulate and concatenate strings, and build new strings with the String-Builder class. In addition, you will find a short introduction to the RegEx class used to match strings based on regular expressions.

Creating Strings

VB.NET treats strings as if they were built-in types. When you declare a VB.NET String using the `String` keyword, you are in fact declaring the object to be of the type System.String, one of the built-in types provided by the .NET Framework Class Library.

In .NET, each String object is an *immutable* sequence of Unicode characters. In other words, methods that appear to change the String actually return a modified copy; the original String remains intact.

The declaration of the System.String class is:

```
NotInheritable Public Class String
    Implements IComparable, ICloneable, IConvertible, IEnumerable
```

This declaration reveals that the class is NotInheritable, meaning that it is not possible to derive from the String class. The class also implements four system interfaces—IComparable, ICloneable, IConvertible, and IEnumerable—which dictate functionality that System.String shares with other classes in the .NET Framework.

The IComparable interface is implemented by types that can be sorted. Strings, for example, can be alphabetized; any given string can be compared with another string to determine which should come first in an ordered list. IComparable classes implement the CompareTo() method.

ICloneable objects can create new instances with the same value as the original instance. In this case, it is possible to clone a String object to produce a new String object with the same values (characters) as the original. ICloneable classes implement the Clone() method.

IConvertible classes provide methods to facilitate conversion to other primitive types; these methods include ToInt32(), ToDouble(), and ToDecimal().

IEnumerable, discussed in Chapter 15, lets you use the For Each construct to enumerate a String as a collection of Chars.

String Literals

The most common way to create a string is to assign a quoted string of characters, known as a *string literal*, to a user-defined variable of type String. The following code declares a string called newString that contains the phrase *This is a string literal*:

```
Dim newString As String = "This is a string literal"
```

The ToString( ) Method

Another common way to create a string is to call the ToString() method on an object and assign the result to a string variable. All the built-in types override this method to simplify the task of converting a value (often a numeric value) to a string representation of that value. In the following example, the ToString() method of an Integer type is called to store its value in a string:

```
Dim myInteger As Integer = 5
Dim integerString As String = myInteger.ToString()
```

The call to myInteger.ToString() returns a String object, which is then assigned to the string variable, integerString.

Strings Are Immutable

While Strings are considered to be reference types, the String objects themselves are immutable. They can not be changed once created. When you appear to be changing a String, what is actually happening is that a new String is being created and the old String destroyed. Thus, suppose you write,

```
Dim myString as String = "Hello"
myString = "GoodBye"
```

The first line creates a String object on the heap with the characters *Hello* and assigns a reference to that string to the variable *myString*. The second line creates a new String object with the characters *GoodBye* and assigns a reference to that new String to the reference myString. The original String is then cleaned up by the garbage collector.

Manipulating Strings

The String class provides a host of methods for comparing, searching, and manipulating strings, the most important of which are shown in Table 16-1.

Table 16-1. String class methods

Method or field	Explanation
Chars	The string indexer
Compare()	Overloaded public shared method that compares two strings
Copy()	Public shared method that creates a new string by copying another
Equals()	Overloaded public shared and instance method that determines if two strings have the same value
Format()	Overloaded public shared method that formats a string using a format specification
Length	The number of characters in the instance
PadLeft()	Right-aligns the characters in the string, padding to the left with spaces or a specified character
PadRight()	Left-aligns the characters in the string, padding to the right with spaces or a specified character
Remove()	Deletes the specified number of characters
Split()	Divides a string, returning the substrings delimited by the specified characters
StartsWith()	Indicates if the string starts with the specified characters
SubString()	Retrieves a substring
ToCharArray()	Copies the characters from the string to a character array
ToLower()	Returns a copy of the string in lowercase
ToUpper()	Returns a copy of the string in uppercase
Trim()	Removes all occurrences of a set of specified characters from beginning and end of the string
TrimEnd()	Behaves like Trim(), but only at the end
TrimStart()	Behaves like Trim(), but only at the start

Comparing Strings

The Compare() method is overloaded. The first version takes two strings and returns a negative number if the first string is alphabetically before the second, a positive number if the first string is alphabetically after the second, and zero if they are equal. The second version works just like the first but is case insensitive. Example 16-1 illustrates the use of Compare().

Example 16-1. Compare() method

```
Namespace StringManipulation
    Class Tester

        Public Sub Run()
            ' create some Strings to work with
            Dim s1 As [String] = "abcd"
            Dim s2 As [String] = "ABCD"
            Dim result As Integer ' hold the results of comparisons
            ' compare two Strings, case sensitive
            result = [String].Compare(s1, s2)
            Console.WriteLine( _
              "compare s1: {0}, s2: {1}, result: {2}" _
              & Environment.NewLine, s1, s2, result)

            ' overloaded compare, takes boolean "ignore case"
            '(true = ignore case)
            result = [String].Compare(s1, s2, True)
            Console.WriteLine("Compare insensitive. result: {0}" _
                & Environment.NewLine, result)
        End Sub 'Run

        Shared Sub Main()
            Dim t As New Tester()
            t.Run()
        End Sub 'Main
    End Class 'Tester
End Namespace 'StringManipulation
```

Output:
```
compare s1: abcd, s2: ABCD, result: -1
Compare insensitive. result: 0
```

 This code uses the Shared NewLine property of the Environment class to create a new line in the output. This is a very general way to ensure that the correct code sequence is sent to create the newline on the current operating system.

Example 16-1 begins by declaring two strings, s1 and s2, initialized with string literals:

```
Dim s1 As [String] = "abcd"
Dim s2 As [String] = "ABCD"
```

Compare() is used with many types. A negative return value indicates that the first parameter is less than the second; a positive result indicates the first parameter is greater than the second, and a zero indicates they are equal.

In Unicode (as in ASCII), a lowercase letter has a smaller value than an uppercase letter. Thus, the output properly indicates that s1 (abcd) is "less than" s2 (ABCB):

```
compare s1: abcd, s2: ABCD, result: -1
```

The second comparison uses an overloaded version of Compare, which takes a third, Boolean parameter, the value of which determines whether case should be ignored in the comparison. If the value of this "ignore case" parameter is true, the comparison is made without regard to case. This time the result is 0, indicating that the two strings are identical (without regard to case):

```
Compare insensitive. result: 0
```

Concatenating Strings

There are a couple ways to concatenate strings in VB.NET. You can use the Concat() method, which is a shared public method of the String class:

```
Dim s3 As String = String.Concat(s1, s2)
```

or you can simply use the concatenation (&) operator:

```
Dim s4 As String = s1 & s2
```

These two methods are demonstrated in Example 16-2.

Example 16-2. Concatenation

```
Option Strict On
Imports System
Namespace StringManipulation
    Class Tester

        Public Sub Run()
            Dim s1 As String = "abcd"
            Dim s2 As String = "ABCD"

            ' concatenation method
            Dim s3 As String = String.Concat(s1, s2)
            Console.WriteLine("s3 concatenated from s1 and s2: {0}", s3)

            ' use the overloaded operator
            Dim s4 As String = s1 & s2
            Console.WriteLine("s4 concatenated from s1 & s2: {0}", s4)
        End Sub 'Run

        Public Shared Sub Main()
            Dim t As New Tester()
            t.Run()
        End Sub 'Main
```

Example 16-2. Concatenation (continued)

```
    End Class 'Tester
End Namespace 'StringManipulation
```

Output:
```
s3 concatenated from s1 and s2: abcdABCD
s4 concatenated from s1 & s2: abcdABCD
```

In Example 16-2, the new string s3 is created by calling the shared Concat() method and passing in s1 and s2, while the string s4 is created by using the overloaded concatenation (&) operator that concatenates two strings and returns a string as a result.

VB.NET supports two concatenation operators (+ and &), however the plus sign is also used for adding numeric values, and Microsoft documentation suggests using the ampersand to reduce ambiguity.

Copying Strings

Similarly, creating a new copy of a string can be accomplished in two ways. First, you can use the shared Copy() method:

```
    Dim s5 As String = String.Copy(s2)
```

or for convenience, you might instead use the assignment operator (=), which will implicitly make a copy:

```
    Dim s6 As String = s5
```

When you assign one string to another, the two reference types refer to the same String in memory. This implies that altering one would alter the other because they refer to the same String object. However, this is not the case. The String type is immutable. Thus, if after assigning s5 to s6, you alter s6, the two strings will actually be different.

Example 16-3 illustrates how to copy strings.

Example 16-3. Copying strings
```
Option Strict On
Imports System
Namespace StringManipulation

    Class Tester

        Public Sub Run()
            Dim s1 As String = "abcd"
            Dim s2 As String = "ABCD"

            ' the String copy method
            Dim s5 As String = String.Copy(s2)
            Console.WriteLine("s5 copied from s2: {0}", s5)
```

Example 16-3. Copying strings (continued)

```
        ' use the overloaded operator
        Dim s6 As String = s5
        Console.WriteLine("s6 = s5: {0}", s6)
    End Sub 'Run


    Public Shared Sub Main()
        Dim t As New Tester()
        t.Run()
    End Sub 'Main
  End Class 'Tester
End Namespace 'StringManipulation
```

Output:
```
s5 copied from s2: ABCD
s6 = s5: ABCD
```

Testing for Equality

The .NET String class provides two ways to test for the equality of two strings. First, you can use the overloaded Equals() method and ask one string (say, s6) directly whether another string (s5) is of equal value:

```
    Console.WriteLine("Does s6.Equals(s5)?: {0}", s6.Equals(s5))
```

A second technique is to pass both strings to the String class's shared method Equals():

```
    Console.WriteLine("Does Equals(s6,s5)?: {0}", _
        String.Equals(s6, s5))
```

In each of these cases, the returned result is a Boolean value (true for equal and false for unequal). These techniques are demonstrated in Example 16-4.

Example 16-4. Are all strings created equal?

```
Option Strict On
Imports System
Namespace StringManipulation

    Class Tester

        Public Sub Run()
            Dim s1 As String = "abcd"
            Dim s2 As String = "ABCD"

            ' the String copy method
            Dim s5 As String = String.Copy(s2)
            Console.WriteLine("s5 copied from s2: {0}", s5)

            ' copy with the overloaded operator
            Dim s6 As String = s5
```

Example 16-4. Are all strings created equal? (continued)

```
            Console.WriteLine("s6 = s5: {0}", s6)

            ' member method
            Console.WriteLine("Does s6.Equals(s5)?: {0}", s6.Equals(s5))

            ' shared method
            Console.WriteLine("Does Equals(s6,s5)?: {0}", _
                String.Equals(s6, s5))

        End Sub 'Run

        Public Shared Sub Main()
            Dim t As New Tester()
            t.Run()
        End Sub 'Main
    End Class 'Tester
End Namespace 'StringManipulation
```

Output:
```
s5 copied from s2: ABCD
s6 = s5: ABCD

Does s6.Equals(s5)?: True
Does Equals(s6,s5)?: True
Does s6==s5?: True
```

Other Useful String Methods

The String class includes a number of useful methods and properties for finding specific characters or substrings within a string, as well as for manipulating the contents of the string. A few such methods are demonstrated in Example 16-5. Following the output is a complete analysis.

Example 16-5. Useful string methods

```
Option Strict On
Imports System
Namespace StringManipulation

    Class Tester

        Public Sub Run()
            Dim s1 As String = "abcd"
            Dim s2 As String = "ABCD"
            Dim s3 As String = "Liberty Associates, Inc. provides "
            s3 = s3 & "custom .NET development"

            ' the String copy method
            Dim s5 As String = String.Copy(s2) '
            Console.WriteLine("s5 copied from s2: {0}", s5)

            ' The length
```

Example 16-5. Useful string methods (continued)

```
            Console.WriteLine("String s3 is {0} characters long. ", _
                s5.Length)

            Console.WriteLine()
            Console.WriteLine("s3: {0}", s3)
            ' test whether a String ends with a set of characters
            Console.WriteLine("s3: ends with Training?: {0}", _
                s3.EndsWith("Training"))
            Console.WriteLine("Ends with developement?: {0}", _
                s3.EndsWith("development"))

            Console.WriteLine()
            ' return the index of the string
            Console.Write("The first occurrence of provides ")
            Console.WriteLine("in s3 is {0}", s3.IndexOf("provides"))

            ' hold the location of provides as an integer
            Dim location As Integer = s3.IndexOf("provides")

            ' insert the word usually before "provides"
            Dim s10 As String = s3.Insert(location, "usually ")
            Console.WriteLine("s10: {0}", s10)

            ' you can combine the two as follows:
            Dim s11 As String = _
                s3.Insert(s3.IndexOf("provides"), "usually ")
            Console.WriteLine("s11: {0}", s11)

            Console.WriteLine()
            'Use the Mid function to replace within the string
            Mid(s11, s11.IndexOf("usually") + 1, 9) = "always!"

            Console.WriteLine("s11 now: {0}", s11)

        End Sub 'Run

        Public Shared Sub Main()
            Dim t As New Tester()
            t.Run()
        End Sub 'Main
    End Class 'Tester
End Namespace 'StringManipulation
```

Output:
```
s5 copied from s2: ABCD
String s3 is 4 characters long.

s3: Liberty Associates, Inc. provides custom .NET development
s3: ends with Training?: False
Ends with developement?: True

The first occurrence of provides in s3 is 25
```

Example 16-5. Useful string methods (continued)

```
s10: Liberty Associates, Inc. usually provides custom .NET development
s11: Liberty Associates, Inc. usually provides custom .NET development

s11 now: Liberty Associates, Inc. always! provides custom .NET development
```

The Length property returns the length of the entire string:

```
Console.WriteLine("String s3 is {0} characters long. ", _
    s5.Length)
```

Here's the output:

```
String s3 is 4 characters long.
```

The EndsWith() method asks a string whether a substring is found at the end of the string. Thus, you might ask s3 first if it ends with "Training" (which it does not) and then if it ends with "Consulting" (which it does):

```
Console.WriteLine("s3: ends with Training?: {0}", _
    s3.EndsWith("Training"))
Console.WriteLine("Ends with developement?: {0}", _
    s3.EndsWith("development"))
```

The output reflects that the first test fails and the second succeeds:

```
s3: ends with Training?: False
Ends with developement?: True
```

The IndexOf() method locates a substring within our string, and the Insert() method inserts a new substring into a copy of the original string. The following code locates the first occurrence of "provides" in s3:

```
Console.Write("The first occurrence of provides ")
Console.WriteLine("in s3 is {0}", s3.IndexOf("provides"))
```

The output indicates that the offset is 25:

```
The first occurrence of provides in s3 is 25
```

You can then use that value to insert the word "usually", followed by a space, into that string. Actually the insertion is into a copy of the string returned by the Insert() method and assigned to s10:

```
Dim s10 As String = s3.Insert(location, "usually ")
Console.WriteLine("s10: {0}", s10)
```

Here's the output:

```
s10: Liberty Associates, Inc. usually provides custom .NET development
```

Finally, you can combine these operations to make a more efficient insertion statement:

```
Dim s11 As String = s3.Insert(s3.IndexOf("provides"), "usually ")
```

Finding Substrings

The String class has methods for finding and extracting substrings. For example, the IndexOf() method returns the index of the first occurrence of a string (or one or more characters) within a target string.

For example, given the definition of the string s1 as:

```
Dim s1 As String = "One Two Three Four"
```

You can find the first instance of the characters "hre" by writing:

```
Dim index as Integer = s1.IndexOf("hre")
```

This code will set the integer variable index to 9, which is the offset of the letters "hre" in the string s1.

Similarly, the LastIndexOf() method returns the index of the *last* occurrence of a string or substring. While the following code:

```
s1.IndexOf("o")
```

will return the value 6 (the first occurrence of the lowercase letter "o" is at the end of the word Two), the method call:

```
s1.LastIndexOf("o")
```

will return the value 15, the last occurrence of "o" is in the word Four.

The Substring() method return a series of characters. You can ask it for all the characters starting at a particular offset and ending either with the end of the string or with an offset you (optionally) provide.

The Substring() method is illustrated in Example 16-6.

Example 16-6. Finding Substrings by index

```
Option Strict On
Imports System
Namespace StringSearch

    Class Tester

        Public Sub Run()
            ' create some strings to work with
            Dim s1 As String = "One Two Three Four"

            Dim index As Integer
            ' get the index of the last space

            index = s1.LastIndexOf(" ")
            ' get the last word.
            Dim s2 As String = s1.Substring((index + 1))

            ' set s1 to the substring starting at 0
            ' and ending at index (the start of the last word
```

Example 16-6. Finding Substrings by index (continued)

```
            ' thus s1 has One Two Three
            s1 = s1.Substring(0, index)

            ' find the last space in s1 (after "Two")
            index = s1.LastIndexOf(" ")

            ' set s3 to the substring starting at
            ' index, the space after "Two" plus one more
            ' thus s3 = "three"
            Dim s3 As String = s1.Substring((index + 1))

            ' reset s1 to the substring starting at 0
            ' and ending at index, thus the String "One Two"
            s1 = s1.Substring(0, index)

            ' reset index to the space between
            ' "One" and "Two"
            index = s1.LastIndexOf(" ")

            ' set s4 to the substring starting one
            ' space after index, thus the substring "Two"
            Dim s4 As String = s1.Substring((index + 1))

            ' reset s1 to the substring starting at 0
            ' and ending at index, thus "One"
            s1 = s1.Substring(0, index)

            ' set index to the last space, but there is
            ' none so index now = -1
            index = s1.LastIndexOf(" ")

            ' set s5 to the substring at one past
            ' the last space. there was no last space
            ' so this sets s5 to the substring starting
            ' at zero
            Dim s5 As String = s1.Substring((index + 1))

            Console.WriteLine("s1: {0}", s1)
            Console.WriteLine("s2: {0}", s2)
            Console.WriteLine("s3: {0}", s3)
            Console.WriteLine("s4: {0}", s4)
            Console.WriteLine("s5: {0}", s5)
        End Sub 'Run

        Public Shared Sub Main()
            Dim t As New Tester()
            t.Run()
        End Sub 'Main
    End Class 'Tester
End Namespace 'StringSearch
```

Example 16-6. Finding Substrings by index (continued)

Output:
```
s1: One
s2: Four
s3: Three
s4: Two
s5: One
```

Example 16-6 is not the most elegant solution to the problem of extracting words from a string, but it is a good first approximation and it illustrates a useful technique. The example begins by creating a string, s1:

```
Dim s1 As String = "One Two Three Four"
```

The local variable index is assigned the value of the *last* space in the string (which comes before the word Four):

```
index = s1.LastIndexOf(" ")
```

The substring that begins one space later is assigned to the new string, s2:

```
Dim s2 As String = s1.Substring((index + 1))
```

This extracts the characters from index +1 to the end of the line (i.e., the string "Four"), assigning the value "Four" to s2.

The next step is to remove the word Four from s1. You can do this by assigning to s1 the substring of s1 that begins at 0 and ends at the index:

```
s1 = s1.SubString(0,index);
```

You reassign index to the last (remaining) space, which points you to the beginning of the word Three. You then extract the characters "Three" into string s3. You can continue like this until you've populated s4 and s5. Finally, you display the results:

```
s1: One
s2: Four
s3: Three
s4: Two
s5: One
```

Splitting Strings

A more effective solution to the problem illustrated in Example 16-6 would be to use the Split() method of String, which parses a string into substrings. To use Split(), you pass in an array of delimiters (characters that will indicate where to divide the words). The method returns an array of substrings, which Example 16-7 illustrates. The complete analysis follows the code.

Example 16-7. The Split() method

```
Option Strict On
Imports System
```

Example 16-7. The Split() method (continued)

```
Namespace StringSearch

    Class Tester

        Public Sub Run()
            ' create some Strings to work with
            Dim s1 As String = "One,Two,Three Liberty Associates, Inc."

            ' constants for the space and comma characters
            Const Space As Char = " "c
            Const Comma As Char = ","c

            ' array of delimiters to split the sentence with
            Dim delimiters() As Char = {Space, Comma}

            Dim output As String = ""
            Dim ctr As Integer = 0

            ' split the String and then iterate over the
            ' resulting array of strings
            Dim resultArray As String() = s1.Split(delimiters)

            Dim subString As String
            For Each subString In resultArray
                ctr = ctr + 1
                output &= ctr.ToString()
                output &= ": "
                output &= subString
                output &= Environment.NewLine
            Next subString
            Console.WriteLine(output)
        End Sub 'Run

        Public Shared Sub Main()
            Dim t As New Tester()
            t.Run()
        End Sub 'Main
    End Class 'Tester
End Namespace 'StringSearch
```

Output:
```
1: One
2: Two
3: Three
4: Liberty
5: Associates
6:
7: Inc.
```

Example 16-7 starts by creating a string to parse:

```
Dim s1 As String = "One,Two,Three Liberty Associates, Inc."
```

The delimiters are set to the space and comma characters:

```
Const Space As Char = " "c
Const Comma As Char = ","c
Dim delimiters() As Char = {Space, Comma}
```

 Double quotes are used in VB.NET to signal a string constant. The c after the string literals establishes that these are characters, not strings.

You then call Split() on the string, passing in the delimiters:

```
Dim resultArray As String() = s1.Split(delimiters)
```

Split() returns an array of the substrings that you can then iterate over using the For Each loop, as explained in Chapter 14.

```
Dim subString As String
For Each subString In resultArray
    ctr = ctr + 1
    output &= ctr.ToString()
    output &= ": "
    output &= subString
    output &= Environment.NewLine
Next subString
```

You increment the counter variable, ctr. Then you build up the output string in four steps. You concatenate the string value of ctr. Next you add the colon, then the substring returned by Split(), then the newline.

```
ctr = ctr  1
output &= ctr.ToString()
output &= ": "
output &= subString
output &= Environment.NewLine
```

With each concatenation, a new copy of the string is made, and all four steps are repeated for each substring found by Split(). This repeated copying of the string is terribly inefficient.

The problem is that the String type is not designed for this kind of operation. What you want is to create a new string by appending a formatted string each time through the loop. The class you need is StringBuilder.

The StringBuilder Class

The System.Text.StringBuilder class is used for creating and modifying strings. Semantically, it is the encapsulation of a constructor for a string. The important members of StringBuilder are summarized in Table 16-2.

Table 16-2. StringBuilder members

Method or property	Explanation
Append()	Overloaded public method that appends a typed object to the end of the current StringBuilder
AppendFormat()	Overloaded public method that replaces format specifiers with the formatted value of an object
EnsureCapacity()	Method that ensures that the current StringBuilder has a capacity at least as large as the specified value
Capacity	Property that retrieves or assigns the number of characters the StringBuilder is capable of holding
Chars	Property that contains the indexer
Insert()	Overloaded public method that inserts an object at the specified position
Length	Property that retrieves or assigns the length of the StringBuilder
MaxCapacity	Property that retrieves the maximum capacity of the StringBuilder
Remove()	Removes the specified characters
Replace()	Overloaded public method that replaces all instances of specified characters with new characters

Unlike the String class, StringBuilder is mutable; when you modify an instance of the StringBuilder class, you modify the actual string, not a copy.

Example 16-8 replaces the String object in Example 16-7 with a StringBuilder object.

Example 16-8. The StringBuilder class

```
Imports System.Text
Namespace StringSearch

    Class Tester

        Public Sub Run()
            ' create some Strings to work with
            Dim s1 As String = "One,Two,Three Liberty Associates, Inc."

            ' constants for the space and comma characters
            Const Space As Char = " "c
            Const Comma As Char = ","c

            ' array of delimiters to split the sentence with
            Dim delimiters() As Char = {Space, Comma}

            Dim output As New StringBuilder()
            Dim ctr As Integer = 0

            ' split the String and then iterate over the
            ' resulting array of Strings
            Dim resultArray As String() = s1.Split(delimiters)

            Dim subString As String
            For Each subString In resultArray
                ctr = ctr + 1
                output.AppendFormat("{0} : {1}" & _
                    Environment.NewLine, ctr, subString)
```

Example 16-8. The StringBuilder class (continued)

```
        Next subString
        Console.WriteLine(output)
    End Sub 'Run

    Public Shared Sub Main()
        Dim t As New Tester()
        t.Run()
    End Sub 'Main
  End Class 'Tester
End Namespace 'StringSearch
```

Only the last part of the program is modified from the previous example. Rather than using the concatenation operator to modify the string, you use the AppendFormat() method of StringBuilder to append new, formatted strings as you create them. This is much easier and far more efficient. The output is identical:

```
1: One
2: Two
3: Three
4: Liberty
5: Associates
6:
7: Inc.
```

Delimiter Limitations

Because you passed in delimiters of both comma and space, the space after the comma between "Associates" and "Inc." is returned as a word, numbered 6 previously. That is not what you want. To eliminate this, you need to tell Split() to match a comma (as between "One", "Two", and "Three") or a space (as between "Liberty" and "Associates") or a comma followed by a space. It is that last bit that is tricky and requires that you use a regular expression.

Regular Expressions

Regular expressions are a powerful language for describing and manipulating text. Underlying regular expressions is a technique called *pattern matching*, which involves comparing one string to another, or comparing a series of wildcards that represent a type of string to a literal string. A regular expression is *applied* to a string—that is, to a set of characters. Often that string is an entire text document.

The result of applying a regular expression to a string is either to return a substring, or to return a new string representing a modification of some part of the original string. (Remember that strings are immutable and so cannot be changed by the regular expression.)

By applying a properly constructed regular expression to the following string:

```
One,Two,Three Liberty Associates, Inc.
```

you can return any or all of its substrings (e.g., Liberty or One), or modified versions of its substrings (e.g., LIBeRtY or OnE). What the regular expression *does* is determined by the syntax of the regular expression itself.

A regular expression consists of two types of characters: *literals* and *metacharacters*. A literal is just a character you want to match in the target string. A metacharacter is a special symbol that acts as a command to the regular expression parser. The parser is the engine responsible for understanding the regular expression. For example, if you create a regular expression:

```
^(From|To|Subject|Date):
```

this will match any substring with the letters "From" or the letters "To" or the letters "Subject" or the letters "Date" so long as those letters start a new line (^) and end with a colon (:).

The caret (^) in this case indicates to the regular expression parser that the string you're searching for must begin a new line. The letters "From" and "To" are literals, and the metacharacters left and right parentheses ((,)) and vertical bar (|) are all used to group sets of literals and indicate that any of the choices should match. Thus you would read the following line as "match any string that begins a new line followed by any of the four literal strings From, To, Subject, or Date followed by a colon":

```
^(From|To|Subject|Date):
```

 A full explanation of regular expressions is beyond the scope of this book, but all the regular expressions used in the examples are explained. For a complete understanding of regular expressions, I highly recommend *Mastering Regular Expressions 2nd Edition* by Jeffrey E. F. Friedl (O'Reilly).

The Regex Class

The .NET Framework provides an object-oriented approach to *regular expression* matching and replacement.

The Framework Class Library namespace System.Text.RegularExpressions is the home to all the .NET Framework objects associated with regular expressions. The central class for regular expression support is Regex, which represents an immutable, compiled regular expression. Example 16-9 rewrites Example 16-8 to use regular expressions and thus solves the problem of searching for more than one type of delimiter.

Example 16-9. Using the Regex class for regular expressions

```
Imports System
Imports System.Text
Imports System.Text.RegularExpressions

Namespace RegularExpressions

    Class Tester

        Public Sub Run()
            Dim s1 As String = "One,Two,Three Liberty Associates, Inc."
            Dim theRegex As New Regex(" |, |,")
            Dim sBuilder As New StringBuilder()
            Dim id As Integer = 1

            Dim subString As String
            For Each subString In theRegex.Split(s1)
                id = id + 1
                sBuilder.AppendFormat("{0}: {1}" _
                    & Environment.NewLine, id, subString)
            Next subString
            Console.WriteLine("{0}", sBuilder)
        End Sub 'Run

        Public Shared Sub Main()
            Dim t As New Tester()
            t.Run()
        End Sub 'Main
    End Class 'Tester
End Namespace 'RegularExpressions
```

Output:
```
1: One
2: Two
3: Three
4: Liberty
5: Associates
6: Inc.
```

Example 16-9 begins by creating a string, s1, identical to the string used in Example 16-8:

```
Dim s1 As String = "One,Two,Three Liberty Associates, Inc."
```

and a regular expression that will be used to search that string:

```
Dim theRegex As New Regex(" |, |,")
```

One of the overloaded constructors for Regex takes a regular expression string as its parameter.

This can be a bit confusing. In the context of a VB.NET program, which is the regular expression: the text passed in to the constructor or the Regex object itself? It is true that the text string passed to the constructor is a regular expression in the traditional sense of the term. From an object-oriented VB.NET point of view, however, the argument to the constructor is just a string of characters; it is the Regex object that is the regular expression object.

The rest of the program proceeds like the earlier Example 16-8, except that rather than calling the Split() method of String on string s1, the Split() method of Regex is called. theRegex.Split() acts in much the same way as String.Split(), returning an array of strings as a result of matching the regular expression pattern within the Regex.

CHAPTER 17

Throwing and Catching Exceptions

VB.NET handles errors and abnormal conditions with *exceptions*. An exception is an object that encapsulates information about an unusual program occurrence, such as running out of memory or losing a network connection. When an exceptional circumstance arises, an exception will be thrown.

Throwing an exception is sometimes called *raising* an exception.

You might throw an exception in your own methods (for example, if you realize that an invalid parameter has been provided) or an exception might be thrown in a class provided by the Framework Class Library (for example, if you try to write to a read-only file). Many exceptions are thrown by the runtime when the program can no longer continue due to an operating system problem (such as a security violation).

VB.NET also provides unstructured exception handling through the use of Error, On Error and Resume statements. This approach is not object oriented and not consistent with how exceptions are handled in other.NET languages. Thus it is discouraged and not shown in this book.

You provide for the possibility of exceptions by adding try/catch blocks in your program. The catch blocks are also called *exception handlers*. The idea is that you *try* potentially dangerous code, and if an exception is thrown you *catch* the exception in your catch block.

Catching an exception is sometimes referred to as *handling* the exception.

Ideally, after the exception is caught the program can fix the problem and continue. Even if your program can't continue, by catching the exception you have an opportunity to print a meaningful error message and terminate gracefully.

It is important to distinguish exceptions from bugs and errors. A *bug* is a programmer mistake that should be fixed before the code is shipped. An exception is not the result of a programmer mistake (though such mistakes can also raise exceptions). Rather, exceptions are raised as a result of predictable but unpreventable problems that arise while your program is running (e.g., a network connection is dropped or you run out of disk space).

An *error* is caused by user action. For example, the user might enter a number where a letter is expected. Once again, an error might cause an exception, but you can prevent that by implementing code to validate user input. Whenever possible, user errors should be anticipated and prevented.

Even if you remove all bugs and anticipate all user errors, you will still run into unavoidable problems, such as running out of memory or attempting to open a file that no longer exists. These are exceptions. You cannot prevent exceptions, but you can handle them so that they do not bring down your program.

Throwing Exceptions

All exceptions will either be of type System.Exception or of types derived from System.Exception. The CLR System namespace includes a number of exception types that can be used by your program. These exception types include ArgumentNullException, InvalidCastException, and OverflowException, as well as many others. You can guess their use based on their name. For example, ArgumentNull exception is thrown when an argument to a method is null when that is not an expected (or acceptable) value.

The current chapter describes how to write your programs to catch and handle exceptions. This chapter will also show you how to use the properties of the Exception class to provide information to the user about what went wrong, and it will show you how to create and use your own custom exception types.

Searching for an Exception Handler

When your program encounters an exceptional circumstance, such as running out of memory, it *throws* (or "raises") an exception. Exceptions must be handled before the program can continue.

The search for an exception handler can unwind the stack. This means that if the currently running function does not handle the exception, the current function will terminate, and the calling function will get a chance to handle the exception. If none of the calling functions handles it, the exception will ultimately be handled by the Common Language Runtime (CLR), which will abruptly terminate your program.

If function A calls function B and function B calls function C, these function calls are all placed on the *stack*. When a programmer talks about "unwinding the stack," what is meant is that you back up from C to B to A, as illustrated in Figure 17-1.

If you must unwind the stack from C to B to A to handle the exception, when you are done you are in A; there is no automatic return to C.

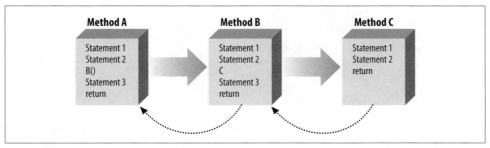

Figure 17-1. *Unwinding the stack*

If you return all the way to the first method (Main) and no exception handler is found, the *default* exception handler (provided by the compiler) will be invoked. The default exception handler just terminates the program.

The Throw Statement

To signal an abnormal condition in a VB.NET program, you throw an exception. To do this, you use the Throw keyword. The following line of code creates a new instance of System.Exception and then throws it:

```
Throw New System.Exception()
```

Example 17-1 illustrates what happens if you throw an exception and there is no try/catch block to catch and handle the exception. In this example, you'll throw an exception even though nothing has actually gone wrong, just to illustrate how an exception can bring your program to a halt.

Example 17-1. *Unhandled exception*

```
Option Strict On
Imports System
Namespace ExceptionHandling

    Class Tester
        Shared Sub Main()
            Console.WriteLine("Enter Main...")
            Dim t As New Tester()
```

Example 17-1. Unhandled exception (continued)

```
            t.Run()
            Console.WriteLine("Exit Main...")
        End Sub 'Main

        Public Sub Run()
            Console.WriteLine("Enter Run...")
            Func1()
            Console.WriteLine("Exit Run...")
        End Sub 'Run
        Public Sub Func1()
            Console.WriteLine("Enter Func1...")
            Func2()
            Console.WriteLine("Exit Func1...")
        End Sub 'Func1
Public Sub Func2()
            Console.WriteLine("Enter Func2...")
            Throw New System.Exception()
            Console.WriteLine("Exit Func2...")
        End Sub 'Func2

    End Class 'Tester
End Namespace 'ExceptionHandling
```

Output:
```
Enter Main...
Enter Run...
Enter Func1...
Enter Func2...

Unhandled Exception: System.Exception: Exception of type System.Exception was thrown.
at DebuggingVB.ExceptionHandling.Tester.Func2() in C:...\Module1.vb:line 27
   at DebuggingVB.ExceptionHandling.Tester.Func1()
   in C:...\Module1.vb:line 21
   at DebuggingVB.ExceptionHandling.Tester.Run()
   in C:...\Module1.vb:line 14
   at DebuggingVB.ExceptionHandling.Tester.Main()
   in C:...\Module1.vb:line 8
```

This simple example writes to the console as it enters and exits each method. Main() calls Run() which in turn calls Func1(). After printing out the Enter Func1 message, Func1() immediately calls Func2(). Func2() prints out the first message and throws an object of type System.Exception.

Execution immediately stops, and the CLR looks to see whether a handler is in Func2(). There is not, and so the runtime unwinds the stack (never printing the exit statement) to Func1(). Again, there is no handler, and the runtime unwinds the stack back to Main(). With no exception handler there, the default handler is called, which prints the error message, and terminates the program.

The Try and Catch Statements

To handle exceptions, you take the following steps:

1. Execute any code that you suspect might throw an exception (such as code that opens a file or allocates memory) within a try block.
2. Catch any exceptions that are thrown in a catch block.

A try block is created using the keyword Try and is ended with the keywords End Try. A catch block is created using the Catch keyword. A catch block can be terminated either by the next use of the Catch keyword or by the End Try statement. These constructs are illustrated in Example 17-2. Note that Example 17-2 is the same as Example 17-1 except that a try/catch block has been added.

Example 17-2. Try and catch blocks

```
Option Strict On
Imports System
Namespace ExceptionHandling

    Class Tester

        Shared Sub Main()
            Console.WriteLine("Enter Main...")
            Dim t As New Tester()
            t.Run()
            Console.WriteLine("Exit Main...")
        End Sub 'Main

        Public Sub Run()
            Console.WriteLine("Enter Run...")
            Func1()
            Console.WriteLine("Exit Run...")
        End Sub 'Run

        Public Sub Func1()
            Console.WriteLine("Enter Func1...")
            Func2()
            Console.WriteLine("Exit Func1...")
        End Sub 'Func1

        Public Sub Func2()
            Console.WriteLine("Enter Func2...")
            Try
                Console.WriteLine("Entering Try block...")
                Throw New System.Exception()
                Console.WriteLine("Exitintg Try block...")
            Catch
                Console.WriteLine("Exception caught and handled")
            End Try
            Console.WriteLine("Exit func2...")
        End Sub 'Func2
```

Example 17-2. Try and catch blocks (continued)

```
    End Class 'Tester

End Namespace 'ExceptionHandling
```

Output:
```
Enter Main...
Enter Run...
Enter Func1...
Enter Func2...
Entering try block...
Exception caught and handled!
Exit Func2...
Exit Func1...
Exit Run...
Exit Main...
```

Following the try statement is a generic catch statement. The catch statement in Example 17-2 is generic because you haven't specified what kind of exceptions to catch. If you don't specify a particular exception type, the catch block will catch any exceptions that are thrown.

Notice that the Exit statements are now written in the output. With the exception handled, execution resumes immediately after the catch block.

In Example 17-2, the catch statement simply reports that the exception has been caught and handled. In a real catch statement, you might take corrective action to fix the problem that caused an exception to be thrown. For example, if the user is trying to open a read-only file, you might invoke a method that allows the user to change the attributes of the file. If the program has run out of memory, you might give the user an opportunity to close other applications. If all else fails, the catch block can print an error message so that the user knows what went wrong. Using catch statements to catch specific types of exceptions is discussed later in this chapter.

How the Call Stack Works

Examine the output of Example 17-2 carefully. You see the code enter Main(), Func1(), Func2(), and the try block. You never see it exit the try block, though it does exit Func2(), Func1(), and Main(). What happened?

When the exception is thrown, execution halts immediately and is handed to the catch block. It *never* returns to the original code path. It never gets to the line that prints the exit statement for the try block. The catch block handles the error, and then execution falls through to the code following the catch block.

Because there is a catch block, the stack does not need to unwind. The exception is now handled; there are no more problems, and the program continues. This becomes a bit clearer if you move the try/catch blocks up to Func1(), as shown in Example 17-3.

Example 17-3. Unwinding the stack by one level

```
Option Strict On
Imports System
Namespace ExceptionHandling

    Class Tester

        Shared Sub Main()
            Console.WriteLine("Enter Main...")
            Dim t As New Tester()
            t.Run()
            Console.WriteLine("Exit Main...")
        End Sub 'Main

        Public Sub Run()
            Console.WriteLine("Enter Run...")
            Func1()
            Console.WriteLine("Exit Run...")
        End Sub 'Run

        Public Sub Func1()
            Console.WriteLine("Enter func1...")
            Try
                Console.WriteLine("Entering Try block...")
                Func2()
                Console.WriteLine("Exiting Try block...")
            Catch
                Console.WriteLine("Exception caught and handled")
            End Try
            Console.WriteLine("Exit func1...")
        End Sub 'Func1

        Public Sub Func2()
            Console.WriteLine("Enter Func2...")
            Throw New System.Exception()
            Console.WriteLine("Exit Func2...")
        End Sub 'Func2

End Class 'Tester
End Namespace 'ExceptionHandling
```

Output:
```
Enter Main...
Enter Run...
Enter Func1...
Entering try block...
Enter Func2...
Exception caught and handled!
Exit Func1...
```

Example 17-3. Unwinding the stack by one level (continued)

```
Exit Run...
Exit Main...
```

This time the exception is not handled in Func2(); it is handled in Func1(). When Func2() is called, it uses Console.WriteLine to display its first milestone:

```
    Enter Func2...
```

Then Func2() throws an exception and execution halts. The runtime looks for a handler in Func2(), but there isn't one. Then the stack begins to unwind, and the runtime looks for a handler in the calling function: Func1(). A catch block is in Func1() so its code is executed, and execution then resumes immediately following the catch statement, printing the Exit statement for Func1() and then for Main().

If you're not entirely sure why the "Exiting Try Block" message and the "Exit Func2" message are not printed, try putting the code into a debugger and then stepping through it.

Creating Dedicated Catch Statements

So far, you've been working only with generic catch statements. You can create dedicated catch statements that handle only some exceptions and not others, based on the type of exception thrown. Example 17-4 illustrates how to specify which exception you'd like to handle.

Example 17-4. Three dedicated catch statements

```
Imports System
Namespace ExceptionHandling

    Class Tester

        Public Sub Run()
            Try
                Dim a As Double = 5
                Dim b As Double = 0
                Console.WriteLine("Dividing {0} by {1}...", a, b)
                Console.WriteLine("{0} / {1} = {2}", _
                    a, b, DoDivide(a, b))

                ' most derived exception type first
            Catch e As System.DivideByZeroException
                Console.WriteLine("DivideByZeroException caught!")

            Catch e As System.ArithmeticException
                Console.WriteLine("ArithmeticException caught!")

                ' generic exception type last
            Catch
```

Example 17-4. Three dedicated catch statements (continued)

```
            Console.WriteLine("Unknown exception caught")
        End Try
    End Sub

    ' do the division if legal
    Public Function DoDivide( _
      ByVal a As Double, ByVal b As Double) As Double
        If b = 0 Then
            Throw New System.DivideByZeroException()
        End If
        If a = 0 Then
            Throw New System.ArithmeticException()
        End If
        Return a / b
    End Function

    Public Shared Sub Main()
        Console.WriteLine("Enter Main...")
        Dim t As Tester = New Tester()
        t.Run()
        Console.WriteLine("Exit Main...")
    End Sub

  End Class
End Namespace
```

Output:
```
Enter Main...
Dividing 5 by 0...
DivideByZeroException caught!
Exit Main...
```

In Example 17-4, the DoDivide() method will not let you divide zero by another number, nor will it let you divide a number by zero. If you try to divide by zero, it throws an instance of DivideByZeroException. If you try to divide zero by another number, there is no appropriate exception: dividing zero by another number is a legal mathematical operation and shouldn't throw an exception at all. However, for the sake of this example, assume you don't want to allow division of zero by any number; you will throw an ArithmeticException.

When the exception is thrown, the runtime examines each exception handler in the order in which they appear in the code and matches the first one it can. When you run this program with a=5 and b=7, the output is:

```
5 / 7 = 0.7142857142857143
```

As you'd expect, no exception is thrown. However, when you change the value of a to 0, the output is:

```
ArithmeticException caught!
```

The exception is thrown, and the runtime examines the first exception, DivideByZeroException. Because this does not match, it goes on to the next handler, ArithmeticException, which does match.

In a final pass through, suppose you change a to 7 and b to 0. This throws the DivideByZeroException.

You have to be particularly careful with the order of the catch statements in this case because the DivideByZeroException is derived from ArithmeticException. If you reverse the catch statements, the DivideByZeroException will match the ArithmeticException handler, and the exception will never get to the DivideByZeroException handler. In fact, if their order is reversed, it will be impossible for *any* exception to reach the DivideByZeroException handler.

Typically, a method will catch every exception it can anticipate for the code it is running. However, it is possible to distribute your try/catch statements, catching some specific exceptions in one function and more generic exceptions in higher, calling functions. Your design goals should dictate the exact design.

Assume you have a Method A that calls another Method B, which in turn calls Method C, which calls Method D, which then calls Method E deep in your code, while methods B and A are higher up. If you anticipate that Method E might throw an exception, you should create a try/catch block deep in your code to catch that exception as close as possible to the place where the problem arises. You might also want to create more general exception handlers higher up in the code in case unanticipated exceptions slip by.

The Finally Statement

In some instances, throwing an exception and unwinding the stack can create a problem. For example, if you have opened a file or otherwise committed a resource, you might need an opportunity to close the file or flush the buffer.

If you *must* take some action, such as closing a file, regardless of whether an exception is thrown, you have two strategies to choose from. One approach is to enclose the dangerous action in a try block and then to perform the necessary action (e.g., close the file) in both the catch and try blocks. However, this is an ugly duplication of code, and it's error prone. VB.NET provides a better alternative in the finally block.

The code in the finally block is guaranteed to be executed regardless of whether an exception is thrown. You create a finally block with the keyword `Finally`, and it ends with the `End Try` statement.

A finally block can be created with or without catch blocks, but a finally block requires a try block to execute. It is an error to exit a finally block with Exit, Throw, Return, or Goto. The TestFunc() method in Example 17-5 simulates opening a file as its first action. The method then undertakes some mathematical operations, and then the file is closed.

It is possible that sometime between opening and closing the file, an exception will be thrown. If this were to occur, it would be possible for the file to remain open. The developer knows that no matter what happens, at the end of this method the file should be closed, so the file close function call is moved to a finally block, where it will be executed regardless of whether an exception is thrown. Example 17-5 uses a finally block.

Example 17-5. Using a Finally block

```
Option Strict On
Imports System
Namespace ExceptionHandling
    Class Tester

        Public Sub Run()
            Try
                Console.WriteLine("Open file here")
                Dim a As Double = 5
                Dim b As Double = 0
                Console.WriteLine("{0} / {1} = {2}", a, b, DoDivide(a, b))
                Console.WriteLine("This line may or may not print")

                ' most derived exception type first
            Catch e As System.DivideByZeroException
                Console.WriteLine("DivideByZeroException caught!")

            Catch
                Console.WriteLine("Unknown exception caught!")

            Finally
                Console.WriteLine("Close file here.")

            End Try
        End Sub 'Run

        ' do the division if legal
        Public Function DoDivide( _
            ByVal a As Double, ByVal b As Double) As Double

            If b = 0 Then
                Throw New System.DivideByZeroException()
            End If

            If a = 0 Then
                Throw New System.ArithmeticException()
```

Example 17-5. Using a Finally block (continued)

```
            End If

            Return a / b
        End Function 'DoDivide

        Shared Sub Main()
            Console.WriteLine("Enter Main...")
            Dim t As New Tester()
            t.Run()
            Console.WriteLine("Exit Main...")
        End Sub 'Main
    End Class 'Tester
End Namespace 'ExceptionHandling
```

Output:
```
Enter Main...
Open file here
DivideByZeroException caught!
Close file here.
Exit Main...
```

In Example 17-5, one of the catch blocks from Example 17-4 has been eliminated to save space, and a finally block has been added. Whether or not an exception is thrown, the finally block is executed; thus, in both examples, the following message is output:

```
    Close file here.
```

Of course, in a real application, you would actually open the file in the try block, and you'd actually close the file in the finally block. The details of file manipulation have been eliminated to simplify the example.

Exception Class Methods and Properties

So far you've been using the exception as a sentinel—that is, the presence of the exception signals the errors—but you haven't touched or examined the Exception object itself. The System.Exception class provides a number of useful methods and properties.

The Message property provides information about the exception, such as why it was thrown. The Message property is read-only; the code throwing the exception can pass in the message as an argument to the exception constructor, but the Message property cannot be modified by any method once set in the constructor.

The HelpLink property provides a link to a help file associated with the exception. This property is read/write. In Example 17-6, the Exception.HelpLink property is set and retrieved to provide information to the user about the DivideByZeroException.

It is generally a good idea to provide a help file link for any exceptions you create, so that the user can learn how to correct the exceptional circumstance.

The read-only StackTrace property is set by the CLR. This property is used to provide a *stack trace* for the error statement. A stack trace is used to display the *call stack*: the series of method calls that lead to the method in which the exception was thrown.

Example 17-6. Inside the Exception class

```
Option Strict On
Imports System
Namespace ExceptionHandling
    Class Tester

        Public Sub Run()
            Try
                Console.WriteLine("Open file here")
                Dim a As Double = 5
                Dim b As Double = 0
                Console.WriteLine("{0} / {1} = {2}", a, b, DoDivide(a, b))
                Console.WriteLine("This line may or may not print")

                ' most derived exception type first
            Catch e As System.DivideByZeroException
                Console.WriteLine( _
                    "DivideByZeroException! Msg: {0}", e.Message)
                Console.WriteLine( _
                    "Helplink: {0}", e.HelpLink)
                Console.WriteLine( _
                    "Stack trace: {0}", e.StackTrace)

            Catch
                Console.WriteLine("Unknown exception caught!")
            Finally
                Console.WriteLine("Close file here.")

            End Try
        End Sub 'Run

        ' do the division if legal
        Public Function DoDivide( _
            ByVal a As Double, ByVal b As Double) As Double
            If b = 0 Then
                Dim e As New System.DivideByZeroException()
                e.HelpLink = "http://www.LibertyAssociates.com"
                Throw e
            End If
            If a = 0 Then
                Throw New System.ArithmeticException()
            End If
            Return a / b
```

Example 17-6. Inside the Exception class (continued)

```
        End Function 'DoDivide

        Shared Sub Main()
            Console.WriteLine("Enter Main...")
            Dim t As New Tester()
            t.Run()
            Console.WriteLine("Exit Main...")
        End Sub 'Main
    End Class 'Tester
End Namespace 'ExceptionHandling
```

Output:
```
Enter Main...
Open file here

DivideByZeroException! Msg: Attempted to divide by zero.

HelpLink: http://www.libertyassociates.com

Here's a stack trace:
  at ExceptionHandling.Tester.DoDivide(Double a, Double b) in ...Module1.vb:line 38
   at ExceptionHandling.Tester.Run() in ...Module1.vb:line 10

Close file here.
Exit Main...
```

In the output of Example 17-6, the stack trace lists the methods in the reverse order in which they were called; by reviewing this order, you can infer that the error occurred in DoDivide(), which was called by Run(). When methods are deeply nested, the stack trace can help you understand the order of method calls and thus track down the point at which the exception occurred.

In this example, rather than simply throwing a DivideByZeroException, you create a new instance of the exception:

```
Dim e As New System.DivideByZeroException()
Throw e
```

You do not pass in a custom message, and so the default message will be printed:

```
DivideByZeroException! Msg: Attempted to divide by zero.
```

 The designer of each Exception class has the option to provide a default message for that exception type. All of the standard exceptions will provide a default message, and it is a good idea to add a default message to your custom exceptions as well (see the section on "Custom Exceptions," later in this chapter).

If you want, you can modify this line of code to pass in a custom message:

```
Dim e As New System.DivideByZeroException( _
  "You tried to divide by zero which is not meaningful")
```

In this case, the output message will reflect the custom message:

```
DivideByZeroException! Msg:
You tried to divide by zero which is not
meaningful
```

Before throwing the exception, you set the HelpLink property:

```
e.HelpLink = "http://www.libertyassociates.com"
```

When this exception is caught, Console.WriteLine() prints both the message and the HelpLink:

```
Catch e As System.DivideByZeroException
    Console.WriteLine( _
      "DivideByZeroException! Msg: {0}", e.Message)
    Console.WriteLine( _
      "Helplink: {0}", e.HelpLink)
```

The Message and HelpLink properties allow you to provide useful information to the user. The exception handler also prints the StackTrace by getting the StackTrace property of the Exception object:

```
Console.WriteLine( _
    "Stack trace: {0}", e.StackTrace)
```

The output of this call reflects a full StackTrace leading to the moment the exception was thrown. In this case, only two methods were executed before the exception, DoDivide() and Run ():

```
Here's a stack trace:
  at ExceptionHandling.Tester.DoDivide(Double a, Double b) in Module1.vb:line 38
   at ExceptionHandling.Tester.Run() in Module1.vb:line 10
```

Note that I've shortened the pathnames, so your printout might look a little different.

Custom Exceptions

The intrinsic exception types the CLR provides, coupled with the custom messages shown in the previous example, will often be all you need to provide extensive information to a catch block when an exception is thrown.

There will be times, however, when you want to provide more extensive information to or need special capabilities in your exception. It is a trivial matter to create your own *custom exception* class; the only restriction is that it must derive (directly or indirectly) from System.ApplicationException. Example 17-7 illustrates the creation of a custom exception.

Example 17-7. A custom exception

```
Option Strict On
Imports System
Namespace ExceptionHandling
    ' custom exception class

    Public Class MyCustomException
        Inherits System.ApplicationException

        Public Sub New(ByVal message As String)
            ' pass the message up to the base class
            MyBase.New(message)
        End Sub 'New

    End Class 'MyCustomException

    Class Tester

        Public Sub Run()
            Try
                Console.WriteLine("Open file here")
                Dim a As Double = 0
                Dim b As Double = 5
                Console.WriteLine("{0} / {1} = {2}", a, b, DoDivide(a, b))
                Console.WriteLine("This line may or may not print")

                ' most derived exception type first
            Catch e As System.DivideByZeroException
                Console.WriteLine( _
                    "DivideByZeroException! Msg: {0}", e.Message)
                Console.WriteLine("HelpLink: {0}", e.HelpLink)

                ' catch custom exception
            Catch e As MyCustomException
                Console.WriteLine( _
                    "MyCustomException! Msg: {0}", e.Message)
                Console.WriteLine("HelpLink: {0}", e.HelpLink)
            Catch ' catch any uncaught exceptions
                Console.WriteLine("Unknown exception caught")
            Finally
                Console.WriteLine("Close file here.")
            End Try
        End Sub 'Run

        ' do the division if legal
        Public Function DoDivide( _
            ByVal a As Double, ByVal b As Double) As Double
            If b = 0 Then
                Dim e As New DivideByZeroException()
                e.HelpLink = "http://www.libertyassociates.com"
                Throw e
            End If
            If a = 0 Then
```

Example 17-7. A custom exception (continued)

```
                ' create a custom exception instance
                Dim e As New _
                  MyCustomException("Can't have zero divisor")
                e.HelpLink = _
                   "http://www.libertyassociates.com/NoZeroDivisor.htm"
                Throw e
            End If
            Return a / b
        End Function 'DoDivide

        Shared Sub Main()
            Console.WriteLine("Enter Main...")
            Dim t As New Tester()
            t.Run()
            Console.WriteLine("Exit Main...")
        End Sub 'Main

    End Class 'Tester

End Namespace 'ExceptionHandling
```

Output:
```
Enter Main...
Open file here
MyCustomException! Msg: Can't have zero divisor
HelpLink: http://www.libertyassociates.com/NoZeroDivisor.htm
Close file here.
Exit Main...
```

MyCustomException is derived from System.ApplicationException and consists of nothing more than a constructor that takes a string message that it passes to its base class.

 Remember that constructors cannot be inherited, so every derived class must have its own constructor.

The advantage of creating this custom exception class is that it better reflects the particular design of the Test class, in which it is not legal to have a zero divisor. Using the ArithmeticException rather than a custom exception would work as well, but it might confuse other programmers because a zero divisor wouldn't normally be considered an arithmetic error.

CHAPTER 18

Applications and Events

Until now you have been creating console applications. Developing these simple programs has allowed you to focus on the fundamentals of the VB.NET language, rather than on the details of creating an interactive user interface. However, the principal purpose of Visual Basic .NET is to help you create Windows and web applications. Windows applications are desktop programs like Word, Excel, and others that you purchase and run on your computer. Web applications are accessed over the Web using a browser. Microsoft provides a set of classes and tools for building Windows applications, called Windows Forms. Windows applications can be very complex, and the details of Windows Forms are well beyond the scope of this book, but this chapter will introduce the fundamentals of creating Windows application, and will show some of the support Visual Studio .NET can provide.

Similarly, Microsoft provides ASP.NET for creating Web applications. The details of this powerful technology could also fill a book, but this chapter will show you how to get started.

Every Windows and web application is driven by program occurrences known as *events*. The current chapter introduces the concept of *events* in the context of developing Windows and web applications.

 For pointers to more advanced books on developing Windows and web applications, as well as other available resources, see Chapter 19.

Creating a Windows Application

To get started building a Windows application, open VS.NET and choose the New Project item from the Projects menu. As you have done throughout this book, choose Visual Basic Projects from the Project Types window, but this time choose Windows Application in the Templates Window, as shown in Figure 18-1.

Choose an appropriate location for your project folder and name the project Hello World.

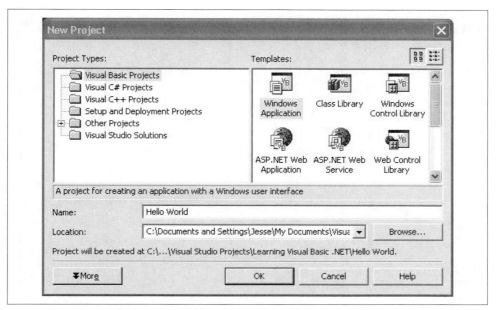

Figure 18-1. Creating the new project Hello World

VS.NET will create a work area for you and will also create an initial form, as shown in Figure 18-2.

The Toolbox should appear docked to the left-hand side of your work area. If not, you can open the toolbox by choosing the Toolbox item from the View menu or by using the keyboard shortcut Ctrl-Alt-X. The toolbox provides easy-to-use widgets for your application.

To get a sense of how this works, click and drag a label from the Toolbox onto the form. Position the label in the upper third of the form. Notice that the label has sizing handles on each side that you can click on and drag to stretch the label to accommodate a fair amount of text.

The Properties window should be docked along the right side of your window. If not, you can open the Properties window by choosing the Properties Window item from the View menu or by using the keyboard shortcut F4. Once the Properties window is open, you can click on the label to display the label's properties in the Properties window.

To see how the Properties window can help you in specifying properties, try setting the label's name to lblOutput. Then set the label's text to:

```
Hello World
```

Now scroll down the Properties window until you come to the Font property. Click the plus sign (+) to expand the Font property, as shown in Figure 18-3.

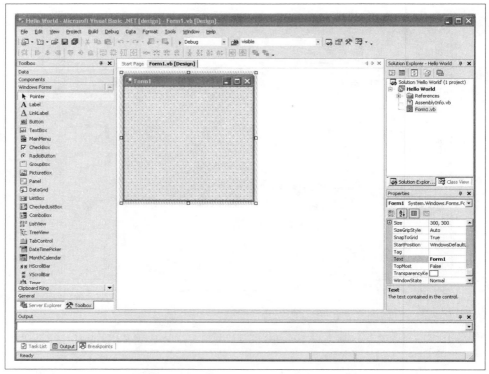

Figure 18-2. Visual Studio .NET initial form

Notice the button following the name of the Font; the button is marked with an ellipsis. Click on this button to open the Font selection window. Set the Font to Verdana, also selecting Bold from the Font style list and 12 (point) from the Size list, as shown in Figure 18-4.

If you look back at the label you created on the initial form, you'll see that the label has been modified in accordance with the properties you've set.

Now go back to the Toolbox and drag a button onto your form; name it btnChange and set its Text property to:

    Change!

Click on the BackColor property. The drop-down menu (which should list "Control" as the default color) opens to reveal a color picker. Click on the Custom tab and choose the red square, as shown (in black and white) in Figure 18-5.

Set the Button's ForeColor property to yellow and then expand the Font property. Set the font to Verdana and set the Bold attribute of the Font to true.

Figure 18-3. The Properties window

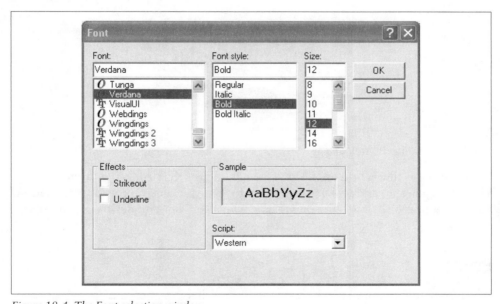

Figure 18-4. The Font selection window

Click on the form and grab the lower righthand corner by clicking and dragging with the mouse. Resize the form to accommodate just the label and the button, as shown in Figure 18-6.

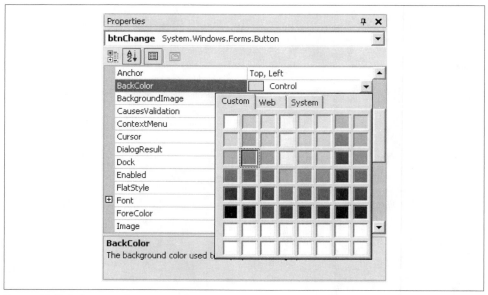

Figure 18-5. Picking a color

Figure 18-6. Making the form smaller

Now run the Hello World application by holding the Control key and pressing F5. The form comes up and looks just great. But when you click on the Change! button, nothing happens. In order to understand why, you must understand a bit about events.

Events

When something happens in a program, we call that occurrence an *event*. Clicking on a button is an event. Closing a window, dropping down a listbox, pressing a key, and moving the mouse are all events. Windows is an event-driven operating system.

How does the operating system know when you've pressed a key? There are, in general, two ways for the system to receive notification. One way is called *polling*. In this approach, the operating system asks the keyboard: "Hey! Do you have a keypress for me? Nope? Okay, I'll check again in few milliseconds." This is very much the same as the way I find out if I have mail. Every few milliseconds, I walk down to the mailbox and look inside. Sometimes there is mail; most of the time it is empty.

The second, much preferable, way to keep the operating system apprised of events is to ask the keyboard to notify the operating system when a key is pressed. This is analogous to how the telephone works. You don't pick up the phone every few minutes to see if you have a call. Instead, you leave the phone alone, and when there is a call, the phone notifies you (typically, just as you sit down to dinner).

This act of notifying you is called *raising an event*. In this case, the event is "a call is ready for you."

VB.NET provides extensive support for handling events such as button clicks. The Button object is declared with the keyword WithEvents. Right-click on your form and choose the View Code item from the pop-up menu. VS.NET will display the code that creates your form, as shown in Figure 18-7.

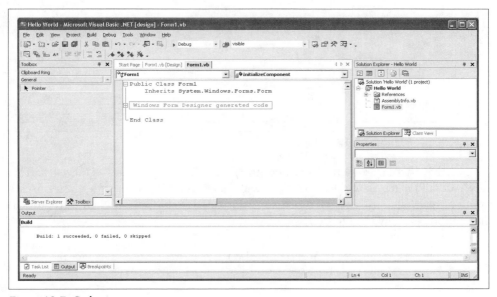

Figure 18-7. Code view

It looks like not much is there. Notice, however, that in the middle of the code a gray box contains the words "Windows Form Designer generated code." To the left of the box is a plus sign. Click on the plus sign to expand this region of code that was created by VS.NET.

Inside this area, shown in Figure 18-8, VS.NET has provided your class with a constructor, a Dispose() method, and various declarations. Just below the Dispose()

method are the declarations of the two controls you've added to your form, the Label and the Button, as shown circled and highlighted in Figure 18-8.

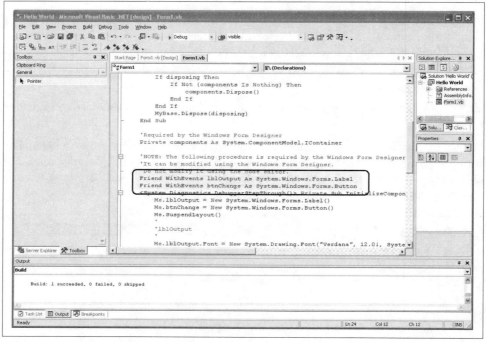

Figure 18-8. The Label and the Button declared

Notice that the declaration of both controls includes the keyword `WithEvents`. This keyword indicates that these controls will raise events. The Button class raises a number of events, as you can discover by looking up the Button class in the documentation, as shown in Figure 18-9.

 Surprisingly, the label control also raises a great many events, though it is uncommon to respond to clicks and mouse movements over a label.

The event we care about is the Button's Click event, which is raised every time the Button is clicked.

Each control has a default event, and the Button's default event is Click. You can create the event handler for the default event by going back to the Design view and then double-clicking on the Button.

Doing so causes VS.NET to create a skeleton event handler for you, in this case a method called btnChange_Click():

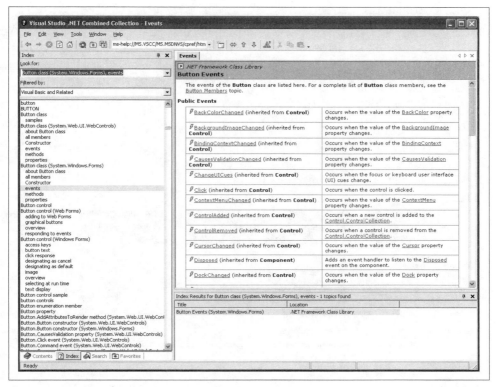

Figure 18-9. Button documentation

```
    Private Sub btnChange_Click( _
        ByVal sender As System.Object, _
        ByVal e As System.EventArgs) _
          Handles btnChange.Click
    End Sub
```

Every event handler takes two parameters. The first is of type Object and is called sender, by convention. This is the control that raised the event. The second is of type EventArgs (or a class derived from EventArgs) and is a structure that contains information about the event. Often this structure has no useful content, but for some events, this structure provides useful information for handling the event. (Structures are discussed in depth in .)

The method declaration includes the keyword Handles followed by the event that the method is designed to handle. In this case, you've declared that the btnChange_Click() method will handle the Click event for the control btnChange.

All you have to do is write the code within the method for whatever is supposed to happen when the button is clicked. In this case, you'd like to change the contents of the label when the button is clicked. Add the following code to the event handler method:

```
Private Sub btnChange_Click( _
    ByVal sender As System.Object, _
    ByVal e As System.EventArgs) _
    Handles btnChange.Click

    lblOutput.Text = "Goodbye!"
    lblOutput.BackColor = Color.Blue
    lblOutput.ForeColor = Color.Yellow

End Sub
```

This code will cause the text of the label to change, along with its background color and foreground color. Run the application with Control-F5. Click on the button. Hey! Presto! The text changes, as shown in Figure 18-10.

Figure 18-10. Testing the event handler

To ensure that you fully understand what is happening with this code, put a breakpoint in the event handler and then run the program in debug mode. When you click on the button, you'll see the program stop at the breakpoint. Creating complex Windows applications now becomes largely a matter of dragging the controls onto the form and wiring up the event handlers to do the work you want when the various events are fired.

Web Applications

One of the most powerful aspects of VS.NET and the .NET platform is that the tools for Rapid Application Development that are provided for creating Windows applications are also available for building Web applications. To see how similar web development is to Windows development, close the current project by choosing the Close Solution item from the File menu. Then choose New Project from the Start menu. This time, rather than choosing a Windows Application as the Project Type, choose an ASP.NET Web Application; then enter a pathname for the Hello World program in the Location box, as shown in Figure 18-11.

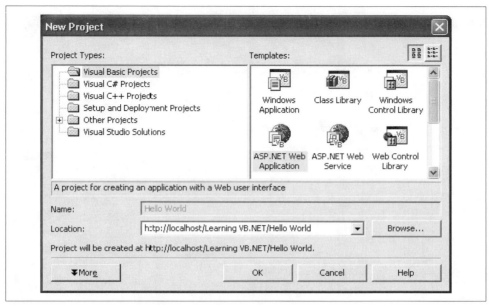

Figure 18-11. Creating Hello World as an ASP.NET application

VS.NET will create a virtual directory for you on your web server (for this example, you'll need to have IIS installed), and will open a development environment not very different from that available for creating Windows applications.

Once again you'll find a Toolbox along the lefthand side of the VS.NET window, and a Properties window docked to the righthand side. ASP.NET applications work by creating an HTML file named with an *.aspx* extension. When you right-click on the form and select View Code, VS.NET also creates an associated *code-behind* file. (Code-behind files are integral to most serious applications but are beyond the scope of this primer. See Chapter 19 for pointers to a number of useful books on advanced VB.NET programming and ASP.NET development.) Your form's default name is *WebForm1.aspx*, and the associated code-behind file will be *WebForm1.aspx.vb*.

From the Toolbox, drag a label onto the form. As you did in the section on Windows applications, set the label's name to lblOutput and its text to "Hello World!" Then click on the Font property and set Bold to true and set the size to x-large. Remember, this program will run in a browser, so the properties are restricted to those supported by HTML and browsers.

Now go back to the Toolbox and drag a button onto the form. Set the button's name to btnChange and its text to "Change!". Set its BackColor property to red and its ForeColor to yellow. Then set the button's font to bold. The results are shown in Figure 18-12.

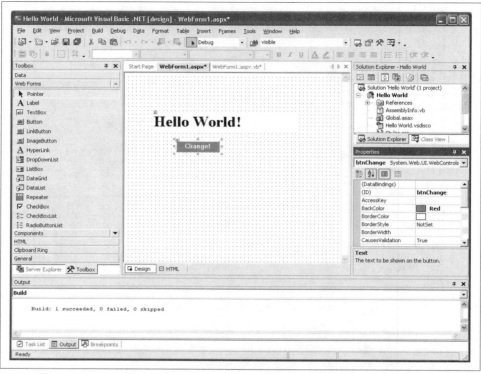

Figure 18-12. Creating the web form

If you double-click on the button, VS.NET creates the code-behind file and takes you to the event handler that it has created for you:

```
Private Sub btnChange_Click( _
ByVal sender As System.Object, _
ByVal e As System.EventArgs) _
Handles btnChange.Click

End Sub
```

Your job is to fill in the code that will be run when the event is fired. You might begin by copying in the code from the event handler you created for the Windows application, earlier in this chapter:

```
Private Sub btnChange_Click( _
ByVal sender As System.Object, _
ByVal e As System.EventArgs) _
Handles btnChange.Click

    lblOutput.Text = "Goodbye!"
    lblOutput.BackColor = Color.Blue
    lblOutput.ForeColor = Color.Yellow

End Sub
```

Now run the application. This time a browser opens to test your application, within which the text and button appear. Click on the button. Hey! Presto! the page is redrawn with the new text and coloring, as shown in Figure 18-13.

Figure 18-13. Handling the event in a browser

Server-Side Code

The output shown in Figure 18-13 is nearly identical to what you saw in the Windows application (Figure 18-10), and in fact the code is also nearly identical.

The actual processing, however, is very different. When you click a button in a Windows application, the event is handled right there, in your code, on the desktop. With a web application, when you click the "Change!" button, the page is submitted to the host, the event is handled on the host, and the new page (with the new text) is sent back to the browser. All of this is done automatically for you by the ASP.NET Framework.

If you start the application again, and select the Source item from the View menu, you'll see that what is actually sent to the browser is just HTML, as shown in Figure 18-14.

All of the code is run on the server; the browser need not have any special functionality. In fact the browser need not even be running on Windows or .NET!

Figure 18-14. Examining the source

CHAPTER 19

Afterword

Congratulations! If you've worked your way to this point in the book, you are now a VB.NET programmer. You should be very proud. Of course, no primer can cover everything there is to know about .NET programming, and you are not at the end, but rather at the beginning of your education. Nonetheless, you've made a very good start.

Where to Go from Here

I intentionally kept this book short to provide you with the fundamentals and not let more difficult topics distract you from the core elements of the language. Now that you've completed the book, however, you may be wondering where to go from here in your pursuit of .NET.

A wealth of information is available, both in books and online. The first task is to decide what you are interested in. Potential topics include:

- Advanced topics in VB.NET programming
- Web (ASP.NET) programming
- Windows (Windows Forms) programming

Sooner or later you'll probably decide to read extensively on all three topics; the only question is which you tackle first. In the next sections, I'll recommend some more advanced books to help you find your way through these topics.

Advanced Topics in VB.NET

If you decide that you want to understand all the nooks and crannies of VB.NET before going on to creating applications, you might consider reading a more advanced guide or a reference work on the language.

O'Reilly offers a few choices: *Programming Visual Basic .NET* is a more advanced book I am writing for release in early 2003, and *VB.NET in a Nutshell*, by Steven Roman, Ron Petrusha, and Paul Lomax is a comprehensive reference work. O'Reilly also has *VB.NET Core Classes* (title?) in a Nutshell by Budi Kurniawan and Ted Neward.

The difference between *Programming Visual Basic .NET* and *Learning Visual Basic .NET* is that the former book is written for the advanced VB6 programmer, and so does not spend as much time on the fundamentals. In exchange, this somewhat longer book does go into more detail and actually gets into the process of developing applications for the .NET platform.

You'll find that all of the material covered in *Learning Visual Basic .NET* is also covered in the first chapters of *Programming Visual Basic .NET*. You may want to skim these chapters anyway, both for review and because some advanced topics do appear in these early chapters.

The next four chapters of *Programming Visual Basic .NET* provide an overview of both ASP.NET and Windows Forms, as well as ADO.NET. ASP.NET is used for programming web applications and web services, while the Windows Forms technology is used to program Windows applications. ADO.NET is the .NET technology for interacting with databases.

The final part of *Programming Visual Basic .NET* covers advanced topics in .NET programming such as assemblies, versioning, attributes and reflection, marshaling and remoting, threads and synchronization, streams, and interoperating with COM.

Assemblies are the basic unit of compilation. The chapter on assemblies and versioning addresses issues that arise when you create large commercial applications. You'll find information about private and shared assemblies, as well as an overview of how you manage the release of multiple versions of your program.

Attributes are metadata; data about your program. *Learning Visual Basic .NET* doesn't cover attributes because this is an advanced topic. However, attributes and custom attributes allow you to control how your program is processed by the tools available in .NET. Reflection is the process of a program examining itself (or another program) and allows you to discover, at runtime, the methods and properties of an object that was not known at compile time.

Threads are created when you want a program to do two things at once. When you have more than one thread operating in your program, you must control synchronization: making sure that access to your data is mediated so that one thread does not corrupt the data created in a second thread. The chapter on *threading* teaches you how to take control of this powerful aspect of .NET and create programs that are highly efficient.

Marshaling is the process of sending an object from one process or computer to another. This allows you to share objects across program boundaries. Remoting is the process of calling a method in a different program. These very advanced topics allow you to build highly distributed programs.

Streams allow you to read and write data both from a file and across the network. The .NET Framework provides extensive stream support, including support for reading and writing data across the standard web protocols such as HTTP.

Finally, many companies have extensive libraries of objects created in COM, the earlier Microsoft technology for building classes and controls. The chapter on COM in *Programming Visual Basic .NET* teaches you how to import these controls and DLL files into your .NET application (or export .NET controls to COM) to preserve your investment.

If you decide that you want to develop expertise in integrating COM with .NET, take a look at Adam Nathan's *.NET and Com* (Sams). I can't think of a more definitive book on this difficult topic.

If you want to go beyond the basics of .NET programming, and get deep into the internals, there is no better book than *Applied Microsoft .NET Framework Programming in Microsoft Visual Basic .NET*, by Jeffrey Richter and Francesco Belena (Microsoft Press, 2002). Richter and Belena are phenomenal writers, and their chapter on delegates alone is worth the cost of the book.

Another key topic in .NET programming is security. For the definitive word on .NET security, you'll want to buy *.NET Framework Security*, by LaMacchia et al (Addison-Wesley).

Web (ASP.NET) Programming

Rather than diving deeper into the recesses of VB.NET, you might decide to get started with building ASP.NET applications. ASP.NET applications can be interactive web sites, portals, or complete applications running on and distributed through the web. For example, Microsoft offers a free sample application, *IBuySpyStore* (http://www.ibuyspystore.com), that demonstrates how you can build a full online store using ASP.NET technology.

VS.NET provides extensive support for building ASP.NET applications, and VB.NET is one of the languages of choice for this development. With what you've learned already, you are well prepared to move on to creating web applications.

I wrote *Programming ASP.NET*, with Dan Hurwitz (O'Reilly) as a comprehensive guide to ASP.NET technology. You'll find extensive coverage of Web Form controls and event handling. You'll also find coverage of advanced programming technique, error handling, and validation. *Programming ASP.NET* devotes more than 150 pages to working with data in your web applications and also provides extensive coverage of web services. Finally, *Programming ASP.NET* offers coverage of such advanced topics as custom controls, security, caching and performance, and deployment-related issues.

Windows Forms Programming

Another alternative is to focus on building rich-client Windows applications, using the new Windows Forms technology. Windows applications allow you to take advantage of the full resources of the operating system, and yet still distribute aspects of your application over the web.

A good starting point for more information on building rich-client applications is an article in the June 2002 MSDN Magazine by Jason Clark. You can read this article online at *http://msdn.microsoft.com/msdnmag/issues/02/06/rich/rich.asp*.

I am currently writing the O'Reilly book *Programming .NET Windows Applications*, again with Dan Hurwitz, to be published in the spring of 2003. *Programming .NET Windows Applications* will be a comprehensive guide to writing Windows applications that includes extensive coverage of Windows Form controls and event handling. As in *Programming ASP.NET*, you'll find coverage of advanced programming techniques, error handling, and validation.

The coverage of data handling will be extensive, and we will also provide complete coverage of advanced topics such as custom controls, security, performance, and deployment-related issues.

Other Resources

Extensive resources are available to the aspiring VB.NET programmer. The most powerful, of course, is the MSDN library available from Microsoft (*http://www.msdn.microsoft.com*), which includes a number of different subscription levels, depending on your needs and resources.

Microsoft also hosts the gotdotnet forum (*http://www.gotdotnet.com*), which provides sample programs, extensive documentation and articles on .NET programming. Dozens of excellent web sites are devoted to .NET programming, not least of which is the O'Reilly site, *http://dotnet.oreilly.com*.

One of the most powerful resources available to VB.NET programmers is the set of extensive mailing lists and newsgroups that have sprung up so quickly. I find the dotnet mailing lists from Developmentor (*http://discuss.develop.com*) and the ASP Friends lists (*http://www.aspfriends.com/aspfriends*) to be particularly useful.

Finally, I provide a FAQ, source code, and related material on my web site: *http://www.LibertyAssociates.com*, where you can also sign up for a private support discussion forum.

Best of luck with VB.NET, and please do keep in touch.

Index

We'd like to hear your suggestions for improving our indexes. Send email to *index@oreilly.com*.

C

Call keyword, 50
call stack, 129, 264–266
Call Stack window (VS.NET debugger), 129
Camel notation, 41
    instantiating objects and, 84
Capacity property
    ArrayList class, 224
    StringBuilder class, 254
caret symbol (^) (see ^, under Symbols)
casting, 45
    to interfaces, 165–170
        Is operator, 167–170
catching exceptions, 259–275
    Catch blocks, 263
    Catch keyword, 263
    catch statements, creating
        dedicated, 266–268
CBool(), 45
CByte(), 46
CChar(), 46
CDate(), 46
CDbl(), 46
CDec(), 46
Char type, 32, 34
    default value, 97
    literal format, 40
Chars property
    String class, 241
    StringBuilder class, 254
CInt(), 46
Class keyword, 83
classes, 11, 82–105
    abstract, 142–145
        instantiating, 142
        interfaces compared to, 158
    base, 146
    client, 19, 158
    clients accessing state through
        properties, 110
    constructors and, 135
    defining, 17, 83–94
        access modifiers, 93
        creating Time class, example, 91
        instantiating objects, 84–86
        memory allocation, 87–91
        Pascal notation and, 84
    derived, 146
        base vs., 20
        deriving new, example, 133
    establishing relationships among, 18
    interface implementation, 157, 163
    modules as, 86
    NotInheritable, 145
    objects and, 84
    overriding interface methods, 174
    public interface vs. private
        implementation, 19
    root, 146
    sharing functionality, 131
    structures compared to, 151
Clear()
    Array class, 199
    ArrayList class, 224
    Queue class, 230
    Stack class, 233
CLng(), 46
CLR (Common Language Runtime), 3
CObj(), 46
Collection class, 226–229
collection interfaces, 212–224
    comparing objects in, 213
    IEnumerable interface, 213–220
    table of, 212
collections
    copying from to arrays, 236–238
    enumerating through, using For Each
        loops, 212
colon (:), 47
combining interfaces, 173
comma (,) (see , under Symbols)
comments, 13
Common Language Runtime (CLR), 3
Compare() (String), 241
compile time, 35
compiler errors, types and, 34–36
compiler warnings, 35
Concat() (String), 243
conditional branching statements, 49, 52–60
    ElseIf statements, 56
    If statements, 52–54
    If…Else statements, 54
    Nested If statements, 55
    Select Case statements, 57–60
conditionals, logical operators within, 77
console applications, 7
    displaying output onscreen, 38
Console class, 147
constants, 39–46
    casting, 45
    enumerations, 42
    literal, 40
    naming conventions, 41
    symbolic, 40–42

constructors, 96–98
    calling base class, 135
    classes and, 135
    copy, 100
    declaring, 97
    naming, with more than one name, 107
    overloading, 107
       signatures, 108
container classes, 215
Contains()
    Queue class, 230
    Stack class, 233
copy constructors, 100
Copy()
    Array class, 199
    String class, 241, 244
copying
    collection types to arrays, 236–238
    strings, 241, 244
CopyTo()
    Queue class, 230
    Stack class, 233
Count property, 224
    Queue class, 230
    Stack class, 233
CShort(), 46
CStr(), 46
CType(), 46, 149
curly braces ({}) (see {}, under Symbols)
Current property (IEnumerator class), 218
custom exceptions, 273–275

D

data, encapsulating with properties, 110–115
    Get/Set accessors, 113
    ReadOnly/WriteOnly properties, 114
Date type, 32, 34
    default value, 39
date/time values, 34
    converting, 46
Debug menu (VS.NET), 122
debugger
    IEnumerable interface/For Each loops
       and, 221–224
debugging, 4, 121–129
    compiler errors and, 35
    setting breakpoints, 121–123
       Debug menu, 124
    (see also debugger)
Decimal type, 32
    literal format, 40
    supporting accounting applications, 34

default property
    indexers and, 202–211
    retrieving, 203
Dequeue() (Queue), 230
derived classes, 146
design time, 35
Developmentor web site, xii, 292
DirectCast(), 149
discussion group, supporting this book, xii
Dispose(), 105
.dll files, 26
Do loops, 61–64
    breaking out of, 64
    caution when looping to specific value, 63
Do While loops, 62
dollar sign ($), 37
double quotes (""), 47
Double type, 32
    as fractional value, 34
    literal format, 40
DrawWindow(), 142

E

ElseIf statements, 56
encapsulating data with properties, 110–115
    Get/Set accessors, 113
EndsWith() (String), 248
Enqueue() (Queue), 230
EnsureCapacity() (StringBuilder), 254
Enum type, 97
enumerations, 42
    advancing to next element, 218
    enumerator list, 42
    incrementing index, 218
    iterating array lists, 224
    retrieving for queues, 230
    setting to initial position, 218
Equals()
    Object class, 146
    String class, 241, 245
errors, 260
    compiler, types and, 34–36
    treating compiler warnings as, 35
event handlers, creating, 282
events, 280–284
    applications and, 276–287
    polling, 280
    raising, 281
Exception class, methods and
       properties, 270–273
exception handlers, 259
    searching for, 260

objects (*continued*)
    current instance of (see Me keyword)
    destroying, 105
    evaluating whether two are equivalent or
        refer to same instance, 146
    instantiating, 84–86
        Camel notation and, 84
        New keyword, 85
    naming conventions, 41
    providing access to type, 146
    providing hash functions for
        collections, 146
    removing from queues, 230
    removing/returning at queue
        beginning, 230
    returning strings with name of class, 146
    tracking specific, 127
    (see also classes)
offsets (see indexes)
one-dimensional arrays, 180
    copying queue elements to, 230
    returning index of first/last instance of
        values, 199
    reversing order of elements in, 199
    sorting values in, 199
operators, 71–81
    assignment, 71
    logical, precedence of, 80
    mathematical, 71–76
        modulus, 75
        precedence of, 80
        simple arithmetical, 72–76
    precedence of, 79–81
    relational, 76
        precedence of, 80
Or operator, 78
overloading
    constructors, 107
        signatures, 108
    methods, 107–110
Overridable keyword, 137
    versioning with, 141
Overrides keyword, 137, 141
    versioning with, 141

P

PadLeft()/PadRight() (String), 241
ParamArray keyword, 189–191
parentheses (()) (see (()), under Symbols)
Pascal notation, 41
    defining classes and, 84
    property names, 111

pattern matching, 255
Peek()
    Queue class, 230
    Stack class, 233
percent sign (%), 37
plus sign (+) (see +, under Symbols)
polymorphism, 21, 136–142
    creating polymorphic methods, 137–141
        runtime and, 139
    creating polymorphic types, 137
Pop() (Stack), 233
precedence of operators, 79–81
Private access modifier, 17, 94, 110, 136
projects (VS.NET), 26
    characters in names of, 26
    solutions and, 26
properties, 17, 83, 107
    Array class, table of, 199
    clients accessing class state, 110
    encapsulating data with, 110–115
        Get/Set accessors, 113
        ReadOnly/WriteOnly properties, 114
    (see also default property)
Properties window (VS.NET), 277
Protected access modifier, 94, 136
Protected Friend access modifier, 94
Public access modifier, 17, 94, 113, 136
Push() (Stack), 233

Q

Queue class, 230–233
    adding object to end, 230
    copying elements to new array, 230
    copying elements to one-dimensional
        arrays, 230
    determining whether element is
        present, 230
    methods and properties, 230
    removing objects from, 230
    removing/returning initial object, 230
    retrieving number of elements from, 230
    returning enumerator for, 230
QuickWatch window (VS.NET), 127

R

RAD (Rapid Application Development), 284
Rank property (Array class), 200
Rapid Application Development (RAD), 284
ReadOnly/WriteOnly properties, 114
rectangular arrays, 192–196

---

reference types, 88
    arrays and, 181
    default values, 97
    passing by value, 117–120
    value types, example illustrating
        differences, 88–91
ReferenceEquals() (Object), 146
Regex class, 256
regular expressions, 239, 255–258
    literals, 256
    metacharacters, 256
    pattern matching, 255
relational operators, 76
    precedence of, 80
Remove()
    String class, 241
    StringBuilder class, 254
RemoveAt() (ArrayList), 224
Replace() (StringBuilder), 254
Reset() (IEnumerator), 218
resources, nonmemory, cleaning up, 146
Reverse()
    Array class, 199–202
    ArrayList class, 224
root classes, 146

S

Select Case statements, 57–60
server-side code, 287
shared members, 102–104
    (see also Me keyword)
shared methods (see shared members)
Short type, 33
    literal format, 40
signature of a method, 108
Single type, 33
    as fractional value, 34
    literal format, 40
.sln files, 26
Solution Explorer (VS.NET IDE), 28
solutions (VS.NET), 25
Sort()
    Array class, 199–202
    ArrayList class, 224
.sou files, 26
source code, 4, 8, 25
specialization, 20, 130–132
    (see also inheritance; polymorphism)
Split()
    Regex class, 258
    String class, 241, 251–253

square brackets ([]) (see [], under Symbols)
the stack
    memory allocation on, 87–91
    unwinding, exception handling and, 261
stack, call (see call stack)
Stack class, 233
    manipulating elements, 236–238
stacks, 233–235
StackTrace property (Exception class), 271
Start Page (VS.NET), 25–27
StartsWith() (String), 241
statements, 47
step commands (VS.NET), 123
String class, 239
string indexer, 208–210
String keyword, 47, 239
string literals, 240
StringBuilder class, 253
strings, 35, 47, 239–258
    aligning, 241
    appending, 254
    comparing, 241
    concatenating, 243
    converting to Boolen, 45
    copying, 241, 244
    copying characters from strings to
        arrays, 241
    creating, 239–241
        string literals, 240
        ToString(), 240
    default value, 39
    deleting characters in, 241
    dividing, 241
    ensuring capacity of, 254
    finding substrings, 248, 249–251
    formatting, 241
    immutability of, 241
    indexing, 241
    indicating initial characters in, 241
    inserting objects in, 254
    inserting substrings in, 248
    length of, 248
    literal format, 40
    locating substrings, 248
    manipulating, 241–255
    pattern matching, 255
    removing characters from, 254
    replacing characters in, 254
    retturning substrings, 241
    returning copy, 241
    splitting, 251–253
    testing for equality, 241, 245

About the Author

Jesse Liberty is the author of a dozen books, including *Programming ASP.NET* and *Programming C#* from O'Reilly. Jesse is the president of Liberty Associates, Inc. (*http://www.LibertyAssociates.com*), where he provides .NET training, contract programming, and consulting. He is a former Vice President of electronic delivery for Citibank, and a former Distinguished Software Engineer and architect for AT&T, Ziff Davis, Xerox, and PBS.

Colophon

Our look is the result of reader comments, our own experimentation, and feedback from distribution channels. Distinctive covers complement our distinctive approach to technical topics, breathing personality and life into potentially dry subjects.

The animal on the cover of *Learning Visual Basic .NET* is a snake-necked turtle. Snake-necked turtles (*Chelodina longicollis*) are found in the southern hemisphere in South America, Australia, and New Guinea. They live in slow-moving, fresh-water environments such as rivers. Sometimes, though not regularly, they migrate in search of new waters in the summertime.

Snake-necked turtles have large, webbed back feet in the back for swimming, and claws on their front feet. Their shells have high bumps, covered with moss and water plants that help them blend in with their surroundings. When seeking prey, the turtle holds its head sideways, waits for prey to come near, and then extends its neck and strikes like a snake. It feeds on insects, worms, frogs, small fish, and crustaceans. The turtle emits a foul-smelling fluid from its musk glands when handled, or when trying to frighten predators.

Darren Kelly was the production editor for *Learning Visual Basic .NET*. Nancy Crumpton provided production services and wrote the index. Emily Quill and Claire Cloutier provided quality control.

Emma Colby designed the cover of this book, based on a series design by Edie Freedman. The cover image is a 19th-century engraving from the Dover Pictorial Archive. Emma Colby produced the cover layout with QuarkXPress 4.1 using Adobe's ITC Garamond font.

David Futato designed the interior layout. This book was converted to FrameMaker 5.5.6 with a format conversion tool created by Erik Ray, Jason McIntosh, Neil Walls, and Mike Sierra that uses Perl and XML technologies. The text font is Linotype Birka; the heading font is Adobe Myriad Condensed; and the code font is Lucas-Font's TheSans Mono Condensed. The illustrations that appear in the book were produced by Robert Romano and Jessamyn Read using Macromedia FreeHand 9 and Adobe Photoshop 6. The tip and warning icons were drawn by Christopher Bing. This colophon was written by Linley Dolby.